The Things that Could Not be Said

ALSO BY FRANK CHIKANE

Eight Days in September: The Removal of Thabo Mbeki (2012)
No Life of My Own: An Autobiography (revised edition, 2012)

The Things that Could Not be Said

FROM A(IDS) TO Z(IMBABWE)

Frank Chikane

PICADOR AFRICA

First published in 2013 by Picador Africa
an imprint of Pan Macmillan South Africa
Private Bag x19, Northlands
Johannesburg, 2116

www.panmacmillan.co.za

ISBN 978-1-77010-225-5
ePub ISBN 978-1-77010-226-2

Editing by Sharon Dell
Proofreading by Sally Hines
Design and typesetting by Triple M Design, Johannesburg
Cover by K4
Front cover photograph by Graeme Williams/South Photographs/
Africa Media Online

Printed and bound by Ultra Litho (Pty) Limited

*This book is dedicated to all the colleagues I worked with
in the presidency and in other departments of state
and to my dear wife, Kagiso Chikane,
who had to endure the absent man who was present.*

'Reverend, you are so damn lucky to be alive.
The stuff was meant to kill!'

STATEMENT BY ONE OF THE SCIENTISTS WHO PRODUCED
THE SUBSTANCE, PARAOXON, USED AGAINST FRANK CHIKANE

CONTENTS

ABBREVIATIONS

ACSA   Airport Company of South Africa
AFP   Agence France-Presse
ANC   African National Congress
APF   Africa Partnership Forum
APRM   African Peer Review Mechanism
AU   African Union
COSATU   Congress of South African Trade Unions
DRC   Democratic Republic of the Congo
DSO   Directorate of Special Operations
GEAR   Growth, Employment and Redistribution
GPA   Global Political Agreement (Zimbabwe)
G8   Group of Canada, France, Germany, Italy, Japan,
            Russia, United Kingdom and the United States
G13   G8 group plus Brazil, China, India, Mexico and
            South Africa
G20   Group of 20 major developing nations
G77   Group of 77 developing nations
ICC   International Criminal Court
IEC   Independent Electoral Commission
IMF   International Monetary Fund
MCC   Medicines Control Council
MDC   Movement for Democratic Change
MEC   member of the executive council
MK   Umkhonto we Sizwe
MTCT   mother-to-child-transmission
NATO   North Atlantic Treaty Organisation
NDPP   national director for public prosecutions

NDR	national democratic revolution
NEC	National Executive Committee (of the ANC)
NEPAD	New Partnership for Africa's Development
NGO	non-governmental organisation
NPA	National Prosecuting Authority
OAU	Organisation of African Unity
RDP	Reconstruction and Development Programme
SA	South Africa
SACC	South African Council of Churches
SACP	South African Communist Party
SADC	Southern African Development Community
SAPS	South African Police Services
TRC	Truth and Reconciliation Commission
UDF	United Democratic Front
UN	United Nations
UNAIDS	Joint United Nations Programme on HIV/AIDS
UNDP	United Nations Development Programme
US	United States of America
WHO	World Health Organisation
WMD	Weapons of Mass Destruction

Introduction

Those who have read *Eight Days in September: The Removal of Thabo Mbeki* will know that I decided that once I left government I would write about the things I could not say while I was in government. I felt that working as a civil servant robbed me of my freedom to express my feelings and views about the developments in the country and the 'things' I dealt with in government. *Eight Days in September* was part of this project and this book, *The Things that Could Not be Said*, is the second part of the same project.

As I mentioned in the first book, I initially thought I would write one book that would be broken into two parts. The first part would focus on the removal of Thabo Mbeki from office as the president of the country and the second part would be about the rest of the things I could not say, but it soon became clear that there was too much material for one book and so I decided to break the project into two parts.

I need to emphasise, as I did in *Eight Days in September*, that these books are not intended as a historical account of the developments within the presidency or government during my incumbency, nor are they a critical analysis of the presidency and whatever it was involved in.

Rather, these books are about my experiences while I was in government. They present these experiences from my perspective as an insider – a player in events – rather than as an observer or spectator on the outside.

Part One lays the foundation for the rest of the text, showing that I am indeed one of the officials in government who could argue that I had seen it all as I was present during the presidency of Nelson Mandela and stayed through that of Thabo Mbeki, Kgalema Motlanthe and up to that of Jacob Zuma. It also reveals that I went into the civil service reluctantly as I was a public advocate for justice and never really wanted to be a civil servant.

Part One also deals with the limitations I still have in telling the story in full because of regulatory issues related to confidentiality and classified information. As a result of these restrictions, a reader will find gaps in some places or a lack of detail on some of the matters where details fall within the scope of classified information. The editors and reviewers who worked on this book tried their best to get me to elaborate on some of these issues but I could not oblige.

In addition, because of the sensitivities involved, many of the characters in the book are missing in the act or are deliberately not mentioned. At times this is not only about the sensitivity of information but is for the safety and security of the players involved. In other cases, names of countries are not mentioned for either diplomatic reasons or because disclosure would compromise sensitive information.

One critical point to be made about this book (and the previous one, *Eight Days in September*) is that it does not conform to the popular perspectives about the presidency and Thabo Mbeki during our incumbency. For some readers who are sold on these popular views and perspectives the book may feel strident or it might strike a discordant note. Indeed, the book is about things that could not be said precisely because they are strident and therefore suppressed or gated. It sharply insists that it be heard even if you do not necessarily agree with what is said.

In particular, Part Two of this book may feel uncomfortable for some readers. It depicts a world that is far from innocent – a cut-throat world of lies, dishonesty, double speak, double standards and distortions of reality – where only the powerful survive and the weak get punished or die.

But this is my experience and I am allowed the freedom to express or reflect on it, however controversial or unpleasant it may feel to some readers. Fear to do so on my part would be limiting my rights as well as denying my experience when I was in government. Saying it otherwise would require me to reinvent myself like an actor who plays different and opposing roles within the same play.

In the name of survival, many of my comrades have successfully remade and remoulded themselves to fit within whatever environment they find themselves in. Like chameleons they change colour depending on the environment and levels of threat. The popular term here would be camouflage. But always to resort to camouflage is precisely what would threaten our future. Without upholding the principles and ideals we stand for, we are bound to lose our future.

Part Four is similar in many respects to Part Two. The titles of the chapters suggest that a reader is going to deal with the traditional subject of HIV and AIDS and Mbeki, which in most publications amounts to 'Mbeki bashing'. But my focus is completely different. It is my experience of and my encounter with Mbeki's views about HIV and AIDS as part of his staff, and what we did to turn a difficult and debilitating discourse into the best policy on HIV and

AIDS that South Africa is proud of today. And it is also an insider account of the issues surrounding drugs, their accessibility and pricing, with HIV and AIDS drugs as the reference point in this regard.

Those who are looking for the popular Mbeki-bashing approach will undoubtedly be disappointed at the end of these chapters. But those who want to understand my insider perspective on Mbeki's mind in this regard will enjoy the reading.

Part Three expresses my grave concerns about the risks and threats facing South Africa. It might also sound strident as it uses the liberation struggle language or the 'national democratic revolution' (which is the language of this struggle for liberation) as a reference point and a yardstick of any form of behaviour and conduct that might threaten the security of the state and the future of the country. Some readers might find this part of the book containing what they would refer to as 'conspiracy theory' material. But from my perspective everything – including my own comrades – seems to be working against the ideal society we struggled for and paid a price for, including even the ultimate price of death paid by many of our comrades. Chapter 10 ('A Solitary Journey'), which deals with my personal quest to find out who poisoned me, explores the contradictions that are confronting our country and government today.

For the 'born frees' it is difficult to imagine the pain that those who made great sacrifices are going through as they watch that which they fought for becoming exactly the opposite of what they expected. Those who passed away during the glorious days of our new democracy went to rest in peace – pleased that what they had sacrificed for was achieved and that their sacrifices were not in vain. But most of the veterans of the struggle who pass away now go with sore hearts as their sacrifices for the new South Africa seem to have been in vain.

Finally, Part Five groups together more of my personal journey, such as in Chapter 15 ('The Pain of the TRC Error'), with other issues that confronted us while I was serving in government. And while each of the subjects touched on in Chapter 16 ('*Sela le Sela*'), the Arms Procurement Programme, GEAR and Lesotho – could have enjoyed its own chapter, I am satisfied to have raised and commented on each of them.

Whatever the readers' perspectives and the text's perceived or real limitations, I invite readers to enjoy the book as well as to engage with it as critically as possible. For those who have strong opposing views or different perspectives my advice would be to publish them, so that readers can have more material to use as a basis to make up their own minds.

PART ONE

CHAPTER 1

Talking about Secrets and Freedom of Expression

Many people who knew me before the 1994 democratic elections expressed their surprise that they did not hear from me during the 1995 to 2009 period when I was in government as much as they did in the 'old days'. Some asked why I was so quiet, especially when 'things were going so badly wrong'. Others pointed out to me their specific areas of concern in our society, government and in the ruling party.

To play on any feelings of guilt I might have they also remarked that they knew me as someone 'who was bold and who could not keep quiet when things went wrong'. They argued that South Africa needed bold people – as of old – who would speak as well as act against wrongdoing, irrespective of who was involved and no matter what the personal cost to the speaker.

On first impressions, this barrage of questions put to me both privately and in public spaces sounded remarkably like nostalgia. It almost felt as if people wanted to return to the past rather than move forward. But the more the questions were posed, the more it became clear that there was serious concern amongst many South Africans about where the country was going.

I tried to answer these questions honestly, without much success. Nobody seemed to understand what I meant when I said that my appointment as director-general in the presidency – as a public servant – limited my freedom to speak in the way I could prior to going into government. Explaining the rules and regulations of public service did not make sense to them either. Worse still was their confusion when I talked about secrecy laws and confidentiality.

Now that I have undertaken to write about 'the things that could not be said' during the thirteen-and-a-half years I served in government, there is little chance that people will believe I am still constrained by some of the rules and regulations that protect classified and confidential information. But in fact, in some cases I will not be able to disclose some of the 'things that could not be said' until they are declassified 20 to 30 years hence. This would mean that I have to live until I am about 80 to 90 years old, and so it is likely that there are some things that will not be disclosed before I go to my grave.

For this reason I felt it was important for me to give the public a better perspective on the scope of what can and cannot be said, and why.

The first thing the public needs to realise is that, by its very nature, a state knows more than ordinary citizens do. With an official information base at its disposal and access to intelligence information, states know a lot about individuals, organisations, companies, countries, both at national and international levels. Most of the information governments have is made available to the public. Some of the information is considered confidential and cannot be disclosed to third parties who have no right to access such information. Confidentiality in this arena builds trust and opens doors to the sharing of more confidential information.

There is, however, the more sensitive area of classified information, which all states or governments possess. There are four normal categories of classification generally used by states or governments, namely, 'restricted', 'confidential', 'secret' and 'top secret'. To maintain the integrity of this system public servants who deal with sensitive information are vetted and are allocated particular levels of secrecy starting from 'restricted' to the highest level of 'top secret'. Whatever classification someone is given determines the sensitivity of information to which that person can have access. Then, like most countries, South Africa has Minimum Information Security Standards that regulate the way in which sensitive information, including classified information, is managed or handled by those who have the relevant level of authority to access such information. The director-general or head of a department or entity of government is responsible for the effective management of security of information in terms of this system.

Sections 3 and 5 of Schedule 2 of the Constitution of the Republic of South Africa provide for 'oaths and solemn affirmations' for members of the executive at both national and provincial levels that include the matter of management and handling of secret information. Members of the executive at national and provincial levels take an oath when they assume office 'to respect and uphold the Constitution and all other laws of the Republic'. They also undertake to 'hold' their office 'with honour and dignity' and 'not to divulge directly or indirectly any secret matter entrusted' to them.

All these rules and regulations are necessary for the proper functioning of the state and for the national security of the country. The rules and regulations ensure that officials at both political and public service levels maintain the integrity of sensitive and classified information in the possession of the state. As secretary of cabinet and the secretary of the National Security Council I was one of the key custodians of such sensitive and classified information at the highest level.

As a result, I had to be even more careful and responsible than most about what I said or communicated in the public arena. In fact, those entrusted with sensitive information do better by talking less, if at all. I spoke publicly only when it was absolutely necessary to do so.

There have been gross violations of these rules and regulations at high levels, which have seriously threatened the security of this country and its people. Some instances of this will be dealt with in the chapters that follow, but other parts of the story will never be told because of the regulatory framework in place.

There is a further requirement in the management of information security that is not clearly legislated for: any discussion with the president is considered privileged and all information acquired during such discussions is treated as confidential unless otherwise stated. No one can disclose this information without the prior approval or consent of the president. Even envoys of the president are expected to treat all the information acquired in the course of their duties as confidential, unless otherwise stated.

In my case, as secretary of the cabinet, chairperson of the National Security Council committee of security-related officials and secretary of the executive-level National Security Council, the bar was set even higher. I operated consistently at a 'top-secret' level – what in Afrikaans is called *streng geheim* – and some things will never be declassified or told during my lifetime. In most instances, this has to do with the security of the state or a threat or risk to people's lives, especially the lives of sources of the information or agents who collect such information.

There is also an international aspect to the management of information security. Friendly states share sensitive information from time to time relating to matters of mutual interest or security. On occasion, this information has to do with combating crime at an international level, or with terrorism. States that share sensitive information on these matters need to be assured that their information will be handled in a manner that assures its integrity. If there is even a suspicion that a state is not able to maintain the integrity of information shared, no one would engage with such a country or government. It is not difficult to understand the implications of such a position for the affected country or government.

Beyond the handling of sensitive and confidential information, there is also the regulatory framework that controls what public servants can and cannot say. Firstly, you can only speak about or represent official positions of government. Your views and personal opinions do not count. Personal opinions that may be construed as 'political' or a critique of one political party or another are not permissible.

Even when you feel that some things are going wrong in the country, you cannot express that feeling or view as you might wish. At desperate times I adopted the cover of pastor of a congregation or church leader to express an opinion. But this was a risk and required me to exercise careful judgement and to choose my words thoughtfully. At times I resorted to rhetorical questions and comments. Sometimes I spoke in parables. And sometimes it was simplest just to pray about the matter. In prayer – one of the age-old weapons of the struggle – I had the latitude to tell God about my concern and to ask God to intervene directly or through whomever God chose as an instrument. But even prayer could be dangerous if used to divulge classified information.

Although public servants are allowed to join parties of their choice and serve in the management committees of such parties, they cannot publicly represent the views of the party or speak in a way that supports their party or opposes another party. For instance, I was a member of the National Executive Committee (NEC) of the African National Congress (ANC), but the fact that I was a civil servant limited my participation in the debates within the ANC in the public sphere. My views and feelings were expressed within the NEC as a closed forum. However, at the general council or the national conference of the party or in public meetings I was limited and avoided public debates that might be construed to be violating the Public Service Regulations. As a result, my freedom to speak, even on those matters I was seriously concerned about, was limited.

Some comrades have raised the question of whether or not it would have been better for the country or even for the ANC if I had played a public political role rather than the role of a public servant, given the events of the last seven years or so, especially as they affect the ANC. Unfortunately, *nkabo* (a Setswana word meaning 'if only') is a speculative proposition that cannot be tested. Batswana say '*Nkabo' ke ngwana was morago*', meaning, 'it's too late'. As English chemist and novelist C.P. Snow says in *Science and Government,* 'The ifs of history are not very profitable'.[1]

The fact that I was a member of the ANC NEC, on the one hand, and a civil servant, on the other, was helpful in terms of understanding the policy framework of the party and the implementation of such policies.

One thing I can say is that my deployment frustrated me significantly at critical moments as the crisis within the ANC intensified. My efforts within the party as a responsible and disciplined cadre of the movement were at times either ignored or simply put aside. As I have explained, the public arena was not open to me. In a sense, I had to *lala ngenceba* (literally, 'sleep on one's wound'). Even today, I am still sleeping on the wounds inflicted by the national and party politics of the last seven or so years.

Another kind of silence hangs over the things that *can* be said but will not be said because of the political and very real personal risks to the sources of such information. At times the political climate determines what 'truth' can be told and what 'truth' must remain unstated.

Power dynamics, fear and risk can distort facts and colour the story. In short, those who are in power can rewrite history, in the same way as the colonists did.

In many instances, the truth one knows to be true cannot be told simply because of a lack of hard evidence. There are many cases in which the community knows about the criminal activities of a particular person or persons and cannot understand why no arrests are made. The challenge is to find evidence that can be tested in a court of law.

So, I venture into this risky territory – to say 'the things that could not be said' – within the bounds of the law on the one hand and to avoid being sued on the other.

One thing beyond dispute is that I am one of the privileged few who has 'seen it all' rather than hearing about it through the grapevine. I have been in the presidency from the time of Mandela to Mbeki, and Motlanthe and Zuma (although the latter was for a short period, except when he was deputy president). The challenge for me is to say 'the things that could not be said' in a responsible way that will help the country to move forwards rather than backwards.

My intention is not to attack individuals, organisations or parties. If there is a reference to any one person or to a party it is because they are part of that story. My objective is not to deal with individuals but to engage with issues of a strategic nature and importance. My overall objective is to assist the nation to avoid the pitfalls of the past and move forward to build a better South Africa that we will all be proud to call home.

CHAPTER 2

I Have Seen it All

There are very few people at a senior level who have had the opportunity and privilege of being in the presidency of the new democratic South Africa from the time of President Nelson Mandela to that of President Jacob Zuma. I happen to be such a person. For me, this amounted to about fourteen years of service, covering the presidencies of Mandela, Mbeki, Motlanthe and Zuma.

I first served during Mandela's presidency as a special adviser to Deputy President Thabo Mbeki and as a director-general in his office from 1995 to 1999. I was then director-general of the presidency from 1999 to 2008 during Mbeki's presidency and for Kgalema Motlanthe's brief stint at the helm. Between 2008 and 2009 I served both presidents Motlanthe and Zuma (although briefly) as a special adviser and director-general to assist with the management of the transitional processes leading up to and beyond the April 2009 national elections. I left the presidency in June 2009, having completed my mission, which included an exit report as part of the handover process to ensure that the transition was as smooth as possible.

This period in my career was both exciting and challenging. It was exciting because it was an opportunity to be part of the reconstruction and development programme of a new society, including the creation of new institutions and structures. It was challenging because it required all of us to think 'outside the box' of normal governance practices and traditions in South Africa and globally.

We came from an apartheid society and were living in a world characterised by failed systems. In order to develop a just and equitable society, we were destined to be creators of new things and new ways of doing things.

Almost everyone who had ideas wanted to have them tested here in South Africa. It was like a theatre of social engineering – in a positive sense rather than a negative colonial sense. The country was like a laboratory in which to experiment with new ideas and theoretical perspectives. Some of the best policies came out of this exercise as we learnt on a global stage from everyone who had gone before us. We became procreators of the new South Africa.

Mistakes were bound to be made, but in the main there were great success stories. We stretched our intellectual, developmental, management, monitoring and evaluation capacities to the limit, and broke new ground. At times, the experience broke some of the players who could not reach beyond their capacities.

Amongst the myriad issues we had to deal with was the political stabilisation of the country following increased levels of violence and conflict just before the political settlement in 1993 and the April 1994 democratic elections. This included dealing with the transformation and integration of the apartheid defence force, the police, intelligence services and the public services. As was to be expected, the process was accompanied by fears, frustrations, unhappiness, discontent, tension and conflict. The Truth and Reconciliation Commission (TRC) was part of this process as it provided a bridge from a violent apartheid system that pursued gross human rights violations to a peaceful and rights-based democratic state.

We participated in the restructuring of the state. First, there was the development of a new democratic constitution, the progressive precepts of which have become the envy of many other countries. The new constitution led to the re-demarcation and establishment of new provinces (from four to nine) and reconfiguration of racially based municipalities to non-racial local governments.

We had to restructure the economy and state assets, transform the skewed apartheid budget into an equitable redistributive budget, and implement the ruling party's new socio-economic policy framework known as the Reconstruction and Development Programme (RDP).

Except in the case of *coups d'état*, there are seldom more thoroughgoing changes to the state as those implemented post the apartheid system. In normal democracies, a change in governments or leaders requires some structural changes in institutions and systems of governance, but seldom do you hear of the systematic transformation of the state itself. Our transformative project ventured into that uncharted territory – where angels fear to tread.

In a complex society such as apartheid South Africa – characterised by racial divisions, many years of exclusive white rule, the oppression and exploitation of the black majority by a white minority resulting in numerous extremely rich whites on the one hand and abject poverty amongst the majority of blacks on the other – a radical and fundamental transitional project of this magnitude was bound to generate fears and foster attempts to either halt the changes or limit their impact.

Even by international standards, ours was a radical project that did not quite 'fit' in the context of a post-Second World War international governance system based on the veto powers of permanent members of the United Nations (UN) Security Council. Nor did it sit comfortably in the geopolitics of the post–Cold War era, which left us with a unipolar or multipolar world (depending on one's perspective about the distribution of global power). For some, this South African 'experiment' – which sought not only a non-racial, non-sexist, democratic society, but just economic and governance systems – was setting a 'bad' example.

Although initially there were accolades both at home and abroad for what was seen to be the miracle of the new South Africa – with Mandela as its iconic face – red warning lights began to flash soon thereafter. Accordingly, the project was closely watched by South Africans and the international community.

The architects of the transformation were very much aware of the risks attendant on the process. Regular assessments were made of the 'balance of forces' to understand better the pressure arrayed against the transformation project, and those that were part of the project of transformation. A way forward was then charted to manoeuvre strategically around these forces and still achieve our objectives. This process of ongoing assessment enabled us to determine the pace and timing of specific changes. Accordingly, there was a high level of consciousness about the need for sophisticated political acumen, strategic thinking and sensitivity in order to properly manage the transition. In a sense, the leadership needed the wisdom of Solomon to survive in a generally hostile environment in order to establish an egalitarian and equitable society, especially where economic justice was concerned.

Essentially, the issues that were always bound to be prominent were race and the unequal distribution of wealth; equity laws and affirmative action; scarce resources and delivery of services to the historically disadvantaged; the Growth, Employment and Redistribution (GEAR) programme and the stabilisation of the economy; arms production, procurement and sales; foreign relations policy positions that were alien to the geopolitics of the day; and HIV and AIDS.

However, two other factors added to our challenges. One was the machinations of some of the former intelligence and security-related characters (both from the old and new orders), some of whom retired voluntarily or were demobilised. These individuals formed complex networks and linkages that threatened the stability of government and the ruling party. On the surface, it seemed odd that their focus, in the main, was the ruling party. But as everyone who really had a problem with the ANC knew, the best way to weaken it was to strike or divide from the inside.

The second factor was the intelligence projects of those outside the country who could never really accept the transition from apartheid to democracy. The knowledge that this radical project was seen as setting a 'bad example' nationally and internationally should have made the ANC more conscious of the risks attendant on this process. It should have expected that external forces could use sinister intelligence projects to destabilise it. It should also have been more alert to the risks of internal disintegration, infighting and competition.

Some would say that the party devised strategies to survive in what was frequently a hostile environment. My view is that it did not do so. If it did, then its efforts in this regard were limited and failed to produce the desired results. My view is that a tsunami of material interests distracted cadres from the critical national strategic responsibility to defend the organisation and strengthen it to be able to pursue the strategic objective of completing the national democratic revolution (NDR). We must accept that we dropped the ball in this regard and allowed reactionary forces within and outside the movement to destroy the organisation from the inside. Who would ever have thought that ANC members would kill each other for control of state power in order to advance their own personal interests or the interests of family, friends and factions?

If this failure had occurred during the time of the liberation struggle we would have considered it a dastardly betrayal of our struggle and the NDR as conceptualised by the movement.

After the ANC had increased its margins of victory over three national elections from just below 66 per cent in 1994 to 70 per cent in 2004 the realisation had grown by those opposed to the ANC nationally and internationally that one of the most effective ways to defeat the ANC, and its project of transformation, was from the inside.

The party was aware of this strategy but it never devised adequate defence mechanisms to deal with the new tactics that were unfolding in this regard, including checking both foreign and national (old order and compromised new order) intelligence elements. Instead, the party was consumed by internal conflicts, power struggles and the temptation of new material interests.

These developments changed the fundamental nature of the revolutionary 'cadre of the movement' that the party talked about at its Port Elizabeth general council meeting in 2000. It was as if the ANC had been hit by a bomb that caused structural damage that would take time to repair. Even today, the project to repair the organisation and the process of healing requires a realisation amongst all the players that the organisation needs extensive repair work, including an overhaul of its engine – and some plastic surgery. The ANC's discussion document on Organisational Renewal tells the story even better.

During ten of the more than thirteen years I served in government I was part of the NEC of the ANC. I painfully witnessed the emergence of the cracks in the relationship between Thabo Mbeki and Jacob Zuma when they were respectively the president and deputy president of both the ANC and the country. The cracks became wider after Schabir Shaik was charged for corruption. As time went by, it became clear that the undeclared tension between Mbeki and Zuma was beginning to affect the performance of government. This raised a serious concern for me, which led me to interact with both principals on the matter. I tried to do what I could, including using my conflict resolution skills, but without much success given the structurally unequal relationship with the president and deputy president on the one hand, and a director-general on the other. Our historical, longstanding, comradely relationships did not count here. In addition, Comrade Kgalema Motlanthe did what he could from his side as the secretary-general of the ANC, also without much success. The details of some of these efforts are contained in my 2012 book, *Eight Days in September.*

Following the removal of the then deputy president of the ANC, Jacob Zuma, as deputy president of the country, and the subsequent corruption charges preferred against him, the undeclared tension reached a boiling point and the NEC was drawn in to try to intervene. But in all situations, both Mbeki and Zuma denied there were problems between the two of them. Their denial was even put in an agreed statement between them that was presented to the NEC.

As time went on, the NEC itself showed signs of divisions. Instead of it holding the fort in the face of the major crisis triggered by the removal of Zuma from his office as the deputy president in government, cracks began to emerge.

Two intelligence projects that I would classify as counter-revolutionary were launched at this time. They were counter-revolutionary for me because they were intent on destabilising and dividing the ANC to make it unable to pursue the NDR as its key strategic objective. The first of these was the production and circulation in 2005 of fake e-mails to leaders of the ANC and to journalists purporting to be communications between those who

worked with Mbeki (including myself) or those who were perceived to be on Mbeki's side and purportedly aimed at sabotaging
Zuma's plans to be president of the country. The intention here was
to create more tensions, distrust and animosity among the leaders
of the ANC, which led to further divisions and weakening of the
organisation.

The second was the Browse Mole report, authored by some
elements within the Scorpions. Both of these interventions were
aimed at exacerbating divisions within the party. It is now history
that, as a result of all this, and the removal of Zuma from cabinet, a
massive campaign was launched within the ANC to remove Mbeki
as president of the ANC and of the country.

Together with my colleagues in government, particularly in the
presidency, I had to manage what could only be called a national
political crisis, especially insofar as it affected government (details
of which are given in *Eight Days in September*). I had to manage
the fall-out after the December 2007 Polokwane Conference, including the removal of Mbeki from office in September 2008, the
moving in of Motlanthe as president for the last seven months of
Mbeki's official term, and the election of Zuma as president. June
2009 ended my journey from Mandela's presidency through Mbeki
and Motlanthe to Zuma's presidency.

It is important to state that I left government by choice rather
than for any other reason. I had given notice two or so years before
Polokwane as I felt I had served for too long in the presidency
and needed a change. This matter is dealt with in detail in a later
chapter, including the way in which I was pressed to stay longer,
notwithstanding my numerous notices to leave the presidency.

As one insightful observer said to me at the end of my time in
government, 'You have seen it all!' Yes, I have. I have seen it all from
the perspective of the secretary of the cabinet, the director-general
in the presidency, the leader of the forum of directors-general, the

secretary of the National Security Council and as an NEC member of the ANC.

The international dimension of my experiences is equally important. I was exposed to policy debates and views about many different groups of issues, including the UN and the UN Security Council; the African Union (AU); the New Partnership for Africa's Development (NEPAD); the African Peer Review Mechanism (APRM); the Africa Partnership Forum; the G8; the Iraq war; control of weapons of mass destruction and related international treaties. I was also involved in conflict resolution and peacemaking in Lesotho, the Democratic Republic of the Congo (DRC), Burundi, Côte d'Ivoire, Zimbabwe and the Middle East. Although our role in peace processes in Palestine and Israel, and in Iraq and Iran (in relation to the nuclear proliferation issues) was peripheral, nonetheless we were drawn in in one way or another to assist.

Given these unique and extraordinary experiences, I felt that I had a responsibility to record them while they were fresh in my mind. My reasons for feeling this responsibility are many.

Firstly, I believe we need to learn to record our history from our own perspectives rather than wait for third parties to do so from their perspectives or from interviews of those who were players during the time. You do not have to be an expert writer to record your history. You should simply offload the information in any language you can master, which is what I have chosen to do.

Secondly, I felt that the people of South Africa and beyond deserved to know from one of the horses' mouths exactly what happened during the time I served in government. It is critical for the nation to hear from someone who was there and who was exposed to a great deal. There is always a question about the objectivity of players who are involved in a particular historical event. Later generations can engage in critical comparative studies or analysis to better understand that history from another vantage point. I simply write about what I know and leave it to others to engage in critical analysis.

Thirdly, it is my considered view that the leadership of South Africa should be given an opportunity to reflect critically on the past since the 1994 democratic elections in order to learn from those experiences, negative or positive. For the sake of posterity we need to learn to avoid mistakes that may have been made. For this reason we have to be brutally honest about our past, however ugly it may be in some instances. The aim here is not to blame one or other person but to present the story as I understand it.

Fourthly, our public service cadres need case studies of our experiences and about specific projects relating to the new democratic government to learn from these experiences and improve their performance in government. The schools of public management and development need this material to be part of their research and training programmes.

Once I left the confines of government I also felt that I needed to share some of the things I could not say while I was in public service in order for me to stay true to my ideals as an advocate for justice.

However, as I have already explained, there are limitations in the extent to which the silence of a public servant can be broken. In my own case, as a result of my high-level positions, the bar of confidentiality and secrecy is high. All this notwithstanding, I decided to navigate through these restrictions to write about my experiences within the limits of the law.

Initially I contracted with the Independent Newspapers group to publish summary articles of various chapters as I was working on them. This was a twofold strategy: to force myself to write, and to reach those who do not buy or read books. The strategy was successful as it forced me to write under enormous pressure in

between my other commitments and the published newspaper articles were widely read and generated conversations about the issues
that are still subjects of discussions today.

The first set of articles, published in July 2010, happened to deal
with the removal of Mbeki as the president of the country. This
attracted an emotional and hostile response from the NEC of the
ANC at the end of July 2010, expressed by ANC secretary-general
Gwede Mantashe at a press conference following a meeting of
the NEC. The fact that I had briefed all the presidents (Mbeki,
Motlanthe and Zuma) as I prepared to write the book seemed not
to matter at that point, and I have no information as to how the
two presidents who were at that meeting intervened (or not) in this
regard.

It is now history that the response of the NEC led to a meeting,
at my request, with top officials of the organisation at its Luthuli
House headquarters to discuss the matter. In the true spirit and culture of the ANC, during the course of this two-hour meeting we
agreed that I had the 'right to write' as well as publish as a member
of the organisation. This was in keeping with the festival of ideas
and freedom of expression the ANC was promoting. The officials
promised to take the matter back to the NEC to settle it there as
well. Unfortunately, no one came back to me in this regard and as
a result I have no idea what the final resolution of the NEC was.
There was also no statement made about our discussions to put the
articles and the books in context or to correct the misperceptions.

What I do know, however, is that although this matter was settled
in an amicable way with the top leadership of the organisation, I
subsequently paid dearly for publishing the articles and *Eight Days
in September*.

As a cadre who is committed to saving the ANC from itself and
to ensuring that what we suffered for and what many died for is
never lost in the stampede of self-interest, I was prepared to take the

pain. I understood now – as I did during the apartheid era – that I could not challenge immoral and unethical behaviour that is antithetical to our NDR, and not pay a price.

We paid the price then (some even unto death) to remove the evil apartheid system, and we have no choice but to pay it again – if needs be – to defend our freedom and the strategic objectives of the NDR. Otherwise, our suffering, sacrifices and the pain we endured during the struggle against the apartheid system would have been in vain. I am prepared to pay the price as all cadres or soldiers who believe in a movement should be prepared to do. The costs are not only political and financial but also extremely personal, particularly because the pain is generated by my own comrades with whom I shared the trenches during the liberation struggle.

What I have found more difficult to deal with is the extension of this pain to my brothers and sisters. My two brothers, Abbey (known as 'Issco' in exile) and Kgotso, who were Umkhonto we Sizwe (MK) cadres of the movement from exile – real 'children' of the ANC – were made targets and blocked in everything they did to try to make a living. From the perspective of these rogue elements of the ANC who were carrying out this reprisal project, the whole of my family had to 'feel the pain' because of what they said I 'had done'.

To the family this felt like an indiscriminate attack, hitting innocent targets purely because they were related to me. The loyalty of the members of my family to the movement and sacrifices they had made during our struggle for liberation did not matter. What mattered was how they 'could get at me' to make me 'feel the pain', as I am told one of them said. I cannot even say that my brothers and sisters were part of collateral damage in a war situation as they were very far from that operational area. My anguish comes from the knowledge that I cannot do much to defend them from these predators who feed on the children of the ANC. Worse still, I cannot do much to mitigate their financial and political losses.

In this regard my pain has been transformed into guilt that the exercise of my freedoms – my right and my commitment to justice – has translated into deprivation for those who are related purely by virtue of their blood relationship with me. Again, this is totally antithetical to the ANC of the past. My brothers and sisters do not deserve this treatment. Only history will tell how much the actions of these rogue elements of the movement have cost me and my immediate family members.

For now the struggle continues (*aluta continua*) and we must constantly defend the gains of our struggle as well as forge ahead to establish a democratic and equitable society. It is for this reason that this book had to be published against the odds.

CHAPTER 3

Into the Presidency
Kicking and Screaming

Before I was roped into public service, I played a public political role – both as part of the leadership of the church (locally,
nationally and internationally) and as part of the political leadership
in the country.

Located within the context of apartheid society, which by design
and law curtailed the freedoms of the black majority, this public political and religious role included a struggle to extend the scope of
freedom of expression and choice. This we achieved after the 1994
democratic elections when a new constitution for the democratic
South Africa was adopted.

But once I was contracted into the public service, first as special
adviser and then as a director-general, my freedom of speech and
expression was curtailed, including the freedom to write what I
would have liked, as Biko would have said.

As explained previously, as director-general in the presidency I
could speak on the policies of government and defend them, but

I could not engage in party political activity in the public arena or express views that might contradict one party or another in public as this would be a breach of my role as a public servant. The Public Service Act rightly regulates the conduct of public servants to ensure that public servants serve the public irrespective of their political parties, views and perspectives.

At the height of the struggle for liberation characterised by extreme forms of repression, the concept of 'sites of struggle' was developed. As political organisations were banned or restricted every activist was expected to be part of one 'site of struggle' or another, mainly in the area of their work and profession (lawyers, nurses, medical doctors, teachers, priests, etc.), and at levels of communities and sectors (community organisations, religious communities, youth, women, etc.) where they found themselves.

Being part of the religious 'site of struggle' involved studying religious forms of struggle throughout history, including theologies of liberation, such as African theology, black theology, political theology, liberation theology, feminist theology, *menjung* theology and so forth. In this way, and given the fact that South Africa is predominantly a religious country, we were able to mobilise religious communities to engage in revolutionary activities to change oppressive and exploitative religious concepts and ideologies as well as regimes of such a nature. Part of the fuel for this movement was apartheid's use of religion to justify its ideology of racism and apartheid.

Besides direct political engagements, such as being part of the leadership of the Soweto Civil Association and the United Democratic Front (UDF), including underground work and being in the trenches with the people, I was involved in student and youth ministries and in the local congregation of my church in Kagiso, Krugersdorp (now Mogale City), at an ecumenical and interfaith level. At the height of the liberation struggle and crisis in the country I engaged in the issues from the beachheads of the Institute of

Contextual Theology and the South African Council of Churches (SACC).

This kind of activity partly explains why Khotso House, the six-floor headquarters of the SACC in De Villiers Street, Johannesburg, was destroyed in 1988 by one of the largest bombs the apartheid regime ever used internally. My poisoning with chemical and biological warfare substances in the same year, an experience that nearly killed me, can also be attributed to the way in which the regime saw the church and religious communities as key centres of resistance to apartheid.

It is for this reason that when I was recruited to serve in government after the 1994 democratic elections some of the activists who worked with me felt that it was a mistake to join the public service as this would neutralise what they saw as a 'prophetic voice' or 'prophetic witness' against injustice, both nationally and internationally. They felt that being in the public service, particularly in the presidency, was like being in the 'belly of the beast', fighting battles within the confines of a system that had the potential to throttle you or oppress and exploit those at the bottom.

Some even believed that my deployment was meant to silence me and keep me away from overt political terrain. At the time of the political settlement in South Africa from 1993 to 1994 there was an unusual but natural political jostling for positions in the new unity government. In this regard, being appointed as a commissioner for the Independent Electoral Commission (IEC) – a permanent body set up by the constitution to ensure free and fair elections – and later as a public servant was seen by some as a deliberate way to sideline me from active politics. Thus the leadership of the Gauteng province of the ANC visited me in January 1994 to discuss my inclusion in the election 'list'. They believed that I should be part of the leadership of the new democratic government, not an IEC commissioner.

Having come to know both Nelson Mandela and Thabo Mbeki well, I am confident that this is far from the truth. Indeed, while there might have been some who welcomed my deployment as helpful in removing me from the contested political leadership terrain, I do not believe that the leaders who appointed me and with whom I worked formed a part of this thinking. In fact, years later when I was nominated as provincial chairperson of the ANC in Gauteng, Mbeki expressed surprise that I had accepted the nomination because he believed that I was fulfilling a much more important and strategic role in the presidency.

Approach by Mandela and Mbeki

The sequence of events leading to me serving as a public servant is as follows.

Sometime in September or October 1995 I was requested to join the presidency to assist with building capacity in the deputy president's office as President Mandela had decided to delegate more responsibilities to the office of Deputy President Mbeki.

I initially resisted the approach precisely because I felt it would limit my freedom to do what I did best. My resistance led to an urgent special meeting with then Deputy President Mbeki one afternoon at his official residence (then at GoedeHoop, Bryntirion Estate, the presidential estate in the capital city of Tshwane).

As I have now learnt over many years, unless it is in written form, Mbeki does not have many words on a matter such as this. He simply wanted to know why I was resisting the request by the leadership.

The call for me to meet the deputy president came on an awkward day. I was due to fly that evening from Cape Town, where I was stationed as senior research officer at the University of Cape Town, to the United States of America to speak at a conference the following day. Instead, I had to travel from Cape Town to Pretoria and back again (a six-hour round trip, including flights out of and into Cape Town and travel time to and from the airports), for a difficult 30-minute discussion, and then still board my flight from Cape Town that night for the US.

The reality, of course, is that if the presidency called, I could not say no. I had to explain within 30 minutes why I did not think it would be the correct thing for me to join the public service. I was of the strong view that I was not cut out to be a public servant but was rather a public advocate for justice and peace; that my role was to promote the common good of all the people of South Africa. There was also my position as a pastor and a church leader that would be affected. Some had said I would be abandoning my ministry if I focused on government.

In reply, Mbeki argued that we had just won the struggle for liberation and what was needed now was capacity to achieve the very objectives we had struggled for and for which many had sacrificed their lives. He emphasised the challenges involved in transforming our society from a racist apartheid society to one that was non-racial, non-sexist and democratic.

In truth, I was one of the few ANC people who had had the opportunity to manage large, formal institutions and the government (and the people) needed my experience. Besides my leadership role in the church at both regional and national levels, I had over many years managed the Institute for Contextual Theology and the SACC. At the height of its ministry, characterised by conflict and extreme forms of violence, assassinations and the imprisonment of those opposed to the apartheid regime, the SACC had 26 regional offices across the country and employed more than 300 staff. It took care of political prisoners, detainees and their dependants, the

33

families of those in exile, the legal costs for those who fell foul of apartheid laws, displaced young people and children and so on.

Given the scope of the work of the SACC, then apartheid Prime Minister P.W. Botha had accused the SACC of acting like it was an 'alternative government' at a time when the masses of our people had embarked on programmes to make the country ungovernable as part of the liberation struggle. The reality was that people had no government to turn to as the de facto government had turned against the people. With all organisations banned or restricted, the SACC was the only organisation that could speak on behalf of the people or take care of their needs.

An intense working lunch with Mandela

As I was discussing this matter with Mbeki, my mind returned to a conversation I had with President Mandela more than a year previously in July or August 1994. Having heard that I was resisting joining government or the public service, Mandela invited me and my dear wife, Kagiso, for lunch at the presidential guest house in Bryntirion.

I had been asked to accept deployment as a South African envoy in Sahrawi, the disputed territory with Morocco, to assist with the resolution of the conflict there. Sahrawi is the Sahrawi Arab Democratic Republic. Another suggestion made was for me to become South Africa's ambassador to Japan.

My wife had good reasons to decline the lunch invitation. She felt I needed to face Mandela alone on the matter and did not want to be used as part of the pressure group wanting me to join government, and especially in a posting outside national borders.

Mary Mxadana, who was personal assistant to President Mandela and one of the senior executive directors at the SACC when I was the general secretary, made arrangements for the lunch. The one-hour meeting with the president went on for 45 minutes before the real subject of the meeting was broached. As the minutes ticked by, I had wondered whether or not the subject would be raised at all. When Mandela was distracted for a moment I signalled to Mary and asked whether or not we were still going to discuss the matter. She advised me simply to wait.

And indeed, during the last fifteen minutes of the luncheon Mandela very directly and in few words put the request to me to join government. I rushed for my carefully prepared response. I told Mandela that being a pastor and a church leader was my main challenge. My concern – based on positions held by my church – was that taking this offer would mean I was abandoning my calling, God's calling, for me to be a pastor, a minister and a servant of the people. This would look like I was turning my back on God's calling. At worst, it could be seen as defiance of God! And, even if I did take on a public service role, I would have to reinvent – suppress – my views, opinions and feelings.

I will never forget Mandela's words. He said that the problem with 'you' [church leaders] is that 'you do not want to soil your hands'. 'You want to stand out there [as spectators or monitors] and wait until we [the political leaders] make mistakes and then condemn us,' he said.

He argued that church leaders had stood together with the liberation movement in the struggle, and he could not understand why we could not now be involved in the more positive task of reconstruction, restoration and the development of the country.

For me (and the church) the challenge was that of party political activity, which would not be advisable for a pastor committed to non-party political service to the people. For Mandela the reconstruction and development of the country was not a party political activity. For him the ANC was not about party political activity; it was a movement for the liberation of all South Africans, blacks and whites.

For Mandela's generation, the ANC was and remained 'the Parliament of the People' as it historically represented the majority of South Africans who were excluded from government. Accordingly, the ANC was not seen as a party in the classical sense of the word as would be the case in a normal democracy. Even after the democratic elections of 1994, the ANC remained and continued to be seen as the representative of the majority of the people, especially those who were historically disadvantaged. Based on this understanding, collaborating with such a government could not be considered by the masses of our people as a 'party political activity'.

Mandela argued further that the new democratic government needed the experience and skills of the clergy and the leadership of the church. As a product of missionary schools himself, he had a great respect for the church and expected more from it in terms of the reconstruction and development of the country. He was also aware of the role the church had played in opposing the apartheid system and the support it gave to victims of this system.

His logic and his argument presented a big challenge for me. I was reminded of his skill as a lawyer as he was systematically able to destroy every defence I had offered thus far for resisting a position in government.

I suggested to Mandela that although the electoral law had been amended, I was not comfortable accepting an appointment so soon after putting the government in place as part of the IEC. The initial electoral law barred those who were commissioners from participating in the government whose election they had presided over. It also prohibited commissioners from being employed as civil servants for at least eighteen months after the elections. The amendments made to the electoral law immediately after the elections

36

to allow members of the IEC to be appointed into government positions were in reality meant mainly for the lawyers that the government wanted to appoint as judges, such as Zac Yacoob, Dikgang Moseneke and others.

In my opinion, the appointment of an individual as a judge was not a problem as it was like a continuation of the independent and objective role of electoral commissioners – as opposed to being appointed into a government position.

For the sake of my own integrity and to avoid misunderstandings, I chose rather to maintain the eighteen-month moratorium for public servants and five-year moratorium for political appointments.

Mandela was sympathetic to the integrity concerns of my case but thought that this could be explained to the people.

In truth, though, at the time of this discussion with Mandela, I was not excited about a possible posting outside South Africa as an ambassador or something similar. I believed I had to be involved in the reconstruction and development of the country inside, albeit from outside government. It would be like being sent into exile. Besides, Kagiso could not imagine abandoning her professional life and occupation as a teacher and following me to a posting outside the country.

During this short discussion I also informed Mandela that I had already started a process of securing a six-month fellowship to the Kennedy School of Government at Harvard University in the US. Harvard was prepared to bend the rules in terms of the time required for such applications and accepted me as a deserving case. At Kennedy I would be exposed to an institution that dealt with the art of governance and would help me gain effective tools to use on my return.

A third part of my submission to Mandela was that I would have to consult my congregation of the Apostolic Faith Mission in

Naledi, Soweto, and the leadership of the church. As a consultative person, who strongly believes in working as a collective in terms of policy issues, Mandela understood this need.

I left the luncheon with Mandela a troubled man. The nature of our discussion robbed me of the pleasure of an exclusive lunch with the man, an experience many would have cherished. I have a vague recollection of how appetising the three-course meal was but the final fifteen minutes disturbed my digestive system.

The ANC leadership ultimately and grudgingly accepted my plea to be allowed at least one year's grace before I would consider joining the public service. So, in September I left for Harvard University and the Kennedy School of Government. I turned the initial six-month fellowship into ten months of mid-career masters' studies in public administration. As the funding provided was not sufficient, I used part of my pension funds to cover my costs. Arrangements were also made for my family to join me for part of the time. Archbishop Desmond Tutu, who knew about my financial challenges, requested the World Council of Churches to find a way of covering part of the costs, which they graciously did. This also heralded the end of my contract with the SACC, which I had served for slightly more than seven years.

The ten months I spent at Harvard was an extraordinary period that gave me a break after a long and torturous struggle against the apartheid regime. Besides learning about the executive management of government, I had the opportunity to reflect on the challenges of reconstruction and development the country was facing and strategies to achieve this.

Having had this unique experience, I wish that all South African activists and leaders could have had the same opportunity immediately after the elections as it would have given all of us a chance to reflect on our new tasks – most of which were new to us. If only we could have hit a 'shut-down' button for the country for one year to give everybody the space to learn before assuming the responsibilities of governing the country. Unfortunately, reality does not allow for such indulgences.

A compromise position with Mbeki

My discussion with Mbeki happened about eighteen months after the 1994 elections and should thus be understood in relation to my earlier conversation with Mandela. The compromise position that I settled on with Mbeki was that I would come as a special adviser rather than a public servant, which left me some room to operate at a political level rather than only as a public servant. The limitations were still there, though, as I could only operate as an adviser and not as an actor beyond the principal I was advising.

For me to take on this challenge a special resolution had to be adopted by my church to second me to government while allowing me to keep my licence as an ordained pastor. This had never happened before in my church. I recall one member of the national executive council of the church urging the council to accept this even if they did not understand it because they did not know what God's intentions and plans were.

As a result, I was able to keep my pastoral credentials and continue with my pastoral work at my church in Naledi while still in government. My ministry to the Naledi Assembly of the Apostolic Faith Mission was a voluntary activity and I was not remunerated for it. In fact, my church as the licensing authority has not paid me for the ministry I have been involved in since August 1976. The first and last stipend I received from the church was paid at the end of July 1976 as the white section of the church, which sponsored the black section, threatened to withdraw its financial support if I was one of the pastors it had to support. In their eyes, I was politically and actively involved in opposing the apartheid system, and that was unacceptable to them.

Thus I served the church from then on without a stipend until March 2010 when the local congregation engaged me on a part-time basis. Like Paul who made tents in order to be able to continue with the mission he was called to undertake, I also worked to take care of my family and support the ministry. This is known as 'tent ministry', taking its name from the way in which Paul undertook his mission and ministry, covering the length and breadth of the world of his time.

The reluctant public servant

The developments after my agreeing to serve as a special adviser show that my engagement as an adviser was simply a way of sucking me in to the public service, as I was made director-general a year later. I accepted, thinking that I would be released in 1999 when the general elections would be held. But this was not to be.

In 1999 I was asked to develop and manage the integration of the offices of the president and the deputy president into one. At the end of my five-year contract the subject of my departure, although raised, was not long entertained. Instead, I was told about the strategic role I was playing in the presidency and in government as a whole, and why the nation needed my services.

About six months before the 2004 general elections, President Mbeki sent a letter to all directors-general. He asked them to share their aspirations, career goals and personal development needs for the next five years to enable the government to 'accommodate the needs of the country' and those of the individual directors-general 'in an optimal manner'. As he had asked for 'an honest reflection' on this matter I thought that it would give me an opportunity to re-emphasise my point of contention in this regard. Here are extracts of my response:

> Mr. President, you will recall that we started a discussion on this matter in May this year, and I indicated that I thought I had served my part in the public service at the time when I was needed to do so, especially because of the transformation project and the need for effective management systems for the presidency. You would also be aware that I invested much of the time since 1998 to work on the integrated system of governance and the executive management of government from the centre, all of which are now reaching maturity.
>
> From the initial discussions we had in October 1995, before I came into government, the president would remember that I never considered being 'a professional public servant' as a career path for me. I did it because the leadership determined that it was necessary at the time. I took it as a 'special deployment' for a 'special task' at a 'particular moment' and not as a form of employment in pursuit of a particular career path. As a disciplined cadre of the movement, I would do it again if the leadership determined that this was the best way I could offer service to the people at a particular time in the history and development of our country.
>
> For now, I am of the view that I have served my part. Staying longer as director-general may just turn this into 'a job' rather than a special task to achieve specific strategic objectives. I also do not believe that holding a chief executive position in an organisation for too long is healthy. This is the longest period I have served as head of an organisation throughout my life. You

would also know that I am of the view that a public service role limits one's extent of engagement at the level of ideas. It stifles political engagement in the continuing struggle for a just, non-racial, non-sexist democratic society. In this regard, one could in a sense say that one's political and public life 'died' with one's deployment as a director-general or a public servant.

Based on the above, I am of the view that a change of roles might assist in allowing me more space for further growth and development in a way that could enable me to serve the nation even better. The possible roles one could play could be a subject of discussion with the leadership once a decision was made that it was time for change.

Accordingly, I would still wish to continue with the discussions we started in May of this year if the President thought it might be helpful.

Once more, thank you very much for opening a door for an 'honest reflection' on this matter to assist in determining the best ways of deploying cadres of the movement.

Again, I was not successful in persuading the president. As the decision was not made 'that it was time for change', the possible roles I could play beyond the public service were not discussed.

In desperation at my failure to have secured my release, I appealed individually to both the secretary-general of the ANC at the time, Kgalema Motlanthe, and to the deputy president of the ANC and the country, Jacob Zuma, to assist me. After more than three months without any response I returned to them and raised the matter again. Both of them told me that they had also failed, as the president was not ready to release me.

The matter was raised again in 2005, but the removal of Deputy President Zuma from the position of deputy president in government made this proposition even more difficult. My leaving would have been interpreted in a manner that would have been false and unhelpful. This took me to October 2007 when my contract was due for renewal for the third time. At this stage I advised that I would not be open to another renewal as I would have been director-general for eleven years – the longest serving director-general of the time – and twelve years if my service as a special adviser was included.

The costs of long service at the highest level

It is at this stage that I tried to make the president understand that being director-general in the presidency for too long was a costly business, not only in terms of the pressures and impact on my personal and family life, but also in financial terms.

At a personal level, I lost both my private life and my privacy. We worked long hours, especially given the fact that Mbeki became more active and productive later in the day and into the night and early hours of the following morning. I missed my family in the same way as I had during the struggle. In fact, the experience felt like playing a stuck record.

At one stage, Kagiso protested about my family missing me as a husband and a father. She said that she could understand having to be alone most of the time at the height of the struggle, including bringing up children single-handedly, but she did not bargain for the same experience in a free and democratic country. As they grew up my children also expressed concerns. At one point one of my sons told me he saw more of me on TV than at home.

As director-general in the presidency I became fair game, an object of pursuit and attack, hunted as if it were a sport. I was called names, such as 'a portly preacher', 'a liar' and so forth, even when

43

there was no lie at all. All the cases in terms of my evidence at the Ginwala Inquiry and the issue of the letter from the Movement for Democratic Change (MDC) that never reached the presidency are dealt with in Chapter 5. There is still an outstanding case with the *Sunday Times* on this matter in which I allege that its description of me and its conclusions were malicious, wrongful, derogatory and defamatory, and impacted negatively on my integrity based on a false logic.

What was even more painful was that in most instances the 'right of reply' was taken away in the name of preserving the integrity of the presidency or in the interests of keeping the presidency 'above these things'. We had to focus on the task ahead and not be distracted by the media or attacks from all sorts of quarters, however unfair and false they might have been.

The remuneration system and structure for directors-general in government also had a limiting effect. It is generally fixed except for annual increments that apply for all public servants. As a result, young public servants who were deputy directors and directors when I was roped in became directors-general over the years and earned either exactly my salary or even more. It has been my experience that at the pinnacle of the public service no one really pays attention to your remuneration. The president has no time to think about salaries. In fact, he should not be involved and the system should have been designed to take care of this but it was not. In this sense it was costly for me to be in the presidency. Interestingly, one performance review after another over the years made recommendations for the salary to be adjusted to match the level of responsibilities of the director-general in the presidency. But all this ended in the files of the presidency.

Whatever the challenges, I continued executing my responsibilities to the best of my abilities. As a director-general, besides heading the presidency, I was responsible for:

1. Assisting the president with the executive management of the rest of government;
2. Serving on and chairing the Forum of National and Provincial Directors-General, which was responsible for strategic planning for government, implementation strategies, monitoring and evaluation of government performance;
3. Managing the National Security Council;
4. Dealing with cabinet business; and
5. The declaration of interests by the president, cabinet members and the public service commissioners.

There was also the necessary regulatory framework to check on the business interests of public servants to avoid abuse of the system as well as conflicts of interest. Serving at the top, I walked the extra mile to avoid anything that might raise any questions or controversy relating to myself or the presidency.

A more compelling reason for me not agreeing to the renewal of my contract was the length of time I had already served in the same position. However, an appeal was made that I stay for another year to give the presidency an opportunity to find a replacement. This was October 2007 and we agreed to enter into a one-year contract, ending October 2008. Incidentally, some media representatives and members of the public in South Africa and elsewhere tend to forget this arrangement, even though it was made public. Instead, they put forward their own interpretations to suggest that I ended my contract in October 2008 because of the ANC conference held in Polokwane in December 2007 or because of the removal of President Mbeki from office. This is far from the truth.

At the end of that year, that is, in October 2008, another appeal was made for me to assist government with the management of transitional processes as elections were due in about six months. To me the situation had become like *pale e tswellang* (a story that has no end). I insisted on a new short-term contract to manage the transition rather than an extension of the normal director-general's contract. This was reluctantly accepted by President Mbeki although it had to be done in a way that would enable the office to phase out my responsibilities as director-general over that period. After the removal of President Mbeki from office, his successor, President Motlanthe, also held the same position in this regard.

The point I want to make is that I had been in a space I had not intended to be in for thirteen-and-a-half years. Having found myself there, I served the nation to the best of my abilities, notwithstanding the costs of doing so at that level. Again, history will tell this story.

PART TWO

CHAPTER 4

Farewell to Innocence

All of us come into the world in a state of innocence. We are open, trusting and unacquainted with evil. Such innocence is a necessary part of our early development. But we grow up and the age of innocence inevitably and painfully comes to an end.

Only the naive retain their innocence and remain unsuspecting in a world of deceit, disinformation and covert intelligence operations that are integral to oppressive regimes and superpowers who have interests in extending their sphere of control and influence. Their strategic objective is to advance self-interests or national interests at all costs, even if it means feeding on their own. In oppressive systems the beneficiaries of such systems retain a form of childlike innocence either because they do not want to know, or they believe in everything that the regime is saying and doing for them. At worst they know but close their eyes to it because of embedded self-interests.

The reaction to my poisoning with chemical and biological

weapons by the apartheid system in the heat of the conflict in the 1980s is a perfect example of this type of innocence. Most whites in South Africa could simply not believe that a so-called Christian government would do such a thing. Even learned leaders within my own church could not believe it and thought of us, the victims, as liars.

It was only after confessions from the scientists who produced the chemicals, and from then Minister of Police, Adriaan Vlok, the three policemen who carried out the operation, and their commander, General Johannes van der Merwe (now retired commissioner of police), that people began to realise how evil the apartheid system was. It is now part of court records that Vlok, Van der Merwe and the three policemen entered into a plea bargain that secured them suspended sentences.

American businessman Bo Bennett says, 'Those who improve with age ... begin to replace youth with wisdom, innocence with understanding.' Some of us in South Africa were prematurely forced to replace our youthfulness with wisdom, and innocence with understanding. We understood that while the regime was running its propaganda campaign against communism, displaying posters and leaflets showing communists torturing Christians, people hanged head down and so forth, the so-called South African Christian government was doing exactly the same against us.

The brutality of the apartheid system and the struggle against it robbed many black children of their childhood and innocence as they were forced to fight the system at an early age.

By the time I arrived in government, I already had a fair idea of what governments were capable of based on my experiences during the struggle for liberation. As part of my master's degree studies at Harvard University I took a course titled 'Pursuit of national interest'. The course used declassified documents, letters, memoranda and so on to show the lengths to which the US and its allies would go to defend their interests. The case of the 1956 Suez Canal crisis was used to expose us to this world. All these experiences deepened my perspectives not to accept things at face value.

Here are a few examples of my experiences that confirmed that one had to bid a final farewell to innocence in order to deal with some of the complexities of governance, both nationally and internationally.

The walls have ears!

President Thabo Mvuyelwa Mbeki was a natural successor to President Nelson Rolihlahla Mandela as president of South Africa and preparations for his takeover started about six months before the June 1999 national elections. As the director-general in Mbeki's office and the deputy secretary of cabinet, it fell to me to take responsibility for the design of the post-Mandela presidency, the management of the transition from Mandela to Mbeki and the handover preparations.

The transition from Mandela to Mbeki was a delicate affair owing to Mandela's formidable reputation. I worked together on the project with the director-general in the president's office, Professor Jakes Gerwel; Mbeki's special advisers, Advocate Mojanku Gumbi (legal), Vusi Mavimbela (political) and Moss Ngoasheng (economics); and the deputy minister in Mbeki's office, Essop Pahad. At the time both Pahad and I were members of the NEC of the ANC, which made coordination between the ruling party and the government much easier.

South Africans' expectations of Mbeki's succession varied along racial lines. For blacks the expectation was that Mbeki would take the country beyond a focus on reconciliation between whites and blacks, political stability and nation-building, and into the terrain of real transformation. This included changes to the economic system to address entrenched historical injustices and inequalities. The project of transforming the society had started during Mandela's presidency but the time had come for the country to pay special attention to the economy and structural inequalities.

Whites were more concerned about possible threats to their security and material interests, particularly the wealth and privileges accumulated during apartheid. In Mandela's emphasis on nation-building and reconciliation, they felt safe. In his warmth and charm, they collectively glowed. However, to attribute the programme of peacemaking, reconciliation and nation-building to Mandela alone was, of course, a distortion of reality. Mandela himself repeatedly stated that he was pursuing the collective decisions of the ANC rather than a personal agenda. But this was not fully understood; hence, the panic at Mandela's departure.

The international community, especially the West, had similar concerns. 'What will happen after Mandela?' was the mantra. They were worried that Mandela's successor could upset the apple cart in terms of their economic and political interests in the country. One of the unexpressed fears was the fate of whites should the new incumbent make radical changes.

Given all these concerns, succeeding Mandela the icon was a real challenge. And Mbeki would somehow need to raise the bar.

There was a second challenge – to make the handover from outgoing to incoming president as smooth as possible without any disruption to the transformation agenda. It was like an athletics relay race in which the techniques in the 'changeover zone' were critical to ensure that there was no loss of time and speed. Mbeki had to achieve maximum acceleration at 'baton exchange point'. Fortunately, the changeover zone for Mbeki was fairly protracted as Mandela had chosen to hand over responsibilities for government to Mbeki much earlier in the race and Mbeki was already running side-by-side with Mandela by the time they reached baton exchange.

As the preparatory team we considered the first moves Mbeki would make to signal that he was dead serious about leading a government committed, firstly, to improving the quality of lives of the people of South Africa, especially the poor, and secondly, to radically change the world's perceptions about Africa and Africans. The 'two-legs' strategy was based on our understanding that South Africa's freedom and prosperity was meaningless without the freedom and prosperity of all Africans. In our generally racist world, all Africans were considered to be the same and were treated with disdain, irrespective of where they came from on the continent or in the Diaspora.

On the home front the metaphors adopted insisted that Mbeki must 'hit the ground running' and accelerate the changes required socially, economically and politically to improve the lives of the poor. Systems, structures and institutions had to be transformed or put in place to translate the policies of the ruling party into reality within as short a period as possible. We had to stretch the bounds of possibilities to the limit, mindful of what we called the 'balance of forces' at the time. This involved an analysis of the balance of forces between those who were committed to changing the system radically and those who wanted to keep the status quo. We had to delicately chip away at the power base of apartheid without causing instability. But this was precisely what was threatening to whites in the country and some sections of the international community.

On the international front the challenge was to change Africa's unequal relations with the world, counter the culture of dependence, and enable the continent to exercise its sovereignty and take its destiny into its own hands. This is where the African Renaissance vision came in. The ANC had already deliberated on this vision as part of its preparations to take over government after the elections in 1994 and details thereof were contained in the 1993 documents of the ANC in relation to its foreign policy perspectives.

Nelson Mandela had already fired the first salvo for this vision at his first Organisation for African Unity (OAU) Summit as president of a democratic South Africa, in Tunisia in June 1994. This speech and its significance were unfortunately missed by many both inside and outside the country because of the euphoria around what was considered South Africa's miraculous political settlement. In my research on the concept of an African Renaissance, and having gone through Mandela's speech in Tunis, I think the excitement being experienced in South Africa and beyond robbed Mandela of the credit he deserved for his contribution to the vision of African renewal. His message was that the new South Africa had come to Tunis not to ask for help as it had during the days of the liberation struggle, but this time to contribute to the rebuilding or Renaissance of the African continent.

Mbeki's powerful 'I am an African' speech, delivered in parliament in May 1996 while he was deputy president, received more prominence and laid the groundwork for the development and implementation of the ruling party's vision for an African Renaissance. Although the concept was part of the ANC's broader foreign relations policy, Mbeki's name became associated with the concept, leading to him being known as 'the African Renaissance man' – at home and abroad.

In our plans to signal the direction of the country's foreign policy, we strategised that Mbeki's first state visit would be to one or more African countries. It was felt that he could not lead the vision for an African Renaissance any other way.

To this end our preparatory team considered Zambia (which had hosted the ANC in exile), Mualimi Nyerere's Tanzania (the home of the first set of leaders who went into exile and the base for strategic thinking about defeating apartheid), Angola (which hosted Umkhonto we Sizwe, the armed wing of the ANC), Algeria (the rearguard support materially and ideologically for the liberation movement), Nigeria (with the largest African population and leadership role on the African continent), Egypt (because of its historical significance and influence on the continent), Kwame Nkrumah's Ghana (the first African country to become independent) and so forth.

Europe and the US were deliberately put on the back burner. Our view was that the African Renaissance required that Africa reassert its sovereignty and its capacity to make its own decisions about its future without the dictates of superpowers. African countries had to stop being 'client states' or 'proxy' governments that governed in the interests of powerful countries and interest groups and not in the interests of the people of Africa or their countries.

As the team was deliberating on these issues and working on an international programme an invitation to the president arrived from the US for an official visit at the beginning of August 1999. The invitation came immediately after the inauguration of Mbeki on 16 June 1999, giving very little notice.

Enormous efforts were made from the beginning in 1994 to normalise the relationship between the newly democratic South Africa and the US, given the negative relationship between the US and the ANC during the liberation struggle. An extraordinary Bi-National Commission at the level of the deputy president (Mbeki) and the vice-president (Gore) had been set up to address this during the Mandela and Clinton presidencies. The commission met twice a year – once in South Africa and the other in the US – and it involved all the ministers and ministries that were relevant to the issues under discussion. It also brought together business people and state institutions to explore possibilities for cooperation and collaboration.

Our thinking behind the sequencing of state visits thus had nothing to do with the nature of this relationship. It was about adhering to a foreign relations strategy that looked at all relations in the light of a commitment to renew the African continent and place it in the international arena as an equal player.

I imagine that for the US the invitation to Mbeki so soon after his inauguration was of a strategic nature in terms of its perspective of the geopolitics of the world in relation to its interests. Both President Clinton and Vice-President Gore knew Mbeki well and did not need a meeting to acquaint themselves. Given the positive relationship between the men one could speculate that Clinton wanted to show support for Mbeki as the new president. He would have wanted to determine the ways and means in which they might strengthen and deepen that relationship for the mutual benefit of both countries and for Africa in general.

What was uppermost in the minds of our team members, however, were the global strategic considerations in relation to Africa and the African Renaissance vision. We understood that we still needed the support of the US and other political and economic powers to achieve our continental strategic objectives. We recognised that a positive relationship with the US was also important for our African Renaissance. Accordingly, a visit of this nature would have been beneficial. However, the overwhelming view of the team was that it would be strategically smarter to start in Africa if we were going to mobilise Africa around an African vision.

Before we could consult with the principals (Mbeki and cabinet) and before we could formulate our response that was going to be in the form of a proposal to postpone, not decline, the visit to the US, we received reports that some organs of the US had got wind of our strategic thinking and were unhappy about it. They expressed particular unhappiness with me as the person they considered 'responsible' for the 'decision'.

Needless to say we were shocked that they had information about our confidential discussions and knew about the proposal to delay the visit even before it had reached our principals. What was more shocking for me, however, was their singling out of me as the person they believed was responsible for it.

Of course, as leader of the strategic team, I take responsibility for whatever we had discussed. But what remained a mystery was how this detailed information reached Washington within such a short space of time. Beyond the mystery, though, was a concern around the real potential for damaged relationships that such premature 'leaks' might provoke.

The next sets of questions were: 'Do we change our position because of what we have heard from the wind?' 'Do we stick to our strategic considerations?' For me it was not difficult to answer these questions. I was in favour of adhering to our strategic and tactical positions as this was about the future of Africa and its identity, rather than things of 'the wind' or *dintho tsa dikhukuni* or *tsa mafifi* (the things of the spies or of the dark). I was convinced that whoever in the US was 'unhappy' would still respect us if we stuck to our principled positions. At the back of my mind was also the suspicion that the information might have been fed into our system precisely to influence our views and perspectives. Singling me out could also have been meant to instil fear, resulting in a panicked response.

After all the backstage drama we emerged from behind the curtain and onto the public stage with the decision, now supported by the principals, that we would accept the US invitation in principle but negotiate for a later, more mutually convenient date, which would give Mbeki a chance to settle into office and look strategically at his international programme.

This event may not seem to be of major importance in the scale of things but it came as a wake-up call to me, reminding me that I was not operating as a free agent concerned with advancing the strategic interests and objectives of the country and the continent. Relationships between countries could be easily jeopardised in the struggle over national interests. It was also clear that one's ability to speak freely would be forever compromised by breaches in confidentiality. In the old days of the struggle, we used to be guided by the principle that the 'walls had ears'. Now, when we were trying to legitimately forge a new democracy, it seemed that the walls were still eavesdropping. This was the beginning of my final farewell bid to innocence within government.

The Iraqi case: Turning innocent citizens into 'collateral damage' for material gain

Any remnants of innocence were lost during the time when we had to deal with the matter of the war against Iraq. The pretext for attacking Iraq was that it had weapons of mass destruction (WMD), particularly chemical and biological weapons, which threatened international peace and security. There was also the claim that Iraq would use these weapons against its own citizens. Heavy propaganda that was known by its proponents to be false was unleashed to ensure that everybody accepted that Iraq qualified as a target for attack. Some media repeatedly showed old pictures of dead people, allegedly killed with chemical and biological weapons by Saddam Hussein.

From our struggle against the apartheid system, however, we learnt not to be so gullible. We used what we called the 'tools of suspicion' to unpack the propaganda and see the story for what it was: a case of major powers with logs in their eyes. It was not as if I was deluded about the potential of states to poison their own people. My own poisoning – related in an earlier book entitled *No Life of My Own: An Autobiography* – was an official attempt by the apartheid regime and decided at the level of the State Security Council to get rid of certain activists in an extra-judicial manner. The State Security Council was normally chaired by the state president (who was then P.W. Botha), and the Ministers of Defence, Police and Justice were members.

Three security branch police were commissioned to deal with me. They ordered the chemicals from top-secret laboratories operating under the auspices of the surgeon general of the South African Defence Force, General D.P. Knobel, applied it to my clothes when I checked in at the then Jan Smuts International Airport (now O.R. Tambo International) with an intention to kill me. The details are now history. The good news is that because of God's providence and my profile at the time, I survived. For this I remain eternally grateful to God. But many others must have died because of these biological and chemical weapons of the apartheid regime and we know that a number of key Western powers assisted apartheid South Africa to acquire such capability and capacity.

In this regard I understand the pain that goes with the use of chemical and biological weapons and what these chemicals can do to people. The use of history and allegations that Iraq used chemical and biological weapons against its people was bound to be an emotive thing that would turn ordinary people around the world against Iraq's leadership.

The tragedy though is that it is now clear to any student of history that the attack on Iraq had nothing to do with WMD, particularly chemical and biological weapons, or a threat to international peace and security, or to the security of the people of Iraq. The interests here were simply political and economic. To be more specific, it was to punish Saddam Hussein, and it was about oil interests. That is why this action could not be authorised or legitimised via the UN. It was a unilateral action with the help of a 'coalition of the willing' as it was called.

Iraq and its neighbouring countries appealed to South Africa to help dissuade the US and Britain from attacking the country and destabilising the region. Its neighbours indicated that they did not believe that Iraq had the chemical and biological weapons and Iraq made the same case. Neighbouring Arab countries felt they could not raise these matters with the US and the United Kingdom (UK) as they felt vulnerable. In our discussions with some of them it was clear that they were telling the US and the UK what those countries wanted to hear, or what was expected from them, rather than the reality on the ground.

Interestingly at that moment in history South Africa had a better grasp of the real feelings in the region given the openness of Iraq and its neighbours to South Africa. In a way, some social scientists would say that South Africa had an epistemological privilege, that is, the advantage of understanding the situation better than interested parties or those who had the option to use power to force opponents to comply.

Given this situation our Arab brothers and sisters believed that South Africa, with its high moral standing and its record of independent thinking on foreign policy, was well placed to raise the matter with the powers that be. As a good and 'innocent' citizen of the world our country responded positively to those appeals and committed itself to raise the issues with the relevant countries, although it was a risky thing to do at the time.

A special operation was undertaken to reach out to the US and the UK as a matter of urgency. However, both the US and the UK insisted that Iraq had WMD and was a threat to international peace and security. Again, as an 'innocent' and dutiful citizen of the world, South Africa looked for other ways to address the matter. Ultimately, an extraordinary decision was made to recall some of the experts who had participated in the top-secret apartheid chemical and biological weapons programme (Project Coast) and constitute them in a high-level technical team with capacity to assess and determine whether or not Iraq still possessed chemical and biological weapons. Iraq agreed to receive our team and to allow it unlimited access to all facilities and storage areas. The inspection was conducted with the knowledge of the US, the UK and the UN.

The irony of the situation was not lost on us. The South African team was made up of people who participated in the top-secret chemical and biological programme that produced chemicals and biological weapons for use against the opponents of the apartheid system, including myself. But we had to do our national duty as well as discharge our international responsibilities. We had to try to save lives if we could and this meant working with people who in the past were our enemies or perceived to be enemies.

The team returned after extensive investigations and reported that there were no chemical and biological weapons in Iraq. The report was communicated to the three interested parties – the US, the UK and the UN. Again we acted as honest and innocent citizens of the world – what some might call 'do-gooders'. We believed that if they received information that was accurate and reliable they would reconsider their plans. At best we thought they would take our information and verify it independently.

The president took a further step and sent delegations to the US and the UK to discuss these matters directly with the countries' respective leaders and to persuade them that an attack on Iraq would not guarantee peace or security for either the people of Iraq or the international community. One delegation went to the US and I accompanied the president to the UK. We spent about four hours or so at Chequers, the prime minister's official country residence. The president had a three-hour one-on-one meeting with Tony Blair and then another hour with some senior officials at which I was present. Besides the issues of WMD, which we submitted did not exist, we discussed tactical issues that also suggested that the war would not in our view produce the desired outcome.

It is now history that within days of our visits the US and the UK started bombarding Iraq using sophisticated modern war machinery that caused as much destruction as some of the WMD they claimed Iraq possessed. Many of the people they asserted Saddam Hussein would kill using chemical and biological weapons were killed during that war. Watching it on international television networks, the war appeared like an opportunity to test modern war machinery. It was like children playing with their newly acquired high-tech toys. But these high-tech machines were striking human beings.

The child who lost her limbs and made international headlines during the attack on Iraq remains a reminder of the destructive and inhuman nature of war and the extent to which innocent people suffer. Like many other citizens of the world I was also traumatised by the picture of that child.

Days before the attacks started, I participated in an informal breakfast discussion with top international business and political leaders. What struck me most was the resignation of these powerful people to the war. As far as they were concerned the matter had gone too far for the major powers to reconsider their positions, whatever the factual situation. The reality was that the US and the UK were determined to wage war at all costs. I sensed a deep feeling of despair and helplessness amongst those powerful people.

Those of us who had been involved in guerrilla warfare argued that if the US and the UK used their superior weaponry to attack Iraq, the Iraqi army could decide to take off its uniform and join a national resistance to the invasion, forcing the US and the UK to bomb the cities and residential areas. This was acceptable in modern warfare. In fact one discussant said that with the weapons at the disposal of the powerful today, the world should never go to war because it is bound to be terribly destructive and devastating.

The discussion led to one of the greatest shocks in my life, that it had to be accepted that there was going to be great loss of life and that it should be considered as unavoidable 'collateral damage'. These comments were accompanied by straight faces as we completed our sumptuous breakfast. That was chilling stuff for me. It felt cold-blooded and lacking in concern for the sanctity of human life. But that is what war is, especially modern warfare.

At the end of that five-star breakfast I left the venue feeling totally disgusted. In Setswana they would say that this discussion *e ntsulafalleditse dijo* (messed up my breakfast). Personally, I reached the lowest depths of despair during that time. I was deeply pained by the fact that we could not do anything to stop the disaster that was about to unfold before our eyes. However senseless the impending action was and however immoral the basis was for the war, we were all powerless to stop it – even their closest powerful allies who did not agree with this approach or logic. There were unprecedented levels of silence in the corridors of the UN in New York – the body formed to safeguard world peace. Worse still, the UN remained silent when the powerful formed their 'coalition of the willing' outside of the UN mandate. If this had been a coalition of less powerful states the 'big brothers' would have stepped in and stopped it. But here there was no 'bigger brother'. I could only hear my own inner voice saying, 'Woe unto those whose elder brothers are delinquent for they shall have no one to protect them or speak a voice of reason to them!'

It is now a historical fact that the powers behind the invasion of Iraq knew beforehand that there were no WMD in Iraq at the time they started the bombardment. Over and above the information supplied by South Africa, it has been confirmed that their intelligence services also had that information. But they went into Iraq regardless. They went in to kill and maim innocent Iraqis. And the UN never lifted a finger.

Even those who innocently believed in the integrity of the US and UK and the reliability of their information relating to Iraq's chemical weapons and its intention to use them against its own citizens now know that they were lied to. Many were incensed about the fact that they were made party to the commission of crimes against ordinary citizens of Iraq.

But no one will be taken to the International Criminal Court (ICC) in The Hague. Those who were involved are beyond and above the jurisdiction of the ICC as an understanding of justice in this case depends on how weak or powerful one is. If one is powerful one can be exempt from becoming a party to the Rome Statute, the treaty that established the ICC. They can also pressurise weaker states to exempt them from the jurisdiction of the ICC.

It is now also a known fact that the story about WMD was a cover for interests other than those publicly articulated. The US and the UK had two strategic objectives. First, they wanted to punish Saddam Hussein because of their embarrassment or humiliation suffered at the hands of Hussein in the Gulf War of 1991. The second, which proved to be the main objective of the war, was access to and control of oil resources in Iraq. Much has been written about this matter and I do not intend to elaborate on it here; suffice to say, like all corrupt systems and deals, tenders or orders were already in place and many made a 'killing' financially over the bodies of innocent Iraqis.

In discussing his memoirs, Alan Greenspan (the former Federal Reserve Chairman who served four US presidents) said: 'I am saddened that it is politically incorrect to acknowledge what everyone knows: the Iraq war is largely about oil.'[2]

He further said: 'If Saddam Hussein had been head of Iraq and there was no oil under those sands our response to him would not have been as strong as it was in the first gulf war. And the second gulf war was as an extension of the first. My view is that Saddam, looking over his 30-year history, very clearly was giving evidence of moving towards controlling the straits of Hormuz where there are 17, 18, 19 million barrels a day passing through.'[3]

The conclusion one draws from this experience is that the world is not as it seems. Firstly, within and between states, lying is permissible if it is in pursuit of 'national interests', even in a narrow sense of this concept. Propaganda machinery is unleashed to make the public believe in the lie and even support it. Secondly, it is not just lying, but a deliberate distortion of reality, including misrepresenting of facts, statistics and so forth. Thirdly, states will go as far as framing others, including innocent people, who at times get killed or eliminated in pursuit of narrow national interests.

There were many other more serious incidents in my thirteen-and-a-half years in government that confirmed these conclusions. To survive I resorted to the old 'tools of suspicion' or 'the art of suspecting' that I learnt from liberation theology during our struggle for liberation.

The starting point of my Christian faith was also an innocent disposition until I learnt that even one's faith can be used as an ideological machine to force one to accept oppression and exploitation. In this situation I discarded 'blind believing' and used 'tools of suspicion' to unpack oppressive forms of faith and embraced a revolutionary form of faith that is based on equal justice for all – individuals, families, communities, nationalities, and even countries or nations.

In liberation theology discourse we used the concept of a 'hermeneutic of suspicion' as a tool to unpack any event or information. A more detailed explanation can be found in Juan Luis Segundo's book, *The Theology of Liberation*, where he asserts that the liberation theologian's 'suspicion is that *anything* and *everything* involving ideas, including theology, is intimately bound up with the existing social situation in at least an unconscious way' (my emphasis). In today's situation I would say that anything and everything that comes our way is intrinsically bound up with the social, political and economic interests of the powerful and dominant forces of society that seek to promote their interests at all costs, even at the expense of those they appear to assist.

My exposure to the concept of a 'farewell to innocence' came from Allan Boesak's classic book, *Farewell to Innocence: A Social Ethical Study of Black Theology and Black Power*.[4] It was indeed a long stretch for a classical, Biblically based reformed theologian like Allan Boesak then to dabble with critical matters like Black Theology, Black Consciousness and Black Power in the 1960s and 1970s in the US. His exposure enabled him to compare the US context with that of South Africa, setting him on a radical path to campaign against the apartheid system. He started from being an 'innocent' reformed evangelical Christian who accepted the status quo, to becoming a radical black theologian who believed that God was on the side of the poor, oppressed and exploited.

If the religious or theological idiom in defining this concept does not resonate, one could read John R. Boekenoogen's novel, also entitled *Farewell to Innocence*.[5] It presents a picture from an artistic perspective of what I am grappling with. The novel is about discovering one's journey in a life that is filled with twists and turns and takes one to places one never thought existed. In the novel 'a young man's life is radically altered when he learns that what seems like ordinary life is far from ordinary'.

Indeed the world in general and on face value seems like an 'ordinary' world and presents itself as such. Each one of us starts with an innocent mind until we are rudely awakened by reality.

CHAPTER 5

The Media: Soft Targets for Manipulation

Every democrat who takes seriously the right of freedom of expression must be concerned about the targeting of the media by intelligence agencies that use the media to pursue the objectives of those who command them. Such 'intelligence projects' not only misrepresent information but manipulate, falsify and distort it to serve the interests of those who deploy them.

Although historically such strategies were used in war times where truth became 'the first casualty', today these strategies are deployed in our day-to-day lives – in political activities and in commercial transactions where commercial intelligence is used to win deals over others, or to compete in the market place. It is also evident in the activities of criminal syndicates seeking to corrupt or compromise their targets and in the management of foreign relations between countries, friendly or otherwise.

Knowing what I know now, I read and listen to media reports with my eyes wide open and I deploy my 'tools of suspicion' to make sure that I am not a victim of misinformation and sophisticated intelligence projects. But many people listen to stories and read without employing critical tools. They consume information innocently and without question. The consequences of this kind of thinking and the views it produces are dangerous.

Of greatest concern is that these projects are executed at 'all and any cost', starting with 'the truth' as 'the first casualty'. When the lives of innocent and unsuspecting citizens are involved, they call it 'collateral damage', which is permissible in the logic of their projects. At worst they even allow the killing of their own to generate anger to achieve these objectives. At times they allow the worst preventable tragedies to happen to achieve their objectives. (Unfortunately, to go into specifics in relation to these assertions would require another book.)

In this situation any genuine democrat or lover of freedom should worry. But those who should perhaps worry most are media practitioners and campaigners for the freedom of the media to ensure that there is no abuse of this medium, which is so critical for our hard-fought democracy.

Attacks on the freedom of the media at this sophisticated level must be considered among the greatest threats to our hard-won freedoms. For this reason we must deploy our 'surface-to-air missiles' to bring down these machinations of intelligence projects in defence of 'the freedom of the press and other media; the freedom to receive or impart information or ideas; freedom of artistic creativity; and academic freedom and freedom of scientific research' as outlined in Section 16(a) of the Constitution of South Africa. Once this freedom is lost and information is not available to enable us to make intelligent decisions, then our democratic rights will also be lost and our capacity to reach our true potential as envisaged in our constitution becomes compromised.

But history has shown that the media can be used equally by

dictatorships and democracies to misinform the public and influence it to make decisions against their own interests or the common good of all of humanity. That is why the (b) part of Section 16 of the Constitution of South Africa contains a limitation, which means the rights protected by Section 16(a) cannot be extended to 'propaganda for war; incitement of imminent violence; or advocacy of hatred that is based on race, ethnicity, gender or religion, and that constitutes incitement to cause harm'.

In classic cases that arise out of this section of the constitution the issues concern how to limit the rights of the media rather than limiting the damage to its credibility that can be caused by the media's reliance – sometimes inadvertently – on propaganda. My experience throughout our struggle for liberation and as an actor in the post-1994 democratic government is that the media is a 'site of struggle', a contested terrain targeted in particular by the powerful seeking to extend their influence nationally, regionally and internationally.

A cursory reading of the experiences of the last century, which will be remembered for major world wars, the Cold War and so forth, shows how schizophrenic humanity can be. Centuries-old democracies in Europe guaranteed freedoms and rights for their people while running oppressive and exploitative colonial systems that caused enormous harm to the citizens of the world beyond Europe. In this regard one only has to recall the UK's military and intelligence operations in the colonial regimes they controlled. The role of the US in the South American struggles for liberation is well documented and highlights some of the best cases about intelligence projects that caused enormous pain to the citizens of those countries.

Hence, the need for the kind of limitation on freedoms outlined in Section 16(b). Limitations to rights may appear as a contradiction. However, the concern I am addressing in this chapter is not about limitation in a traditional sense; it is about the greater threat to the freedom of the media occasioned by its manipulation by powerful forces internationally to achieve their own objectives, which in most instances are not in the interests of the poorer countries and its marginalised peoples. There can be no comparison between the capacity of rich and powerful countries and poor countries to manipulate information in their favour. The Iraq and US matter, dealt with earlier, is a case in point.

This greater threat to media freedom eludes most media practitioners and campaigners for the freedom of the media. But none of the media houses, and no self-respecting journalist, would want to be manipulated through covert intelligence operations that cause them to report falsified information that might affect their credibility. Nor would any media practitioner worth his or her salt want to work with moles who extract information from them for use against the interests of the media or to try to influence their colleagues.

All should agree that the manipulation of the media is a violation of everybody's right to freedom of choice and of thought.

Those who were involved in the struggle for liberation learnt, sometimes the hard way, that the media was not exempt from the machinations of apartheid and international intelligence operatives. The strategy of the operatives who were involved in these intelligence projects was, firstly, to compromise serving journalists in order to advance their interests and, secondly, to plant their 'journalist' agents to achieve the same objectives. The success of the liberation movement in drawing the media over to its side spurred the apartheid regime to focus more on the media, even if this was simply aimed at collecting information or knowing what was to be published well in advance.

As part of its legacy, the apartheid system left us with a number of moles that, like all moles within the liberation movement or the old-order intelligence operations, either remained dormant, abandoned the mission, or were left on the ledge by their handlers. Some were creative and set up their own risk assessment companies. Others formed disguised intelligence collection entities, and many formed security companies to continue using their skills and trade. Some became freelance journalists with a wealth of information networks that placed their reports in high demand.

The challenge with this legacy is that it is possible for some of these elements to be reactivated or roped into similar sinister operations, especially in conflict situations. In South Africa some have become part of disinformation campaigns to try to destabilise the new government and the ANC. In the instances discussed below the players involve 'old-order' security and intelligence elements and operatives, on the one hand, and moles within the liberation movements and those who were compromised by the system, on the other hand.

Examples of these types of activities post-democracy are, firstly, the fake 1998 'Meiring Report', which claimed that left-wing elements were planning a coup against the young new state. The second was the hoax e-mails saga, which falsely implicated senior ANC leaders in a conspiracy to oust Jacob Zuma. The third was the Browse Mole 'intelligence' report, which described a plot to support Zuma in his bid for the presidency. All of the above were aimed at destabilising both the government and ruling party, and, in the case of the latter, create tensions with other countries.

Investigations relating to these cases show that the common element in all of them was the involvement and collaboration of former apartheid security, intelligence operatives and compromised new-order intelligence operatives or historical moles within the liberation movement. Investigations also show that there were elements within the media who were part of these projects. In one of the cases an old-order intelligence operative who worked as a freelance journalist was at the centre of a case where he provided information to three blocks of people who were at loggerheads with each other on the one hand, and, the prosecution authority on the other. He became a resource person or source of information to all of them and manipulated the information in a manner that intensified the conflict. To make it more dramatic he released 'bits and pieces' of the information to the media to electrify the playing field and make the players react in a particular manner with the objective of influencing their perspectives about the problem and intensifying the conflict.

Surprisingly the intention was not to reinstate the old order or to create conditions conducive for old-order elements to take control of the government. It was clear to them that returning South Africa to exclusive white rule was no longer a viable option given global political developments. Given this reality they seem to have decided that the best way to stop the new democratic government from achieving its objectives was to destabilise it and empower compromised elements within the liberation movement who could ensure that individual interests were secured rather than the objectives of the NDR.

As time went by and the power of the old-order edifice faded, as did the threat of prosecution of the former leadership, commanders and foot soldiers of the apartheid system, these agents began to work as free agents with personal and criminal motives. Even the handling of their sources or agents within the liberation movement became privatised. In some cases the 'handler' became the 'handled' and the 'handled' became the 'handler' as power relations shifted. Generally, the more powerful in criminal stakes became the centre of command, even for those who were in government. In this context, basic criminality came to play a pervasive role in South African politics.

The objectives of these 'free agents' switched from securing

political power for their old masters to creating conditions conducive for criminal elements to control the country and use it for
their interests. The strategy involved compromising the existing
leadership or promoting to positions of power those compromised
leaders who served the interests of criminal syndicates, gangs and
foreign intelligence.

The warning signs of this type of development are the same as
in organised crime syndicates or in criminal gangs. They include
the murders of possible sources and witnesses to criminal activities,
graduating finally into political assassinations. These warning signs
flickered right from the beginning, mainly in the Mpumalanga area
and more recently in KwaZulu-Natal, which should be a cause for
great concern given the history of violence in that region before
and after the democratic elections in 1994.

Before we know it this fire could engulf the whole country as
those who have committed crimes that are known about by comrades begin to perceive such comrades as a threat. Once this culture
takes root our democracy will become more vulnerable as leaders
will do everything possible to remain in power and secure their
personal, family or 'gang' interests. In the long term a dynasty of
criminal 'gangs' will be lined up to secure their interests into the
future.

This reality is not a uniquely South African phenomenon; it is
a common characteristic of post-war and conflict states. Similarly,
the focus on and interest in the media is also not the preserve
of the apartheid and post-apartheid systems. It is a worldwide
phenomenon.

Most intelligence entities, especially those of dictatorships and
superpowers, make the media a particular focus or target of their
intelligence activities. Whenever they have an intelligence project,
they factor the media into their planning. Many democracies that
guarantee freedom of expression and a free press have not figured

out how they can protect the media from the machinations of these forces, which, in turn, negatively affect freedom of the press. Smaller and weaker states are always on the receiving end of these machinations. Also at risk are civil society groups that are infiltrated and used to achieve the objectives of the powerful.

The standard approach of these agents is to identify grievances and build strategies around such grievances, presenting the agents as friends to the aggrieved party. Intelligence services of many major democracies have made this aspect of intelligence operations a major preoccupation in the training programmes of their operatives.

One of the best recent examples of the use of the media for propaganda purposes was the Iraqi war. The strategy to control the oil resources in Iraq after Saddam Hussein had broken ranks with the US and other Western powers was to generate a war with the objective of effecting regime change. And to justify this war, massive propaganda machinery was unleashed to present Hussein as a menacing threat to his own people and the West. Footage of dead Iraqis killed by Hussein were repeatedly displayed around the world and false intelligence reports were generated to show that Iraq had WMDs when, as I illustrated in the previous chapter, the truth was quite the opposite.

What is pertinent here is that the media was fed blatant falsehoods about the WMDs – and they accepted them – over a protracted period until everyone believed that there were indeed WMD in Iraq, which were a threat to the world and to Hussein's own people. When the war started the media was invited to accompany the American and British forces and their allies to report on events and win the propaganda war internationally. This approach gave us some new vocabulary in the form of 'embedded journalism'. The brutality visited on innocent Iraqis was discounted as 'collateral damage' and the media in the main accepted this eventuality. Accordingly, there were no consequences for those who falsified intelligence information or who knew the truth but continued with the war regardless.

Another area of interest in relation to the media and covert operations was Zimbabwe during the 2000s when the country faced its worst crisis since independence in 1980. The details about this crisis are presented in a later chapter on Zimbabwe. For now it is enough to say that the crisis was initially an economic one that later became a political one.

The trigger for the political crisis was the land question, a resolution to which was still outstanding long after the Lancaster House political settlement. The long and short of it is that both the UK and the US had promised to pay for the land, which would be 'returned' to Zimbabweans while the Zimbabwean government would pay for development on the land.

One of the items on the agenda of the 1998 international donor conference on Zimbabwe was the land question. At the conference, the UK again committed to the agreements following the Lancaster House political settlement. But later (almost within a year) the UK withdrew (or, as others would say, reneged) on its commitment to pay for the land. The reason given was that the Zimbabwean government was corrupt and could not be relied on to manage the funds. When an alternative plan was forged to actualise this commitment via the UN this was sabotaged and never saw the light of the day. It is this position that led to the occupation of land by what were known as Zimbabwe's 'war veterans'.

It is now history that the occupation of land resulted in violent conflicts that characterised Zimbabwe in the 2000s. As the land question was tied to the so-called Lancaster House constitution, attempts were made to amend the constitution and this led to further violent conflicts over a referendum about the issue. The conflict spilled over into the subsequent national elections, and continued up to the 2008 elections, which were based on the Global Political

Agreement (GPA) facilitated by President Thabo Mbeki. For almost a decade, from 1999 to 2009 until the 'inclusive government'
was constituted in terms of the GPA, Zimbabwe was politically
destabilised to such an extent that the thriving economy of the
1980s and 1990s had totally collapsed. Food disappeared from su-
permarket shelves. Even those who had money could not buy it.

Recently I had a discussion with some Zimbabweans who
lived through that decade and who categorically agreed that no
one would want to go through that kind of situation again. People
had to cross the borders to Botswana, South Africa, Mozambique,
Malawi, and Zambia just to find food. Some drove across the borders simply to have a meal. Many left the country for greener pas-
tures or to survive.

For historical reasons and in pursuit of their national interests,
the UK and the US took a direct interest in the developments in
Zimbabwe. For the UK relations with Zimbabwe went back to
colonial days through the Lancaster settlement, including the land
issue. There are also citizens of Zimbabwe who were of British
descent and held dual citizenship. The US became party to the
resolution of the land issue and shared an interest in the future of
Zimbabwe.

They openly took sides with the opposition parties and some
civil society groups against the ZANU-PF government, particularly its president and the president of the country, Robert Mugabe.
They were highly critical about the violation of human rights and
election processes that were not free and fair. The opposition to
the ZANU-PF government and its president was mounted as a
regime-change strategy, which opposition parties and some civil
society groups became part of.

Amongst the strategies unleashed to achieve this objectives were:
1. sanctions against the president, specific individuals within
government and some corporate entities. This ended up

affecting the whole country as the sanctions were applied indiscriminately, notwithstanding the intended specificity thereof; and

2. all forms of covert operations and propaganda focusing on Mugabe, ZANU-PF, opposition parties, civil society, the Southern African Development Community (SADC) facilitator (President Mbeki) and his facilitation team (former minister Sydney Mufamadi; Mbeki's legal adviser, Advocate Mojanku Gumbi; and myself, as director-general in the presidency and secretary of cabinet); the governments of the SADC region; and the rest of the leadership of the African continent.

The regime change campaign and sanctions deepened the economic crisis and forced many Zimbabweans to leave the country as 'economic refugees' and 'exiles'.

It was in the heat of this crisis that Mbeki was requested by his SADC peers and fellow presidents to facilitate a resolution of the conflict. Mufamadi, Gumbi and I formed the facilitation team that assisted the president with this task.

The mission was challenging because there were conflicting expectations of the outcomes of the facilitation process. The SADC mandate, which was endorsed by the AU, was for Mbeki to facilitate a political settlement between the government and opposition parties. The settlement was expected to lead to free and fair elections to give the people of Zimbabwe the right to determine their own destiny, including the choice of leadership. On the other hand, some non-governmental entities and foreign countries (particularly the UK and the US) wanted regime change. No other outcome other than that of the removal of Mugabe from office was acceptable.

The facilitator and his facilitation team clung to the mandate of SADC against all odds. The key aim was to create conducive conditions for the people of Zimbabwe to determine their own destiny, including the election of leaders of their choice. Based on this principle, African leaders were generally opposed to the foreign and undemocratic concept of regime change that was reminiscent of what major Western countries did in some of the Eastern European countries following the collapse of the Soviet Union.

As one would have expected, these principles did not help to protect the facilitator and his team. Mbeki became a target of attack by all entities seeking regime change, including the South African and international media. In this regard a highly organised media campaign was unleashed against Mbeki and efforts were made through covert operations to destabilise the dialogue between the affected parties, especially when the direction of the facilitation process seemed to be heading for a political settlement that was not going to result in the removal of Mugabe as president.

The negotiation processes were closely monitored, both overtly and covertly. This included cyberspace operations to monitor all communication between the parties to the negotiations and related players. Moles were placed in some of the delegations to monitor negotiation processes from inside, and diplomats hovered around the negotiating venues or around specific delegations. In this situation one did not need sophisticated intelligence capability to perceive the covert machinations of some of these countries. I often say that the weakness of power is that it assumes that nobody else matters. The powerful tend to take others for granted and end up becoming more careless and covertly transparent.

Throughout the process of facilitating dialogue between parties we worked on the understanding that all delegations were infiltrated, rendering everything we discussed during the dialogue knowable to the superpowers who had a direct interest in developments. The media was no exception. Many media acted like the propaganda machinery of the Western powers while a few supported the Zimbabwean president to the hilt.

Two specific incidents relating to the media stand out in the Zimbabwe negotiation processes. The first was the publicity around a document allegedly leaked during the 2007 SADC conference in Lusaka and which the media turned into an 'Mbeki report' without any basis whatsoever. The second was a 'letter' from the leader of one of the formations of the MDC, Morgan Tsvangirai, to President Mbeki that was supposed to ask Mbeki to recuse himself from being the facilitator. The letter alleged that the MDC felt he was biased against them. The letter never reached the presidency but there was much in the media to suggest it had. A statement denying the presidency had received such a letter was not accepted by the media although it could not produce evidence to the contrary.

More details of these incidents are set out below.

The mysterious Lusaka document

The SADC summit in Lusaka in 2007 was the scene of sophisticated intelligence operations aimed at destabilising the dialogue between the parties in Zimbabwe and the facilitator, and to influence the SADC leadership to adopt the 'regime change' approach.

Both Mbeki and the SADC, seen as obstacles to achieving this objective, qualified as targets for certain countries' intelligence activities. Another objective was to break the cordial relationship between the UK and South Africa (which was at its best during the Mbeki-Blair era) as the UK was seen not to be taking a hard stand against Mbeki.

All this was because the direction of the facilitation process was that of a global political settlement that would give Zimbabweans an opportunity to decide on their leadership. This was not leading to 'regime change' and was not in terms of their strategic objective.

Accordingly it had to be stopped, and stopped by all means however dirty these would be. As it is often said, the first casualty in a war is the truth. Lies become the order of the day even if it leads to the deaths of innocent people.

The bizarre story of an Mbeki report attacking the UK's position on the Zimbabwe crisis was a classic, dirty tricks, intelligence activity. None of the media that reported on it could provide an evidential basis for their stories, nor could they subsequently provide an explanation for why they played along with it. In the case I present below, I cannot, unfortunately, use classified intelligence material. Instead, I rely heavily on Robert Brand's critique of the manner in which the UK's *Guardian* newspaper handled the matter and the response of Chris McGreal (a *Guardian* journalist) to this critique.[6] (Robert Brand is an experienced journalist who teaches media law, ethics and economic journalism at Rhodes University.)

A Lusaka-based stringer, who was acting as a freelance journalist for a number of media outlets, got hold of a document that he first said was a Zimbabwean document in the initial story and soon after presented it as a South African document. His first report was filed with Agence France-Presse (AFP) and it specifically said that the document, which attacked Britain, originated from Zimbabwe. A few hours later (about four hours) the same story was published by Reuters but the document had now become an 'Mbeki report', despite the fact that the language, including its form, structure and style, of the report was distinctly un-Mbeki.

Next, huge headlines appeared in the UK about Mbeki attacking Britain for its position on Zimbabwe. The *Guardian* led the pack. A report by McGreal referred to 'a South African document circulating among diplomats ahead of [the SADC] summit' in Lusaka that 'blamed Britain for the deepening crisis in Zimbabwe by accusing the UK of leading a campaign to "strangle" the beleaguered African state's economy'. The report claimed that the document was a 'draft of the report South African president [Mbeki] is expected to present at the meeting'.

In his critique of McGreal's report Brand notes that there was 'no indication' in McGreal's report that he 'attempted to contact the South African government or Presidency to verify that the report was in fact a draft of Mbeki's report to the SADC, or to obtain comment'.

The South African media followed swiftly with reports, based either on the *Guardian* reports or the Reuters' story, claiming that Mbeki had attacked Britain or had been criticised by political analysts for blaming Britain for the crisis in Zimbabwe. These reports appeared in the *Business Day* and the Independent Newspapers, amongst others, and there was no indication that either of the newspapers checked the source of the reports or whether the document was genuine.

My interaction with some of the South African journalists indicated that they had not seen the actual document and had relied entirely on what had appeared as agency copy on the news wires. Their attitude towards Mbeki and their obvious disagreement with his handling of the Zimbabwe situation did not help. It was clear they came to the event with preconceived ideas and had expected Mbeki to differ with Britain as a matter of course. In a sense they had an *a priori* position that blunted their professionalism and ethics.

To date we have not been able to obtain an adequate explanation from the stringer as to what happened between the time that AFP published the story stating the report originated from Zimbabwe, and the time the stringer gave the story to Reuters, which attributed its authorship to Mbeki.

This mystery alone should have been sufficient to raise an alarm for any serious journalist. But this did not happen as most never took the trouble to do what journalists should do: check the information, its origin and source. Instead, they lapped the story up without question.

We raised the matter with Reuters as we were concerned that the agency might also have been a victim of manipulation of which they were unaware. I handled the matter personally at a higher level with an experienced communications adviser in the presidency who had vast experience as a journalist and editor. This journey took us as high as the agency's Africa bureau chief. He took the trouble to come and discuss the matter with us after understanding our concern – which was not only about the story but the way in which the media could be fed with incorrect information by forces that had interests other than those of Reuters at heart, and could discredit the news agency.

Initially the Reuters' representative maintained the standard view that their source was 'very credible' and could not have fed false information into the network. There was also some reluctance to share with us a copy of the document that was said to be Mbeki's report. The representative felt that he needed to check the facts about the case as he did not handle the story directly given that he was operating at a different level. By the time of our follow-up meeting we had found a way of securing a copy of the document and were able to confirm its source as a Zimbabwean report. We offered Reuters an opportunity to compare the document we had with the one in their possession.

At the end of our discussion the agency representative accepted that something had gone wrong, which was unusual for them, and they agreed not only to correct the story but to expunge it from all their records in a manner that our communications adviser thought appropriate.

Unfortunately, we could not exercise the same influence at home as people believed what they got through the wires. Levels of gullibility were such that even if what appeared on the wires was part of an intelligence project it would be lapped up without question. We tried hard to suggest to the South African media that they might be victims of sophisticated intelligence operations but they would not buy it. They stuck to their traditional view that they were not obliged to reveal their sources.

The surprising thing is that even the *Guardian* failed to do what a respectable paper was expected to do to avoid being caught by such a scam. In his critique, Brand asks: 'How does that square with the *Guardian*'s editorial code, which is strong on accuracy, fairness and admitting mistakes?' But this is precisely the havoc intelligence projects can cause. Either someone knew about the project and promoted it or it did not make sense. The *Guardian* should not have done such a thing. But they did. They carried the story and even defended it.

About three days after McGreal's report, the *Guardian* published an opinion piece by Simon Tisdall about 'Mbeki's attempt to blame Britain for Zimbabwe's problems' and his sources were now from 'leaks to the South African media'. On enquiring, no one could indicate who 'leaked' the story to the South African media. The presidency was incapable of doing so as it had no knowledge of such a 'South African document'. In his critique, Brand says that the statements from the South African government were 'widely reported'. However, the *Guardian* ignored them. 'Instead', Brand says, 'the *Guardian Unlimited* [ran] a report by Fred Attewill that Mbeki "would back Mr Mugabe's claims that UK-orchestrated sanctions were the principal cause of Zimbabwe's woes".'

Brand reaches some conclusions that, in my opinion, are devastating for any journalist or media house aspiring to quality and accountability, and are worth quoting in full:

> McGreal and Attewill's reports were shoddy, to say the least.
> Neither made any effort to verify that the 'leaked report' was

in fact an official South African document. Neither made any attempt to obtain comment from the South African government or Presidency. Neither published the comments offered by the South African government and Presidency.

Brand continues:

> The so-called 'leaked report' story originated with the *Guardian,* yet within a day or two the newspaper managed to disown its own story and attribute it to 'South African media'. As is clear from my analysis ... the South African media followed, not originated, the *Guardian*'s reports. The story has turned out to be wrong – yet the *Guardian* has made no attempt to correct the record.

McGreal's response to Brand did not help much. In fact in some instances it made matters worse. He says: 'The original report did not appear in the *Guardian*. It appeared on Reuters five days before my own, and a version appeared in South Africa's *Sunday Independent* a day before.'

I would argue that if Reuters published the story five days before McGreal's then he should have had enough time to verify the story. His defence that the *Guardian* did 'indeed run an article saying that the South African government denies knowledge of the document', did not help either as this was done 'three days' after Brand posted his piece and 'NINE days after the government first denied knowledge of the report,' as Brand argues.

This was one of the most surprising stories I had handled in my position. As part of the facilitation team on the Zimbabwe Dialogue, as secretary of the National Security Council and having general access to intelligence information, I knew that there was no such report from South Africa or the presidency. My first suspicion was that if it existed it would be the creation of other agents that were intent on opposing any form of agreement in Zimbabwe that would not secure 'regime change'. Following our investigation it became clear that whoever was involved chose to turn a Zimbabwean document into a South African document and succeeded in getting the media to report it as such.

From a government perspective I was struck by the silence of the British government. I never saw a response from them to the reports. One could speculate that there was no response either because they knew about the origins of the report or they did not think it was important enough to worry about. But I am sure that with their intelligence capacity they would have known that the report was false and did not want to be involved or be seen to be showing interest.

The mystery letter from the MDC that never reached Mbeki

One of the most controversial issues that ended up with me suing the *Sunday Times* for defamation involved the alleged letter from the president of the MDC, Morgan Tsvangirai, to President Thabo Mbeki, which to my knowledge never reached the presidency or Mbeki. This occurred at the height of the political dialogue between the opposition parties (the two MDC formations, led by Tsvangirai and Arthur Mutambara respectively) and ZANU-PF. A massive campaign both in South Africa and internationally was unleashed against Mbeki as facilitator of the Zimbabwe Dialogue, as they believed that he was biased against the MDC.

Mbeki's SADC mandate, which did not include regime change in it, was such that he always appeared to be taking sides with the ZANU-PF government against the MDC. The MDC was already unhappy about the terms of the SADC mandate, which sought a dialogue to create conditions conducive for a free and fair election. To do this would require a political agreement, including a constitution and new laws. This was not what the MDC wanted. For them the removal of Mugabe and ZANU-PF from government was the first prize and they were not in the mood for compromise. To do so would mean loss of support for the party. At one stage the party embarked on a protest programme and strategy called the 'Final Push', which was meant to topple the government or force it out of office. Some civil society groups shared this view and made even more radical demands in this regard.

The approach of the US and Britain complicated matters. The Zimbabwean land invasions, which had deteriorated into violent conflicts and resulted in attacks on white farmers, some of whom were tragically killed, calcified the view of the US and Britain: Mugabe had to go!

For their part, Mugabe and ZANU-PF perceived the national and international forces arrayed against them as a strategy to re-colonise Zimbabwe, which had to be resisted at all costs. In this regard they saw the MDC as 'unpatriotic' and an 'agent' of foreign interests – a treasonable act. In the process the genuine grievances of the Zimbabwean people got lost in the emotions and war of words.

A massive international communications strategy was unleashed to force Mbeki to deviate from or abandon the SADC mandate and join the regime change campaign to remove Mugabe. In resisting this approach Mbeki became the target of a multiplicity of complex intelligence projects aimed at forcing him to abandon the SADC mission and adopt his own approach – or to force him out as a facilitator.

The strategy involved the media and other covert operations directed not only at Mbeki but at the Zimbabwean government, opposition parties, as well as SADC and AU leaders to influence them against the SADC mandate. Unfortunately, the details relating to this massive covert operation, involving major foreign intelligence entities, falls within the realm of classified information. Those who were involved in these projects know exactly what I am referring to.

The campaign was so intense that even 'shaking hands' with Mugabe at the airport made headline news and commentators made it a major subject of discussion. As far as the media was concerned Mbeki was supposed to isolate Mugabe and force him out of office.

The campaign was also carried out on South African soil and included the mobilisation of the ANC's alliance partners to attack Mbeki and the facilitation team. Such measures included expressing solidarity with the MDC. Some church groups were also mobilised in the same manner.

But when it became clear that Mbeki was not going to cave in and deviate from the SADC mandate, the campaign turned to removing him as facilitator. Again, the details here fall within the realm of classified information. One incident though that became a public matter was the letter of MDC president, Morgan Tsvangirai, which was supposed to inform Mbeki that the MDC had decided that Mbeki should resign or recuse himself as facilitator because of bias. Obviously there was enormous pressure on the MDC internally and internationally to withdraw from the talks and force a change in facilitator because the dialogue process, as it was then structured, was never going to secure Mugabe's removal the way they wanted it to happen.

A public announcement by an MDC spokesperson was released concerning the letter, driving the media to the office of the presidency to confirm its receipt. The media ran headlines that suggested that Tsvangirai had sent the letter to Mbeki but had received no response. Our response that the letter had not been received was dismissed, but no one could prove otherwise.

We had checked all our records and our carefully managed registry. We also checked with our embassy in Harare in case the letter had been delivered there, but we found no trace of it. Using our own information gathering system we discovered that the person allocated the responsibility of delivering it had not done so out of concern that it would result in a collapse of the negotiation process and a return to intensified conflict; in other words, more violence and disaster for Zimbabweans.

As director-general in the presidency, I addressed a press conference at which I categorically stated that the presidency had not received the letter. Despite this statement, the media insisted that their 'sources' had confirmed that the letter was delivered.

In response to their persistence, I advised the journalists present that they needed to be careful with their sources as they could be part of an intelligence operation involving those who wished to jeopardise the negotiations. I also suggested that they go back to their sources rather than spend more time debating whether or not the letter was delivered when we knew categorically it was not.

Instead of taking my advice, a set of journalists from the *Sunday Times* attacked my person by calling me names in a defamatory manner. They called me a 'liar', a 'portly priest', questioned my integrity and even asked questions concerning what I 'preach' on Sundays. This was hurtful, especially because I knew the letter had not been delivered and was still sitting in someone's bag. The newspaper's Hogarth column then added salt to the wounds by making fun of me and repeated the 'portly priest' who 'lies' story.

There was no evidence to suggest that we had received the letter, nor could any of those journalists prove we had. It was almost as if they had the right to reach conclusions and make injurious statements without a moral responsibility to test their facts. It seemed to me then that journalists had a licence to accuse and judge a person without the burden of proof.

At one stage an undisclosed source handed over a copy of the missing letter to the media and *The Times* published it as proof that the letter existed. We tried our best to indicate that the fact that the letter existed, if it was in fact an authentic version, still did not prove that the presidency had received it. Instead of logically evaluating and applying their minds to what we were saying, some of the journalists continued to call me and the presidency liars.

To resolve this matter we suggested that the MDC leadership deliver another copy of the letter in question either to the presidency or to our embassy in Harare. The spokesperson of the MDC accepted the challenge and promised to deliver the letter to the embassy by the Friday of that week. Friday came and went, and no letter was delivered. We enquired again but the letter still never came. I left the presidency in June 2009 and I do not recall the letter ever being delivered or received.

This did not stop the *Sunday Times* repeating its injurious attacks on my person. We tried to get the *Sunday Times* to correct their statements without any success. That is why I was ultimately forced to appeal to the courts for relief. The matter is still outstanding.

For those of us in privileged positions it is painful to see journalists refusing any advice, especially about the covert operations of other countries, which could negatively affect not only our country, the region and the rest of the continent, but the credibility of the media itself.

CHAPTER 6

Zimbabwe Facilitation: Caught in the Crossfire

Articles on this chapter published in the media in 2010 and the publication of *Eight Days in September* attracted attacks from those who felt I had not done justice to the Zimbabwe matter. What was clear to me, however, was that they all missed the point. This chapter is not about the history of the conflict in Zimbabwe or about issues of human rights. Rather, it is about my experiences as part of the facilitation team that assisted then President Thabo Mbeki to fulfil the mandate of the SADC leadership. What follows is a reflection on my experiences as part of the facilitation team on the dialogue between the three main political parties in Zimbabwe.

Mbeki is known for his commitment to the vision of an African Renaissance. He understood that the freedom of South Africa would not be fully realised without the renewal of the African continent. Pessimism about Africa and its people had to end and this could be achieved only by changing the political, social and economic conditions on the continent. Change on the continent was one side of the coin. The other was a change of attitude towards Africa and Africans. The power relations between Africa and the rest of the world, especially those countries that have interests in the African continent, had to change to give Africans the sovereign right to determine their own destinies.

In pursuance of this vision and mission Mbeki invested much of his time as deputy president and then as president working on renewal to change the quality of life of all Africans on the continent and in the Diaspora, which includes South Africa. Besides a programme to popularise the vision of the African Renaissance as well as mobilise the leadership of the African continent to work together to achieve strategic objectives, Mbeki's starting point was to end wars and conflicts on the continent. There was a common understanding that there could be no development where there were conflicts, wars and instability. The change from the OAU to the AU came at the right time to lay the basis for stabilising the continent politically as well as pursuing its developmental strategies. The development and adoption of the New Programme for Africa's Development (NEPAD), which is the basis for the developmental strategies of the continent, and the African Peer Review Mechanism (APRM) were part of the overall strategy for the renewal of the continent.

Zimbabwe was one of the countries Mbeki focused on. The rumblings and conflicts between various parties, including interested international parties, were threatening to reverse the enormous gains Zimbabwe had made since its independence. After independence Zimbabwe had become the bright light of the southern African region and a reversal of its gains would impact negatively on the development of the rest of the region. In fact, it would be like turning off the light that gave hope to the region and the rest of the continent. In my opinion, Mbeki's role as a facilitator of the Zimbabwe Dialogue to assist the main political parties reach an agreement to end the conflict will go into the annals of history as one of the key elements of his legacy on the continent.

What we are dealing with here is Mbeki's particular approach in conflict resolution, which fell within the overall perspective of the rights of people and nations to determine their own destiny. But for Africans and people of the developing world Mbeki's facilitation approach, which was in line with the decisions of the SADC and the AU, was the best hope for Zimbabweans and the region. The approach respected the sovereign right of Zimbabweans to independently make their own decisions about the future of their country, rather than be dictated to by outsiders. The key strategic focus of this facilitation process was to create conducive conditions that would allow Zimbabweans freely and democratically to decide on the constitution they would like to have to govern their country, and then allow them to elect leaders of their choice rather than having leaders imposed on them from outside.

From this perspective the facilitator had to play the role of 'enabler', and 'mediator', rather than a 'dictator' there to enforce specific perspectives or impose solutions from outside.

As discussed in the previous chapter, this principled approach, or call it a particular form of diplomacy, incensed those who wanted to pursue the 'regime change' strategy, which Mbeki refused to be pressured into. Those who pursued the 'regime change' agenda included major powers like Britain and the US, which rendered the contest comparable to that between Goliath and David. As stated, a multiplicity of strategies were unleashed, including various communications strategies and intelligence projects, to get the public to buy into the 'regime change' approach against the wishes of the SADC and AU member countries.

The media avalanche was unbelievable. Africa lost the public battle of ideas and Mbeki was left as the embodiment of a strategy considered to be unacceptable.

The reality, however, is that Zimbabwe's Global Political Agreement (GPA) facilitated by Mbeki assisted Zimbabweans to stabilise the situation and gave them an opportunity to produce a new constitution and a regulatory framework that will together create conditions conducive for free and fair elections.

Whatever the views and perspectives about Mbeki's facilitation of the Zimbabwe Dialogue, the reality is that even those who were sceptical at the time about the GPA now accept that conditions in Zimbabwe have changed for the better since the inclusive government was formed on the basis of the GPA. The execution of the GPA is indeed a challenge and will be completed when a new constitution is adopted and free and fair elections are held.

Mbeki's commitment to assist Zimbabwe in resolving its problems pre-dates the SADC mandate he received later in the process. His initial involvement was based on early warning signals in the late 1990s that Zimbabwe was heading for a crisis. He understood that the crisis could impact negatively on the region and the rest of the continent. This would include a negative effect on the vision of the African Renaissance and the African renewal programme.

The SADC's mandate for him to facilitate dialogue between political parties in Zimbabwe was based on the fact that he was already involved as a neighbour and that he understood the political dynamics. He had already made his mark through his leadership of the processes that gave birth to NEPAD and the APRM.

Mbeki also had a track record in conflict resolution on the continent in countries such as the Democratic Republic of the Congo (DRC), Burundi, Côte d'Ivoire, Lesotho and others. It is because of this role and others that many leaders in the SADC and the rest of the continent have great respect for Mbeki. He has a reputation for being an extraordinarily patient facilitator, who never gives up until agreement is reached. No amount of insult or attack by the parties in the negotiations or outside the negotiations would deter him from pressing on until an agreement was reached.

The SADC and AU leaders also had respect for him as a peace-maker. His appointment by the AU in March 2009 to lead the AU high-level panel to assist Sudan in securing peace, justice and reconciliation illustrated the confidence of the African leadership in him. This appointment was made notwithstanding his removal as president of South Africa six months earlier. In this regard some have said that the saying, 'a prophet has no honour in his own country', seemed applicable in this case.

Although Mbeki is credited with the success of facilitating the GPA in Zimbabwe, there are those who did not like the manner in which he conducted the process, let alone the outcomes of the negotiations. Amongst these were some civil society groups inside and outside Zimbabwe. But the major challenge came from some of the major Western countries, which are members of the UNs Security Council. Key amongst these were the US and the UK. The European Union was also mobilised to take a stand, which defied the views and feelings of some of the Zimbabwean political parties, the leadership of the southern African states and the rest of the continent. They gave no credit to Mbeki for the facilitation of the GPA as they did not agree with the original SADC mandate. Consequentially, they also rejected the outcomes. In the main they measured success or justice against objectives they set for themselves – regime change – notwithstanding the SADC mandate.

The concept of regime change was popularised during the changes that occurred in the former Soviet Union countries. It consisted of an internal revolt, leading to the collapse of a government. Some of it was induced from outside through a multiplicity of strategies, the details of which go way beyond the scope of this chapter. In some cases it was called an 'Orange Revolution'. For those who supported regime change, any agreement that included

Mugabe in the inclusive government was unacceptable, even if this was agreed by the Zimbabwean parties.

Instead of making the SADC and its mandate the target for its unhappiness, Mugabe's detractors targeted Mbeki who, as facilitator, was turned into a punching bag for Britain, the US, some regional and international civil society groups, and some of the media, which served as the mouthpiece for this perspective.

Thus the campaign made 'regime change' not just the desired outcome from the facilitator but the 'right' one. In a sense, this became their measuring stick for success. Anything else was not acceptable. That is why even shaking hands, holding hands or smiling with President Mugabe when the facilitator was received at the airport made headlines and was seen as reprehensible.

For the media it was a betrayal of the people of Zimbabwe if one did not participate in the campaign to isolate President Mugabe or remove him from power. In this regard a vicious campaign was unleashed against the facilitator that presented him as an enemy of justice and peace in Zimbabwe, a 'protector' of the 'dictator', a supporter of human rights violations and so forth. In a campaign of this nature misrepresentation of facts and distortion of reality become permissible as long as it advances the cause people were pursuing. The saying that 'truth is the first causality of war' proved correct. People lied or accepted lies with straight faces and without any moral qualms.

The campaign was not only an overt one. As time went by an elaborate covert operation was unleashed to achieve a number of objectives. The first was to undermine the facilitator and what the facilitator was doing. This included special intelligence projects by various foreign intelligence entities. The second was to mobilise public opinion against the facilitator both within South Africa and abroad. Those who had the means deployed their technical capabilities and human resources to monitor every key player in the dialogue processes and meetings held in this regard. The objective was to influence the outcomes or intervene in or disrupt processes that seemed to be heading in the direction that may not be compatible with the policy objectives of those who wanted 'regime change'. That is why we had agreements one night and the following day the positions had changed. The third objective was to discredit the outcomes of the facilitation processes before the process was completed.

As we endured this tortuous journey I was reminded of the DRC Sun City negotiations in 2002. Before the DRC delegates arrived at the hotel, foreign intelligence agents checked into the hotel for the sole purpose of monitoring the talks and being close enough to the parties they needed to influence. The worst of these cases were overt 'handlers' who made sure that even if the delegates had made decisions in the interests of their country these positions were later reversed.

In Zimbabwe, apart from the targeting of the media – the effects of which are highlighted in the previous chapter – the regime change campaign also involved the lobbying of heads of state and AU leaders. Every effort was made to divide SADC leaders in particular and African leaders in general. In some instances the lobbying went beyond acceptable diplomatic practice to threats involving the withdrawal of development assistance to some of the more vulnerable countries. The discussions about these were at presidential levels and cannot be detailed. To the surprise of many, SADC leaders and other African leaders resisted the pressure and maintained their positions irrespective of the consequences or possible repercussions. I will elaborate later on this bold stand by the leaders that led to the failure of this strategy.

As a facilitation team we decided to stick with the SADC mandate, not just because it was binding on the facilitator, but also because it was the best way in which a resolution of the conflict in Zimbabwe could be found. A 'win–win' solution for Zimbabwe held better prospects than a 'win–lose' solution at the time. The regime change approach wanted a 'win–lose' solution but it never stated clearly how this was to be achieved. An 'Orange Revolution' was not possible in the Zimbabwe situation at that time. Elections had failed to produce universally accepted results and the MDC's 'Final Push' campaign had proved that the opposition did not have the support it needed, for whatever reasons, to force a regime change.

The only other way would have been the use of force. This was too radical an option in the Zimbabwean context, given its history. The 'balance of forces' as we would say in South Africa were such that it would be suicidal to try such an option, although some contemplated it. Some mad people even thought of crazy and unthinkable things like an invasion by foreign forces. Any military strategist with a sound mind could not even think of this as it would lead to a catastrophic disaster for the people of Zimbabwe and the region resulting in untold pain and suffering for a long period. The Iraqi experience is a case in point. More people have died since the removal of Saddam Hussein and up to now the pain and suffering of the people continues. The same happened in Libya causing enormous pain to ordinary citizens of the country.

For any rational person, dialogue amongst Zimbabweans was the only way to resolve the crisis. Because we believed this, we were determined to hold the course.

As would be expected the negotiating parties also came to the table in a fighting mood. The language was bellicose. At times it felt like, as the facilitation team, we were the only ones who wanted peace for Zimbabwe. Representatives of the people of Zimbabwe seemed ready to continue to fight and halt the talks. Negotiators came armed with extreme positions that seemed irreconcilable. Everyone appeared to be eager to faithfully represent the positions of their parties. But as time went by, the dialogue partners

– consisting of representatives of the three major Zimbabwean parties, namely, ZANU-PF and the two MDC formations – began to realise that war, conflict and sectarian party interests could not save Zimbabwe and the only way to peace was through talking.

The challenge that then faced the dialogue partners was to get their own constituencies to understand this new perspective, which was at odds with the way in which they had initially been mobilised.

This is a classic problem of political negotiations: as those involved in the negotiation process begin to understand each other better, the people they lead continue to hold extreme positions. Thus we had to tolerate statements issued outside of the negotiation room that contradicted the substance of agreements made inside. We understood that the negotiating parties had to keep their credibility intact and maintain unity among their constituencies. The problem with these postures was that they created more difficulties for the parties later, both within and outside their constituencies. The media, on the other hand, accepted the statements as gospel and later used them against the political parties, deepening the crisis within and outside their constituencies.

Interestingly, once the dialogue partners came to accept negotiation as the only way to save their country, they preferred to talk amongst themselves rather than through or with us. Most of the documents that formed the greater part of the GPA were produced by the parties themselves and we simply presided during reporting sessions. They had their own drafting teams, and where the matters were sensitive, they did the drafting themselves. It was only when they faced sticky 'make-or-break' issues that they consulted us. A common thread among the negotiating parties was pride they felt as Zimbabweans who could solve their problems without outside help. But so much water had passed under the bridge, and in this regard, there were difficult issues for which they needed the facilitator's assistance.

The political parties reached a settlement on 11 September 2008 and signed the GPA on 15 September 2008. What the GPA did was provide for an interim constitution on the basis of which an inclusive government was formed to jointly manage government while a new constitution was developed. This would culminate in a free and fair election based on the constitution accepted by Zimbabweans through a referendum. Obviously, as South Africans well know, negotiated settlements come with compromises for everyone and it was to be expected that all the parties were not entirely happy with all aspects of the agreement.

Following the signing of the GPA many Zimbabweans celebrated the achievement, which gave them renewed hope. But the regime-change campaigners rejected it. The fact that it was a settlement agreed to by all the Zimbabwean political parties did not matter. For some of the major Western countries, what really mattered were their national interests or simply the supremacy of their views, feelings and wishes that took precedence above those of Zimbabweans or, at least, their political parties. The mandate of the negotiating parties to negotiate on behalf of the people of Zimbabwe was questioned, but they were legitimate groups, voted into parliament in the 2008 national election.

There are different perspectives about these elections as they happened under difficult conditions marred by violence, and it is hard for the public to make a difference between the presidential elections, the results of which were not accepted, and the parliamentary election results that were ultimately accepted as the best representation of the strength of the parties involved after some contestation.

If one revisited the two events without preconceived positions one would understand that notwithstanding the delay in releasing the results the outcome was widely accepted as the best representation of the parties' performance in the election. What guaranteed the credibility of this election was Form 11, which recorded the count and results at voting station level and was signed off by party agents at the voting station. Where there were doubts was in the case where some parties were not able to be at the particular voting station either because of violence or because they had no resources to reach such places.

The three major parties shared the parliamentary seats as follows: MDC (T): 100; ZANU-PF: 99 and MDC (N): 10. The parliamentary results of this election were used as a basis for constructing the GPA and the current parliament. The results of the first round of the presidential elections were 48 per cent to Tsvangirai and 43 per cent to Mugabe.

Hell broke loose in relation to the 27 June second-round of presidential elections, which were marred by violence leading to MDC presidential candidate, Tsvangirai, withdrawing from the elections. No one, including the SADC and its facilitator Mbeki, recognised the outcome of this election, and as a result, only the outcomes of the March 2008 elections were used for the GPA. President Mugabe was left in office, but Tsvangirai became prime minister based on the interim constitution.

None of this mattered for the regime-change campaigners. In fact the views, feelings and wishes of Zimbabweans were not a concern. For those of us who were victims of colonialism and white racist apartheid rule this felt like a return of those hated 'isms'. Here, power (or the powerful) determined what was right and wrong for its subjects or slaves. Even when a joint call by all parties in the inclusive government was made for the lifting of sanctions to normalise the country's economic situation and better the lives of the people of Zimbabwe, the call was either rejected or ignored.

One has to acknowledge that there were Zimbabweans as well who were not happy about the negotiations and the outcomes thereof. For them too, any agreement that left Mugabe part of the government was unacceptable. It reminded me of my own reaction when I learnt that the ANC had decide to have F.W. de Klerk as one of the deputy presidents of the new democratic order. I had not been consulted on the issue and I was in Boston, Massachusetts, and I was about to address a public meeting on the situation in South Africa. I had to think carefully about how to explain this development to the meeting, and I took it on like a cadre of the movement ready to defend its rationale.

Back in Zimbabwe, some civil society groups were too angry to live with the compromise deal. They chose to discredit the agreement, including the parties to the agreement which used to be on the same side as them. They argued that they had not been adequately consulted by the political parties that had taken the decisions. Despite attempts by these groups to be included directly in the negotiation, they were not accommodated because the decision of the SADC was concerned with dialogue between 'political parties', that is, elected representatives of their people.

The facilitation team created at least two formal opportunities for civil society groups to make representation. The team also interacted with concerned individuals from time to time to hear their views and better understand their issues.

Although the team was not mandated to meet these groups, it did share their views with the dialogue partners. Except for the way in which the challenges facing Zimbabwe were characterised and articulated and apart from the levels of anger, the concerns and proposed solutions between the two sides, that is, civil society groups and the two MDC formations, were almost identical.

It was only when compromises were made at the negotiation table that radically divergent positions emerged and were defended. The reality, of course, is that where there are no 'victors' and 'vanquished', compromises have to be made. But where there are 'victors' and 'vanquished' there are no negotiations in any case. Power that is in the hands of the 'victors' determines what happens. A classic example is the Second World War. The US and its allies won and, as a result, dictated the terms of the settlement and the nature of the post-war world. That is why the Nuremburg Trials continued for a long time after the war. Some Nazi-related individuals were still being hunted not so long ago.

South Africans learnt the bitter lesson of compromise during the negotiation and transitional processes that gave birth to our new democracy. The ringing slogan during the height of the struggle for liberation was the 'seizure of power' but we ended up with a negotiated settlement. Initially we spoke of a two-sided negotiation, with all the collaborators on the side of the apartheid regime. But, we ended up with a 'round table'. We expected a straightforward victory in a winner-takes-all scenario and we ended up with a Government of National Unity in partnership with parties that were our enemies. Moreover, those parties had a very low share of the vote.

The findings of the Truth and Reconciliation Commission (TRC) remain for me a classic example of an outcome with which both sides were unhappy. The results were difficult to accept because they were based on compromise positions.

The proposal to have a TRC came from the mass democratic movement; the apartheid regime was against it. Following intensive negotiations that dealt with matters of disclosure of gross human rights violations, reparations and amnesty, amongst many others, the parties agreed on the TRC Act – a compromise that none of them liked. In fact, both the major parties (the ANC and the National Party) rejected some of the key findings of the commission. But the commission achieved its purpose and helped South Africa to cross the bridge from war to peace.

The historical lessons of compromise notwithstanding, South Africans were also divided over Zimbabwe. The close geographical, economic and historical relationship between Zimbabwe and South Africa tended to complicate matters.

The first problem for some South Africans was the Zimbabwean redistribution of land programme, originally set out in the terms of the Lancaster House Agreement.

There was a great deal of fear, particularly on the part of white South Africans that the new South Africa would go the route of Zimbabwe in terms of land redistribution. Nothing would convince them that what was happening in Zimbabwe could not happen in South Africa because of our constitutional framework and laws. But there were fears that the constitution and the laws could be changed.

I remember being told about a discussion between President Mwalimu Julius Nyerere of Tanzania, President Kenneth Kaunda of Zambia and ANC President O.R. Tambo in the late 1980s. Apparently, they had a talk about the developments in Zimbabwe a decade or so after their independence. At that time the moratorium on land restitution and restoration was about to lapse. That meant that they would now be able to deal with the land issue, which was a major part of their own liberation struggle. But this was at the same time that South Africa was preparing for negotiations to end the apartheid system. Nyerere and Kaunda were concerned about the coincidence in timing. Having analysed political developments within the region, they made a special plea to Mugabe to delay action on the land matter until South Africa had concluded its negotiation processes. The fear here was that if Zimbabwe acted on the land issue, South African whites would be so terrified that the envisaged talks with the liberation movement could be jeopardised. Mugabe, I am told, graciously accepted the plea from the regional leadership and agreed to delay the redistribution of land in Zimbabwe for a while to save the envisaged peace processes in South Africa.

The story surprised me. If it was part of our history, why did so few know about it? Clearly, Zimbabweans were expected to make a huge sacrifice for the sake of peace and liberation in South Africa. Moreover, it must have been an enormous political challenge for Mugabe to convince his comrades within ZANU-PF and the people of Zimbabwe that it was of strategic importance to further delay the planned land redistribution programme.

Emotions still expressed a decade later show how strategic the decision to delay the programme had been. In all our deliberations on the land reform programme of Zimbabwe we have maintained that the restoration of land to those dispossessed of it during colonialism is a legitimate expectation. Zimbabwe cannot be an exception. The challenge with Zimbabwe, however, was the problematic way in which it was done – the invasions of farms and their repossession by force, including the use of violence. I will return to this matter later. For now it suffices to say that the land redistribution programme in Zimbabwe impacted directly on South Africa.

Another challenge was the 'kith and kin' concept that Mbeki addressed in the newsletter, *ANC Today*, a concept that explored the ethnic, racial and cultural ties that existed between white Zimbabweans and the West. Many of the farmers who were affected by the Zimbabwe land redistribution programme were of British origin or descent. Some were absentee farmers who kept their farms in Zimbabwe while living in South Africa, so there were linkages between the two countries even at that level. Internationally, the footage of just one white person being beaten up by blacks on TV networks was bound to cost Zimbabwe dearly and raise the 'kith and kin' matter even more sharply. Another challenge was that the media, which had chosen to bid for the 'regime change', allowed no room for contrary views on the issues. Any dissenting voice was silenced by the dominant voices that were given the space to articulate their views.

The media's portrayal of the issues is one of the reasons Mbeki's detractors still cannot see anything good that Mbeki has done. They still find it difficult to acknowledge that the current inclusive government was constituted on the basis of the GPA Mbeki facilitated. They also ignore the fact that the GPA was adopted by a duly elected parliament of Zimbabwe. Publicly, it became difficult to say anything positive about the man without being branded a 'follower of Mbeki'. This classification was costly. It made one an enemy of those who had different views about Mbeki. I believe that one day – however long it takes – the world will acknowledge the efforts Mbeki made to help Zimbabwe to return to normality.

The Zimbabwe crisis provoked deep and emotional views. Some still continue to hold on to those views irrespective of the developments of the last four years or so, which show that the inclusive government is holding and that progress is being made to normalise the situation. Having been thrown into the deep end of it as part of the facilitation team I often felt that many approached the crisis of Zimbabwe the way blind men would feel an elephant. Their views depended entirely on the angle or perspective from which they approached the beast. A particular view of the animal, which is not the whole truth about the totality of the elephant, becomes the 'absolute truth'. Some can see the whole of the elephant but their perspectives are blinded by their prejudices or the context from which they view the elephant.

Based on a critical contextual analysis it was not difficult for us as facilitators to understand the positions from which the various parties to the Zimbabwean negotiations came, even if we did not agree with their perspectives. Their starting points coloured their views about Zimbabwe to such an extent that facts did not matter. Their *a priori* positions blinded their vision and closed their ears and minds to any reasoning that did not fall within their previously determined positions.

This was also the case with the world's major Western powers – the US and the UK.

The government in which Mbeki served during Mandela's presidency and during Mbeki's own time as president had walked many extra miles to create better relationships with Britain and the US despite the fact that they never recognised the ANC during the struggle, or supported it. Instead they supported the apartheid government, and almost to its death bed. The support included assistance with WMD such as nuclear weapons, and chemical and biological weapons.

Interestingly, the white South African regime was amongst the few countries of the South which fought on the side of the US and British forces during the Second World War, leading to it becoming part of the founding members of the UN. In fact, Jan Smuts, who was the prime minister of the Union of South Africa, is said to have written the preamble of the UN Charter. In the Cold War against the Soviet Union – what was packaged as a war against communism – apartheid South Africa was the key ally of the US and Britain.

In this regard there was some logic behind their support of the apartheid regime, irrespective of its wicked policies. Accordingly, for them, the ANC was a terrorist organisation. Prime Minister Margret Thatcher refused to meet the ANC until she left office, notwithstanding the fact that the Tambo family lived in Britain during their exile years. The US on the other hand never received any delegation of the ANC until the late 1980s. It was not surprising therefore that the relationship between the ANC-led government and some of the major Western countries was either cool or simply a relationship of convenience as was the case with many other governments that became independent before us. President Mandela's public statement during Bill Clinton's state visit in 1994 – that the aid we received from the US was 'peanuts' – explains this relationship a little better.

Among its many tasks, the new South Africa had to determine what future relationships it would craft with foreign states to create a peaceful co-existence with them. Having learnt from the experiences of all our brothers and sisters on the continent and elsewhere, the ANC-led government understood that it would not benefit the people of South Africa, especially the poor, if negative relationships with the UK and the US were maintained after the 1994 democratic elections. There was also the larger vision of the African Renaissance, which developed out of an understanding that the development of South Africa was bound up with the rest of the continent. With the African Renaissance as its major foreign relations policy, healthy relationships with the major powers in the world became even more critical. In this regard, building of a new relationship with the US and Britain to end the estrangement with the ANC was regarded to be of strategic importance.

Regarding the US, a special Bi-National Commission was constituted at the level of the deputy president (at the time, Mbeki) and the US vice-president (then Al Gore), who were co-chairs of the commission. The Bi-National Commission met twice a year: once in South Africa and once in the US. It involved a considerable number of cabinet ministers on both sides, and for each Bi-National Commission meeting there was a meeting with the president of the country concerned to report on progress.

A different route was followed in normalising the relationship with Britain. Tony Blair had just been elected prime minister. He visited South Africa and a close relationship between him and Deputy President Mbeki was established. This helped to cut through the bureaucracy to speed up the process of normalising the relationship between the two countries. At a formal level, a bilateral commission was constituted.

By the time Mbeki assumed responsibility for the facilitation in Zimbabwe, South Africa's relationships with the UK and the US were at their best and were managed carefully. US President Bush even called Mbeki their 'point man' on Zimbabwe during his state visit to South Africa.

However, these relationships were marred by the radical differences between Mbeki and the SADC on the one hand and the US and UK on the other hand in relation to Zimbabwe. The big guns were sent to SADC and AU summits to lobby them to change their views about Zimbabwe without much success. The battle raged on until it reached the UN Security Council where both the US and Britain pushed for sanctions against Zimbabwe. The US and the UK lost twice on this matter against positions held by South Africa (as a country) supported by the SADC and AU leadership. Tiny South Africa was not even a permanent member of the Security Council. This again felt like the David and Goliath story. The veto of other UN Security Council members was useful to the course of letting Africans solve their problems without hindrance. In this regard China and Russia chose to support the SADC and AU positions.

The one thing that the international community failed to understand was why the SADC and the AU held to their positions against the odds and until the end. They essentially underestimated the depth of resistance to colonialism, in all its forms. Africa and the southern African region in particular had just gone through about 50 years of anti-colonial wars of one form or another and they were not going to allow anyone to colonise them again; that included colonising their minds. They resented any activity that suggested that someone, particularly Western countries, wanted to tell them what to do with their lives. What united them most was the 'regime change' obsession of the US and Britain that threatened the very existence of these leaders or the positions they held. If the major powers could determine who should be part of the government of Zimbabwe then all of the countries in the region were vulnerable.

They were of the view that if they let the policy of 'regime change' succeed in Zimbabwe it would be used against them as well. As a result the policy had to be fought at all costs, even if it meant impoverishment.

Some commentators have criticised this position, arguing that regional leaders were so obsessed with past experiences they were ready to ignore gross violations of human rights. The same logic was frequently used against South Africa's foreign policy perspectives, especially during the time when South Africa served in the UN Security Council. However, at stake were bigger issues: humanity and human dignity; the right to self-determination; the right to make choices without being dictated to by one powerful country or another; and, importantly, sovereignty – the power to protect the rights of one's own citizens and be free from outside control or domination.

How did Mbeki land up with the daunting responsibility of resolving Zimbabwe's crisis? The answer lies in his awareness of the need for the renewal of the continent. He needed to create conditions conducive for this renewal programme.

As part of his commitment to the vision of an African Renaissance, Mbeki had a way of picking up developments within our sister African countries that had the potential of creating conditions of instability. He had his ear to the ground and was ready to respond. The South African ambassadors in the affected countries were critical in this regard. The intelligence services – at the level of sharing information – were also helpful. But the key sources of his information were his peers and other organs of civil society. At times he was ahead of the intelligence services and his ambassadors because of his network of relationships with heads of state, government leaders and other institutions of civil society. Mbeki also frequently consulted the Elders of Africa, that is, former presidents who served their countries and the continent well. He consulted them to better understand some of the dynamics on the continent. Nyerere was one such leader.

Mbeki is known as a prolific reader, which gave him an edge in relation to his colleagues and peers. For his staff, especially those who had to draft speeches for him, he was a difficult taskmaster. His article on Somalia in *ANC Today* shows beyond doubt that he is one of the most informed leaders on African affairs. It is very difficult for many to believe that his seminal 'I am an African' speech was written between 1 a.m. and about 8 a.m. on the day he delivered it. When the last staff member left his residence at 1 a.m. there was not even a draft. His advantage was his vast knowledge about the African continent and the world.

He also had a graphic mind. Mbeki had travelled extensively when he was responsible for the information and international relations department of the ANC. He travelled extensively with O.R. Tambo in his international campaign against the apartheid regime.

We tried during his term to create a formal early warning system to assist him in his troubleshooting endeavours. Unfortunately, conflicting interests within and between departments failed him and the facility created was not of a standard that could ever meet his needs. He simply walked away from it and relied on his own devices to address crises. He also went beyond the African continent to deal with challenges, for example, to the Middle East and Haiti when he was invited to do so.

On the matter of Zimbabwe, his own personal early warning system began to show red lights during the late 1990s. This was specifically over the 'land issue'. The agreements reached at Lancaster had delayed the resolution of land question by about ten years as part of the transitional arrangements to assist Zimbabweans to move into the future. As indicated earlier this was delayed further by another ten years or so to give South Africa space to negotiate a political settlement. About four years into South Africa's new democratic government Zimbabwe began to review its policies on land restitution as well as develop strategies to redistribute the land. An international conference was held in 1998, which included donor countries and developmental partners. An agreement was reached at this conference that the donor countries, particularly Britain and the US, would raise money to pay for the land that had to be redistributed or restored to indigenous Zimbabweans who were dispossessed of their land centuries ago. The Zimbabwean government would pay for the improvements and infrastructure on the land. This was a restitution and reparation programme that made sense and it raised high expectations amongst Zimbabweans.

About a year later a new Labour government was elected in the UK. As indicated in an earlier chapter one of its first decisions was to withdraw the offer on the basis that the Zimbabwean government was corrupt.

As one would expect, this response was not received kindly by the leadership in Zimbabwe nor those expecting land. I imagine that the 'war veterans' were the first to respond because they were amongst those who had been waiting for about twenty years to receive their portions of land.

This triggered further protests that were joined by other Zimbabweans. It was the occupation of white-owned farms that turned the peaceful protest into a violent one. Many people were injured and some were killed. The violence did not only affect white farmers but the black workers as well. For me, this is what went wrong in what started as a legitimate protest action: violence against the farmers and the workers.

Allegations made during that time were that neither the government nor police intervened or protected the targets of the protest action. They also did not remove those who occupied land.

The view of the government was that if Britain refused to meet their part of the deal the government would take the legally pre-scribed portions of the land and only compensate farmers for the improvements and infrastructure on the land — which was their part of the deal. The compensation for the land, they would get from Britain. If all the white farmers were British or of British origin this approach would have made sense, as Britain would have compensated the farmers directly without going through the Zimbabwean government. But some of the farmers were not British or of British origin, even if they were white. For instance, there were a considerable number of South Africans who lost farms without any compensation. Some of them appealed to the South African government to protect them and others resorted to the courts, both within South Africa and at the SADC tribunal. There was also the problem that once the protestors began to oc-cupy land, the determination of which land had to be restored to indigenous Zimbabweans, and how much of it, could not be im-plemented according to the plan.

To understand this political crisis in Zimbabwe that is normally associated with land reform (or land grabs as some would call it), one has to start with the economy, as Mbeki's paper on the crisis in Zimbabwe shows. Interestingly, the economic crisis was occasioned by the good intentions of the post-independence democratic gov-ernment, which was 'pro-poor' and 'pro-people'.

Over fifteen to twenty years Zimbabwe pumped much of its revenues into social services to improve the social conditions of the people, especially the poor. They put money into schools and today Zimbabwe has one of the most educated and skilled population. The number of skilled Zimbabweans in strategic industries in South Africa is evidence of the efforts of post-independence Zimbabwe. The region and the world are beneficiaries of this effort. Zimbabwe also invested enormous resources in the health system and other social services. Although this was commendable, the downside was that social expenditure went beyond the revenue available and created a large budget deficit. The only way to relieve the situation was either to take more loans or increase tax levels, or both. Whichever way, the effect would be to crowd out the private sector in terms of availability of capital. But higher levels of taxation also crowd out private sector investment and results in capital flight. An increase in loan finance when one cannot pay back the capital and the interest simply invites the International Monetary Fund (IMF).

The combination of all these factors had the effect of slowing down the economy, which in turn resulted in the reduction of state revenue. Accordingly, the state could no longer meet the social needs of the people in the way in which it did before.

As anticipated, the IMF gave Zimbabwe a prescription to resolve its fiscal crisis. But this led to increases in the prices of basic commodities. This naturally resulted in protests against high prices. It was this economic crisis that made the land issue more urgent and critical.

The need for the redistribution of land in Zimbabwe has never been in doubt. The region and the international community understood that one of the greatest injustices occasioned by colonialism and racism was the dispossession of the indigenous people of their land. In Zimbabwe the question of land was more pertinent as the war of independence was mainly about land and the war was waged largely in rural areas. Even today many Zimbabweans still live in rural areas.

Mbeki was deeply concerned about the Zimbabwean situation, which had the potential to escalate into a crisis that would affect the region. In this regard, Mbeki held discussions with the governments of Zimbabwe and the UK to find an amicable solution. The most urgent matter was to resolve the crisis related to the occupation of land by the 'war veterans' as this had become a highly emotive issue that was used to mobilise the world against Zimbabwe.

The immediate solution was to raise money to purchase land to which the 'war veterans' would be relocated while dealing with the greater challenge of managing the land reform process. If my memory serves me correctly, the costs for acquiring land to relocate the war veterans was about £9 million. Initially, when Mbeki discussed this matter with the British government it seemed open to finding the funds. A delegation from the Zimbabwean government also visited Britain to discuss the best way in which this crisis could be resolved, including a discussion of this fund. The expectation from the Zimbabwean delegation was that the British government would make available the £9 million as an initial gesture. Unfortunately, there was a breakdown in the talks, which led to more occupation of land and violent acts.

Given this crisis, Mbeki interacted with other donor countries in order to raise funds. Although they responded positively to Mbeki's appeal, they were concerned about how the money would be distributed in Zimbabwe and who would do it and, secondly, how Mbeki would make sure the funds reached the affected farmers? Although these questions were irritating to the Zimbabwean leadership they were prepared to engage with Mbeki to find an amicable way in which this matter could be dealt with. Mbeki also interacted with the UN to ask for help in this regard.

An agreement was reached that the money would be processed through the United Nations Development Programme (UNDP) to reach the affected farmers. As fate would have it the UNDP official who had to deal with this matter was British and the approach he took muddied the waters rather than helped to resolve the problem. This complicated the matter and the programme was stillborn and never executed.

Parallel to the unfolding land crisis was a programme to amend the constitution of the country, not only to free it of the temporary transitional constructs, but to improve it to serve the people of Zimbabwe better. All went well until clauses on land restitution were included. A campaign ensued against the new constitution that was subjected to a referendum, which the ruling party lost. The irony is that the civil society groups and their related parties effectively campaigned against a better constitution than the old one, simply because of a cluster of clauses of which they did not approve. The government on the other hand lost both its draft constitution and the clauses on land restitution.

This was a classic zero-sum game. Everyone came out losers. From here on the civil society groups, together with the MDC, campaigned for a new constitution and against human rights abuses. Where the new constitution they voted against could have protected them, the old-order constitution was used against them. The government pushed on with the land reform programme, in the process drastically resulting in the reduction of agricultural production as a result of the conflict. Suddenly a nation that was able to feed itself and share food with its neighbours was without sustenance. Emergency food support programmes were mobilised to feed the people as if there was a severe draught. Again, a zero-sum game.

The major Western powers landed their weight on the side of the MDC and applied unilateral sanctions against Zimbabwe to worsen the situation. In a period of about eight years the economy was ground down and its economic base was almost destroyed. There was no foreign currency and the Zimbabwean dollar became worthless. By the time the inclusive government was formed, the Zimbabwean dollar had been abandoned and foreign currencies like the South African rand and the US dollar were used. Many Zimbabweans voted with their feet, particularly Zimbabweans with skills. Many more left in search of better prospects for their future and the future of their children. Today we talk of a large Zimbabwean Diaspora, which is scattered throughout the world.

CHAPTER 7

Colonialism in a New Guise

The chapters on 'Farewell to Innocence' and the 'Zimbabwe Facilitation' show beyond doubt that our post-Second World War international governance system – which has not changed much since it was implemented – leaves much to be desired, especially from the perspective of the victims of past imperial and colonial systems. The chapters also show that the world is not 'innocent' at all. If it cannot do its primitive and backward things in the old ways it does them in a new guise.

The post-Second World War governance system was mapped out by the victors in the Second World War, namely, the US, Britain, France, Russia and China, who became veto-wielding permanent members of the UN Security Council. The current fault lines of this system originate from the unequal power relations between the 'victors' and the 'vanquished', and the rest of the colonised and developing world of the time. China, as the only developing country among them, always remained a unique partner in this geopolitical dynamic.

For the victims of the colonial system, the manner in which the Security Council was structured fell squarely within the definition of colonialism and imperialism. This was not surprising as the system was constructed at a time when colonial systems, with their racist characteristics, still persisted. Some of the leading powers that presided over the creation of the UN were colonising countries that also presided over the oppression and exploitation of millions of people around the world.

In a paper entitled '"There is no New Deal for the Blackman in San Francisco": African Attempts to Influence the Founding Conference of the United Nations, April–July 1945', Marika Sherwood deals with efforts made by colonised people of the time and black Americans 'to have their voices heard' and to put 'the freeing of colonies' onto the UN's agenda, but these efforts were ignored.[7] It was like the pain of the colonised was in one window, which was closed, while for the victors the only open window concerned the spoils of the war. The fact that some black Africans participated in the war was not apparent through their open window.

It is interesting from a South African perspective that racist South Africa – one of the three African countries represented at the 1945 UN conference in San Francisco – played an important role at the conference. Its racist practices did not matter for the Second World War victors. Instead its prime minister, Jan Smuts, was considered a great statesman, which he was within that context.

The rights of other nations and those of individuals outside the victors' own allies were not in the colonial powers' minds, let alone the right to self-determination and the efficacy of democratic systems. Their definition of rights applied to their own people and allies rather than that of all of humanity.

Outside this club the victims of the colonial system were used to some of these powers playing 'human rights' and 'democracy' games at home while doing just the opposite in the colonies or foreign territories they controlled. If the victims had the English word 'schizophrenia' in their vocabulary they would have described this behaviour thus, in the original Greek sense of a 'split' (*skhizein*) 'mind' (*phren*) or 'splitting of the mind'. On the one hand they promote democratic values at home while denying democracy and freedoms to others in the colonised world.

This schizophrenic approach was only possible within a racist perspective. Otherwise it would be '*bohlanya*' in Sesotho, which has a deeper meaning than simply, 'mad people'. The victims of the colonial systems also understood the colonisers as *bo senwa madi* (bloodsuckers) as they advanced their own interests at all costs, including plundering resources, exploiting subjects, treating others as less than human, and even killing. The popular name for this behaviour became that of 'racism' and its effect was 'racial exploitation'.

Hence, the UN Security Council was constructed on the basis of power and influence rather than on equal sovereign rights for all. It is almost like the traditional 'elder brother' concept with a racist slant. It is bad enough to create a paternalistic or dependent relationship of unequal rights, but to have an 'elder brother' who does not have the interests of the siblings (the 'other') at heart but instead protects his own interests at the expense of his siblings is worse.

Historical records for each permanent Security Council member show that right from the beginning permanent members used their veto powers to advance their national interests or the interests of their allies rather than the interests of the community of nations, particularly the weakest amongst them.

President Truman's closing words at the San Francisco conference seem to have landed on deaf ears: He said: 'If we fail to use it [the Charter of the United Nations] we shall have betrayed all those who have died' and 'if we seek to *use it selfishly – for the advancement of any one nation ...* we shall be equally guilty of that betrayal' (emphasis added). From the record it is clear that the betrayal of those who died started immediately after the conference ended.

Besides the protests Sherwood referred to, there were objections by smaller nations at the conference about the provision of the veto for the 'Big Five', that is, the permanent members of the security council. The concerns were twofold: one was that given the veto power, if one of the 'Big Five' threatened international peace the Security Council would be powerless to act; the second was that if there was a clash between two powers beyond the 'Big Five', they could act arbitrarily. These objections were also ignored. The results of this of course are clear. One just has to contrast the intervention of the veto-wielding US in oil-rich Kuwait in 1991 to 'protect' the Kuwaitis, with the dismal failure to lift a finger to stop the genocide in 'resource-poor' Rwanda. The former chair of the Westminster United Nations Association, Titus Alexander, aptly described the Security Council as 'a pillar of global apartheid'.[8]

Even the resolution adopted in April 2006 concerning the responsibility of the UN to protect populations from genocide, war crimes, ethnic cleansing and crimes against humanity is blatantly abused to advance the national strategic interests of the powerful or the Security Council. The intervention by North Atlantic Treaty Organisation (NATO) forces in Libya based on a resolution of the Security Council has become a classic example of how the powerful can use UN resolutions to advance their interests, and they do so at any cost. The resolution was purportedly intended to protect citizens against Muammar Gaddafi's forces but it ended up being used to provide military support for the rebels to achieve the objective of regime change.

The ultimate interest of some of the NATO partners was access to oil resources or to secure their oil interests in Libya. Rebel leaders made it clear those countries that supported them – notably Britain and France – 'should expect to be treated favourably once the dust of war had settled'.[9] The French Foreign Minister for instance was quoted as saying, 'What I know is that the NTC [National Transitional Council] said officially that concerning the reconstruction of Libya it would turn in preference to those who helped it.' That seems 'fair and logical to me', he said.

Whatever one thinks about Gaddafi or however right the cause of some of the rebel groups, at the end of the day those who wield power used the pain of others to achieve their strategic objectives at the expense of the innocent citizens of Libya who were bombarded with sophisticated war machinery and lost their houses and their businesses. Some were maimed, killed, displaced or sent into exile. Long after the bombs of NATO have gone silent the Libyan people are still caught in a spiral of violence, which for some of them may seem worse than that experienced during Gaddafi's time.

The relationship between the Security Council and the International Criminal Court (ICC) dramatises the contradictions inherent in the international governance system. In terms of the Rome Statutes, the ICC's jurisdiction covers crimes of genocide, crimes against humanity, war crimes and the crime of aggression.

Two functions of the Security Council are provided for in the Rome Statute in relation to this court. The first is that the Security Council can refer cases of countries (or leaders of countries) that are not signatories to the Rome Statute to the ICC for prosecution. Secondly, the Security Council can ask the court to defer cases that the ICC has decided to prosecute independently. The contradiction here is that three of the five members of the Security Council, namely, China, Russia and the US are not signatories to the Rome Statute but they are expected to participate in the business of the court by either intervening or referring cases to the court via the Security Council.

What is really bizarre about this is that the members who themselves are not signatories to the statute and therefore not subject to the court but have the veto power to stop it from being used against them can refer other non-signatory parties to it. What is worse is that some of them, like the US, tried not only to lobby internationally to get consent to exempt them from subscribing to the ICC, but went further to indicate consequences for those who did not act as expected.

As South Africa takes its sovereignty seriously, we maintained that in relation to the exemption of some powerful countries to ICC's jurisdiction, we could not be coerced into agreeing to something we did not believe in or which was contrary to our policy perspectives. As far as South Africa was concerned every country should ratify the Rome Statute. For this standpoint, we were made to pay a price: a grant amounting to millions of dollars was immediately withheld. For poorer countries without their own resources, this kind of punishment could be devastating.

Notwithstanding the bizarre situation concerning the role of the Security Council in relation to the ICC, the Security Council exercised its mandate by referring Sudan president, Omar al-Bashir, and others within his government, to the ICC for investigation and prosecution. The same was done with Libya. It would be interesting to know how the deliberations went within the Security Council and what motivation they would have made to refer these countries to a court whose authority over some of them was not recognised.

Comparatively speaking one might have thought that the invasion of Iraq justified on the basis of WMD – the weapons of which it was known by its aggressors not to possess – might have attracted the attention of the ICC. The pain and suffering visited on ordinary innocent Iraqi civilians, the killings and the torture of prisoners alone falls squarely within the definition of crimes against humanity, which is within the mandate of the ICC. One would have expected the Security Council at the very least to have debated the matter and let the matter be settled by a vote. But apparently these have not been raised. This recent history serves to underscore the concerns of the smaller powers at the San Francisco conference back in 1945.

Given its blatant injustice, one would have expected the whole of humanity to take to the streets and protest against the system of international governance. But the world has either submitted to the might of the powerful or has become used to the status quo. Clearly the world is resigned to the reality that the powerful can do whatever they wish with impunity while the weak and powerless are punished for any misdeeds.

Another gross injustice of our time at an international level is Guantanamo Bay. The world knows about the prisoners at the Guantanamo Bay camp who have been in detention without trial for many years. Some of them have been there since the 9/11 attacks on the US. There is evidence of severe torture of detainees in the camp. But not much has been done internationally to stop it or to seek justice for those wronged. All attempts that have been made have not produced any results.

To his credit, President Barack Obama has tried to close Guantanamo Bay detention centre since he came into power, but also without much success. In the words of the US Secretary of Defence in a testimony before the US Senate Armed Services Committee, in February 2011, 'The prospects of closing Guantanamo as best I can tell are very, very low given very broad opposition to doing that here in the Congress.'[10] I would imagine that the 'opposition in the Congress' is a reflection of where their constituencies are in this regard. Indeed, one understands the pain and suffering visited against Americans in relation to the 9/11 attacks, but that cannot justify injustice against others, especially because they have not been tried for any crime.

Again, all this has been attended by little protest, notwithstanding the fact that they are clear, gross violations of human rights and international laws.

Sometime in February 2006 the UN called for the closure of Guantanamo Bay camp, following a report of five inspectors from the UN Commissioner for Human Rights. The report called on the US to put all detainees on trial or release them. It reminded me of the 'charge or release detainees' campaign at the height of our resistance against the apartheid regime. We campaigned against what was then called 'preventative detention' whereby people were detained for long periods of time without being charged. Those of us who have been victims of arbitrary detentions without any trial and those of us who have been subjected to extreme forms of torture cannot be expected to lightly accept the actions of the US in Guantanamo Bay.

On the matter of Guantanamo, former UN Secretary General, Kofi Annan, said: 'Sooner or later there will be a need to close Guantanamo Bay [camp].' It was a strong statement, especially against a superpower, but the 'later' in it was cause for concern because it opened the door to delays. If it were not a superpower involved, an ultimatum would have been given to the state to release the prisoners or face serious consequences. The question is: what would be serious consequences for a superpower?

Annan went further to say that he opposed the holding of people 'in perpetuity'.[11] But still, there has been no indication of a change in the US. Human Rights Watch and Amnesty International have tried to make some noise without much effect. As of September 2012, 167 detainees were still reported to be in Guantanamo Bay camp.

The same global inconsistencies pertain in the Non-Proliferation of Weapons of Mass Destruction campaign. The Treaty on the Non-Proliferation of Nuclear Weapons is an international treaty that stands on three pillars:

(1) prevention of the spread of nuclear weapons;

(2) promotion of cooperation in the peaceful uses of nuclear energy; and

(3) nuclear disarmament.

Unlike the Rome Statute of the ICC, veto-wielding permanent members of the Security Council who are also nuclear powers have ratified the treaty. Four countries that are known or believed to have nuclear weapons but are not signatories are India, Israel, North Korea and Pakistan.

Again, the issue of power and privilege is pertinent. The pillar that some of the Security Council veto-holders pursue at all costs is the first: non-proliferation. On this issue, most signatories of the treaty agree, except that they are concerned about nuclear countries who are not signatories. Regarding the second pillar – the promotion of cooperation in the peaceful uses of nuclear energy – there are two difficulties. The first is that although the development and use of nuclear energy is not prohibited there is fear that once a country has the capability to enrich uranium and has plutonium reprocessing technology it can use this capability to produce fissile material, which virtually puts them at the door of capability to produce nuclear weapons. This is where most of the challenges on the peaceful use of nuclear energy are, especially as it affects Iran.

The critique of the nuclear powers referred to earlier is that they have not moved sufficiently on the third pillar – nuclear disarmament. Their harping on pillars one and two and spending inordinate time monitoring and curbing the proliferation of nuclear weapons suggests that their strategic objective is to block anyone else from acquiring the capability – leaving them as an exclusive club. What is more worrying is that their activism is based on their narrow national interests rather than the common interests of humanity, which is the spirit of the treaty.

Secondly, their pressure on those who differ from them while they remain quiet about those who are considered their allies does not help their case. In fact it discredits the cause and works against the very objectives of the treaty.

One needs a high moral ground to be able to make a meaningful contribution in this critical subject that affects the future of all humanity, a ground the superpowers do not have.

Out of sheer anxiety about South Africa's weapons landing in the 'wrong' hands after democracy, the final leaders of apartheid disposed of the country's nuclear arsenal and turned the biological and chemical weapons programme into a strictly defensive capability. Although unintended, this pre-emptive move gave the new democracy an edge when it came to credibility.

Fortunately, the ANC had campaigned consistently against the WMD possessed by the apartheid regime and against all the major Western countries that collaborated with it to develop this capability. The ANC had called for the dismantling of the weapons as its policy was that of a 'nuclear-free Africa'. When the apartheid regime decided to disarm, the ANC welcomed the action and saw it as a victory for the liberation movement. Thus, the biological and chemical weapons programme became a defensive rather than an offensive capability.

Having personally been a target of the regime's chemical and biological weapons, I found this development highly significant. Not only was I the only victim of such 'warfare' who survived to tell the story, but I lived to witness those involved in trying to murder me stand in court and accept culpability. These were the then Minister of Police, Adriaan Vlok, former commissioner of police, Johannes van der Merwe, and three policemen who carried out the operation. It was somewhat ironic that I went on to assist two presidents in the new democracy to manage the control and regulation of this capability. I felt proud to witness the preparations of a specialised police unit to deal defensively with any possible chemical and biological weapons attack during the World Cup held in South Africa in 2010.

Having disarmed 'voluntarily', South Africa met the ultimate objective – pillar three – of the treaty for the non-proliferation of WMD. This gave the country the credibility and confidence to speak on the subject of the non-proliferation. To this day, it is able to take a stand against the nuclear powers whenever they step out of the line and encourage those who strive to acquire uranium en-richment capability to do so within the limits of the treaty. South Africa has also been able to push the nuclear powers to work to-wards the objective of disarmament.

Our unique position put South Africa at the centre of efforts to deal with Iran's insistence on its right to develop nuclear energy, on the one hand, and the fears of the US that this would bring Iran close to acquiring nuclear power status, on the other hand. This tension has become a major bone of contention among friends and foes alike. Fortunately, we were in the privileged position of being able to talk to all the parties involved, without any suspicion of an agenda, to help to narrow the points of difference between the conflicting parties. The challenge, however, is that we also got lobbied by all the parties, including third parties to the conflict. The lobbying tried to divide our government to take contradic-tory positions or to influence us. But, we were able to maintain our sanity and balance to make sure that justice was done and all countries were treated in the same manner. However, this unique position – which recognises the right of Iran to use nuclear energy for peaceful purposes while understanding the fears of those who felt that Iran could develop into a nuclear state - has not put us in a favourable position with some of the nuclear powers as we attempted to achieve justice for all, irrespective of how powerful some countries might be.

The skewed international governance system bequeathed to us

by the victors of the Second World War extended to the economic sphere through the Bretton Woods system, which set up rules, institutions and procedures to govern monetary relations amongst nation states. Interestingly, the vision of the Bretton Woods institutions was not a consequence of the Second World War but it was conceived earlier after the Great Depression of the 1930s. The institutions established in this regard under the auspices of the UN were the IMF and the International Bank for Reconstruction and Development. The latter became part of a larger group called the World Bank Group.

Like the Security Council, these institutions were designed to serve the 'independent nation-states' of the time. This meant that those states that were not independent or were still colonised were excluded from participating in them. When colonised states became independent the institutions were firmly under the control of the US and Europe. In the midst of the Cold War divide between the capitalist West and the communist East these institutions were experienced by the newly independent states as instruments of the West to control the economies of the 'lesser' countries for the benefit of the West as well as promote the capitalist mode of production and the free market system.

For many African countries the IMF and World Bank were seen as instruments to advance policies and economic models that promoted the capitalist system in opposition to the communist or socialist systems of the time. Most of the prescriptions given to developing states in the 1970s and 1980s were generally ill-fated and did not help the development of those countries. A more ideological critique was that they promoted neo-liberal economic theories that did not serve the interests of the poor and marginalised.

To this day, the governance structures and systems of the IMF and World Bank expose their imperialist and colonialist origins. Unfortunately, there is no space to go into the details of their history for the last 68 years or so. For our purposes it should suffice to say that the institutions were designed under the influence of the allies of the Second World War and essentially reflect the thinking of the time. Even when the colonial system collapsed, however, and more countries became independent and joined these institutions, their structures remained largely the same. Both representation and voting powers are weighted in favour of the developed countries, particularly the victors of the Second World War against the developing countries.

What sells them as real colonial institutions though is the choice of who leads them. For instance, and to date, the president of the World Bank has always been an American and still is. He (or she) is nominated by the US as the bank's largest shareholder and his or her appointment is confirmed by the board of directors. The managing director of the IMF as well has always been a European appointed by the executive board of directors. In the last round of appointments there were protests from some major developing countries and moves to change the exclusive domination of these institutions, but they were left as they were.

The voting system is also skewed in favour of the developed countries. This is absurd given the fact that most of the countries serviced by these institutions, particularly by the World Bank, are developing countries. If this does not convince anyone that the governance system prevailing during this twenty-first century is an old colonial system, then nothing will.

In general the Cold War worsened the situation for developing countries as it divided the globe into two blocs. The formation in 1961 of the Non-Aligned Movement – a group of states that chose not to side with either power bloc, did not help much either. Much of the Western world saw the Non-Aligned Movement as another protest group that posed as an enemy. Outside of the power blocs one chose sides or paid dearly. This was like '*kgomo ya moshate: wa ikgapa o molato; wa e tlogela omolato*' (a catch-22 situation). No one could escape this. It felt like the primitive days when smaller communities or nations subjected themselves to the domination of the better resourced nation, just to be on the safe side. This did not mean that the one you chose to subject yourself to was any less of an oppressor. It was more about survival, life in the jungle.

When the colonial systems were wiped out they were substituted by neo-colonial systems that were very much the same systems in another guise. The former colonial powers had client states that governed either on behalf of the former colonial power or acted as proxy governments. The IMF and the World Bank were used to pursue the interests of the colonial powers rather than the interests of the people, as already indicated. Thus, unequal relations were perpetuated. If colonialism is defined as a policy and exercise of power that extends its control over weaker peoples or areas, driven in the main by a feeling of superiority, then the current system fits the bill.

While in government, I was concerned about another manifestation of these unequal power relations: the use of resources to beat poorer countries into submission. Many developing countries do not have resources to finance their own national budget. As a result they rely on donor agencies and countries.

I remember sitting in a meeting during which a head of state declared: 'Mr President, we are making progress. Our budget is no longer made up of 70% foreign funding; it is now 60%.' That depressed me, because it suggested that even that country's army was foreign funded. In such a situation the country holding the purse strings must call the shots. It's a case of: 'He who pays the piper calls the tune.' Whenever there are competing candidates for a position in international organisations, poorer countries are visited by those who bankroll them in the guise of lobbying. But what it turns out to be is either an offer to support the country or an individual

– which essentially is corruption – or the application of subtle pressure, or even more overt threats, over the withdrawal of financial support should a 'favourable' position not be taken.

Thus, basic extortion, fraud and corruption move easily to the level of international extortion, fraud and corruption.

In a case that bordered on what I call 'terrorism' at the highest levels, during a discussion South Africa pursued at a presidential level, the leader of a small and poor country refused on principle to support the 'Coalition of the Willing' – the grouping of countries in favour of the attack on Iraq. But when the members of the coalition were made public, the said country was on the list. It was shocking to say the least.

When confronted on it, the president of the country responded: 'Mr President, I received a call during the night and I was told that if I did not support the Coalition of the Willing, our entire foreign-funded budget would be withdrawn. That would mean a collapse of my government and I would not even be able to pay the army.' These are the 'things of darkness' (*ntho tsa bosiu*). During the day you are okay; in the night you are under attack. This is real state-on-state terrorism!

In every way – in form, appearance and in substance – these actions cannot be said to be democratic, participatory or even consultative. Even if you are consulted, final decisions are made 'after consultation with' rather than 'in consultation with'. It is a straight-forward dictatorship of the powerful. To maintain this position the powerful have to make sure that no one comes close to their power. To achieve this, a regulatory system is put in place that applies to everyone else except those who have the power. The powerful can violate the law but the rest must respect the law, otherwise they get punished, and punished severely.

In this regime – that is, the UN governance system – there is no separation of powers between the judiciary, the executive and parliament. The security council is all in all the prosecutor, the judge and the executor.

Sitting in the Union Buildings trying to assist the president to manage this international system with the help of the Department of Foreign Affairs, I often wondered how all of us could allow such a system to continue. It was like growing up in an apartheid system and wondering how and why your parents could subject themselves to such a crude and blatantly racist system without taking it on. How could they have allowed white *'pikininis'* (children) to call them 'boys' and 'girls' up to their graves while they were expected to address whites as *'groot baas'* and *'klein baas'*.

My own initiation into the apartheid system came just after the age of sixteen and introduced me to the concept of two separate rule systems for blacks and whites. At that age you had to have a 'passbook' to control your movements, including where you will live, where you will go to school or university, where you will work and so forth. After applying for the 'passbook' you got what was called a *'dublicate'* (in an Africanised way), which was a duplicate of the application form that was given as a receipt for the application. One had to keep that piece of paper daily to produce it whenever the police asked for it.

Six months later the *'dublicate'* was in bad shape and I had tried to keep it together with a *saloteipi* (sellotape). As I emerged from the Westgate train station in Johannesburg to go to the 'pass office' to check whether or not my passbook was ready I met a contingent of young white policemen who promptly demanded my pass. I responded by producing my *'dublicate'*. One young white policeman said, *'Hoekom is jou duplikaart so stukkend?'* ('Why is your duplicate card so damaged?') My innocent response was to start by addressing him as *'Meneer'* ('Sir') to show respect as I was taught at school. I was beaten up for that. He said, *'Ek is nie jou meneer; ek is jou baas!'* ('I am not your Sir [equal]; I am your boss!')

This incident, which was an everyday experience for black people, taught me that even the Afrikaans I learnt at school was not applicable in an apartheid society. Here, you must also behave differently. So, there were two sets of rules, one for blacks and one for whites. And here, the rule of law did not apply. You could not lay charges against the '*klein baas*'!

As I pulled back from the past I realised that my aversion to this international system was informed by the struggle we waged against the apartheid system. I was simply not prepared to accept that we had just come out of an apartheid system into another world that looks exactly like it, with '*groot base*' and '*klein base*' on the one hand, and 'boys' and 'girls' on the other.

A cursory study of the development of humanity over the centuries and from one generation to another shows that humans are just 'children of their times' and are prone to repeating mistakes of the past unconsciously as if they were never made before. Everyone cannot believe today that we ever allowed systems like slavery and slave trade, a colonial system or apartheid. We also wonder how the Nazis were part of humanity or a product of humanity. There are wars we all wonder how we could have fought.

But this is exactly where we are. Generations to come will wonder how our generation could allow such an unjust and archaic system that belongs to the discredited era of colonialism to persist without challenging it effectively and forcing it to change. When they ask questions we will look stupid – like we do with apartheid today. The questions will sound like this: 'How did you accept a world of '*groot baas*' (the superpowers) with '*klein baas*' (the untouchable states that do what they like under the protection of the superpowers), on the one hand, and on the other hand, 'boys' and 'girls' who are dictated to by the '*groot baas*' and the '*klein baas*'.

It is for this reason that the ANC determined well before our first democratic elections in 1994 to go back to the concept of the African Renaissance and start with the renewal of the African continent. The ANC understood that South Africa could never be free unless the rest of the African continent was free, and that South Africa would never defeat racism in the world without changing the economic conditions of Africans on the African continent and in the Diaspora. It understood that South Africa could not be fully developed without the development of the rest of the African continent. From the beginning the ANC saw itself as an African national congress and not just a South African congress. That is why it changed its name soon after its launch from the South African Native Congress to the African National Congress. The author of the anthem, '*Nkosi Sikelele i'Afrika*', which the ANC adopted as its own, conceptualised it as an African anthem rather than a South African anthem. The 1906 speech of Pixley ka Seme, one of the ANC's founders, says it all. He starts in the same way Mbeki did: 'I am an African.' A reading of the speech leaves one in no doubt that the African (South African) leaders of old thought of the whole African continent as one facing the same challenges.

The path to renewal starts from the recognition that the African continent was the most affected by centuries of slavery, colonialism, neo-colonialism and the present international governance system that reaffirms the old imperial and colonial systems. But it also recognises that it is Africa that needs to lead its own renewal, and the renewal of the entire global system. We understood as we developed the concept that there could be no renewal of the African continent without the renewal of the global political and economic systems.

Thus, the renewal of the continent could not depend on outsiders but on ourselves. We learnt from history that freedom is never given on a platter, and that oppressors never surrender power freely and voluntarily. For this reason we had to strategise and develop a programme to pursue our objective.

As I said earlier, although many missed it, the idea of the African

Renaissance was launched by the first president of democratic South Africa, Nelson Mandela, at the OAU Summit in Tunis, May 1994, but the man who popularised the vision and put it on the global map was Thabo Mbeki, starting with the famous 'I am an African' speech he presented at the South African Parliament in May 1996.

A team had been constituted in Mbeki's office, which was then the deputy president's office, consisting of his special advisers Vusi Mavimbela, Moss Ngoasheng and Mojanku Gumbi, the then parliamentary adviser, Essop Pahad, and myself as the head of the deputy president's office. Its task was to 'download' the vision from Mbeki's mind, as we used to say, and this was done within the broader policy framework of the ruling party. A plan of action was developed and presented to cabinet for approval. From there on Mbeki made the vision of the African Renaissance the centre of everything he did during his term as the deputy president and during his presidency.

Firstly, the vision had to be sold to South Africans, through consultative conferences and meetings involving as many stakeholders as possible, and this lead to the publication of a number of books. The second part of this step was to engage with the South African government at all levels, including national, provincial and local departments in order to make it a pivotal point for all government programmes.

The second step was to mobilise the leadership of the African continent in order to sell the African Renaissance as a continent-wide vision. This had to be managed with sensitivity. We wanted the idea to grow from its roots as an African vision and programme. The natural starting point for this overture was the chair of the OAU, Abdelazia Bouteflika, president of Algeria at the time. I accompanied Mbeki (who was by then the president of South Africa), to Algeria, armed with a document called the Millennium Partnership for the African Recovery Programme, which outlined the vision and which was then taken to the OAU in Summit in Togo in July 2000.

Strategically, two African state presidents were then leaders of the Group of 77 developing nations and the Non-Aligned Movement, namely, Olusegun Obasanjo of Nigeria and Thabo Mbeki. Together with the OAU chair, they were tasked by the OAU to present this vision – as an African vision – to the Okinawa G8 Summit in Japan in 2000.

A development framework for Africa – NEPAD – was also conceptualised and presented to all international fora, including the G8, to make sure that all engagements with Africa took place within the framework that Africans had developed for themselves. New forms of partnerships were developed leading to the formation of the Africa Partnership Forum (APF), after the 2003 Evian G8 Summit, and to broaden the dialogue between the G8 and NEPAD so as to include other African institutions and Africa's major bilateral and multilateral development partners.

The APF was conceptualised as a partnership of equals with the objective of enhancing actions on both sides of the partnership in support of Africa's development. It has four co-chairs: two from Africa and two from the development partners.

The APF meets twice a year and focuses on key political issues affecting Africa. One of its functions is to make 'recommendations to leaders on decisions which needed to be taken in key regional and global processes, including the G8 and G20, the AU and the UN, in support of Africa's development'. The APF is also concerned with the monitoring and evaluation of the 'delivery of commitments on both sides of the partnership'.

As part of Africa's own performance monitoring mechanism for African countries the Peer Review Mechanism (APRM) was established in 2003 to 'encourage conformity in regard to political, economic and corporate governance values, codes and standards

... and the objectives in socio-economic development' within the NEPAD framework.[12]

These developments are highlighted to illustrate the efforts made by African leaders to shift the philosophy and ideological positions of the international governance systems. The idea is for developing and developed countries to be regarded as equal partners as well as ensure that the concerns of African countries are represented at all significant international fora and that no decisions are made without their participation.

Since the intervention of the OAU (now AU) at the Okinawa Summit of the G8 countries, the summit has held no meetings without the participation of leaders from the African countries. Other key countries from developing regions like Asia, South America and others have also been invited to participate, leading into a proposal for the formation of a new group of thirteen countries (the G13), that is a G8 plus Five Group, which would include five leading emerging economies, namely Brazil, China, India, Mexico and South Africa. The idea had not been implemented because of resistance amongst some of the G8 countries who would like to reserve membership of the club for the privileged and powerful.

Interestingly, on climate change issues this forum was found to be useful. At the 31st G8 Summit held at Gleneagles, Scotland, in 2005, the leading emerging countries were invited to join the talks on climate change with the hope of forming a more representative network on trade issues and wider cooperation on climate change. Following this meeting the G8 plus Five countries issued a statement that expressed a vision to build a 'new paradigm for international cooperation' in the future.

The positive aspect of these developments is that they have raised the need for a broader forum for cooperation and have shed some light on the need for a 'new paradigm for international cooperation'.

For now we stand at the gate of these new ideas and visions.

Ahead of us, we can see the land of promises. These are promises that could fundamentally change the world. They are based on simple principles: the common good of all of humanity, the destruction of narrow nationalistic interests and the establishment of a world in which we can all live in peace and prosperity, sharing the common interests of all humanity.

PART THREE

CHAPTER 8

Warning Lights

S outh Africa is a great country to live in! We started well in 1994 with international icons like Madiba. We were considered to be a miracle, a marvel of the world. With expectations very high we did our best to create a new South Africa that was non-racial, non-sexist, just, democratic, equitable and prosperous. We all know that we are not there yet but it is a work in progress.

Extraordinary achievements were made in many areas since 1994, but there are still great challenges facing our country. These are summed up in three words: poverty, unemployment and inequality. One could argue that there are many other challenges outside these three, but clearly our greatest challenge is in the area of the economy, integral to improving the quality of life of the people of South Africa.

This challenge was anticipated and was expressed in the form of the NDR from the early days of the life of the ANC and concretised at the first National Consultative Conference held in Morogoro, Tanzania in 1969, and other conferences thereafter.

The strategic objective of the NDR was to construct a social order in which the legacy and consequences of national and gender oppression and economic exploitation of blacks in general and Africans in particular are 'liquidated'.[13] At the Morogoro conference the NDR was understood as 'a dialectical resolution of the class, gender and national contradictions'. In simple terms the NDR would be realised when the ills of our society are not defined or expressed in racial and gender terms. As long as poverty, unemployment and inequality manifest themselves in racial and gender terms we are far from achieving the objectives of the NDR.

With this perspective in mind, counter-revolution was understood as any activity aimed at resisting this change or reinforcing these contradictions. To ensure that the forces of counter-revolution did not negate this project we regularly held analytical sessions on the 'balance of forces' on the basis of which we identified opportunities to advance the objectives of the NDR. Based on this strategy we were able to weave our way through the challenges we faced nationally and internationally to achieve many of our objectives.

The fatal weakness of this strategy, however, is that its analysis of the 'balance of forces' focused on external forces and factors and ignored internal dangers and threats that could cause an implosion within and amongst the motive (driving) forces of the NDR. The ANC, the party of revolution, did not look strategically at the reality that counter-revolutionary forces could have infiltrated the organisation over the years and that such elements would come back to life at strategic moments during the execution of the NDR in order to negate it from within, derail the movement and then pursue their own interests and not the interests of the people. The party of revolution also did not anticipate that its own cadres would be corruptible and compromised in many ways, to the extent that they would not be able to pursue the objectives of the NDR.

Based on my experience as a member of the NEC of the ANC and my years in government, I am of the view that the ANC as a liberation movement and a ruling party was adequately prepared to deal with attacks from outside but was not sufficiently prepared for this attack from the inside and on its cadres.

For me one of the most heartbreaking experiences of my ten years as a member of the NEC of the ANC and my thirteen-and a-half years in government was watching the warning lights on the dashboard turning red without being able to do much to save the situation.

Like any driver I saw the warning lights switch on, but as a civil servant I did not have unencumbered authority to apply breaks, change course or direct the car to a garage or service station. The vehicle's computerised messages were clear but somehow those who had the authority were paralysed by circumstances either of their own making or beyond their control. Some simply did not have the capacity or the will to intervene.

I made two interventions to try to save the situation, but without much success. The first was made soon after I joined the government. It took me only a year to discover that our comrades who were prepared to govern from the crucible of the struggle were also corruptible and material interests could change the nature and character of a person – even the best of the cadres of the movement – within a very short space of time.

The mistake we made was that we glorified the ANC-led movement to such an extent that we missed the realities that would confront the movement once in government. One just needs to go back into history and analyse what really drew people into the struggle or sent them into exile. There are those who joined the struggle because of their commitment to justice, for which they were prepared to die. However, others joined it because they were part of the dynasty of the movement but had no commitment to justice. Some went into exile because they had committed a crime and were not prepared to go to jail. Yet others got involved simply because they hated being treated like a lesser being or were not allowed participating fully in the economy because of the apartheid system. Others hated the racist apartheid system and wanted it gone.

Apart from the first reason for joining the struggle, the other motives do not necessarily lead to a commitment to the course of justice. Some people really wanted a chance to participate in the game rather than change without being disadvantaged by the colour of their skin.

Another of my discoveries was that the 'old' was corrupting the 'new', which did not make sense in the beginning. My expectation was that the players from the 'old order', that is the apartheid system, would watch the 'new' incumbents from the liberation movement like hawks and expose them for corruption and other ills. But the opposite was true. The security for those who were corrupt or those who wanted to loot lay in corrupting the new; because once the newcomers were corrupted, they could not act against the old.

Corruption is devastating. It can compromise leaders to such an extent that they abandon their mission to serve the people and instead serve their own interests or the interests of those who have compromised them or those who know that they have been compromised.

Having grasped the strategy of the 'old' corrupting the 'new', I rushed for the panic button. As I was then in the office of the deputy president and because of the seriousness with which I took this matter my concern took the form of a letter to President Nelson Mandela, and I copied it to Deputy President Thabo Mbeki. And, the message was as clear as an alarm bell: THE 'OLD' IS CORRUPTING

THE 'NEW' and this trend should be stopped in its tracks or it would consume the new like an uncontrollable cancer.

Unfortunately, I cannot publish the letter as it was classified because of its sensitivity at the time, especially because it was about the 'old' and the 'new', the relationship between which was then still very precarious. It was also sensitive and required discretion because those who were involved had the capacity to neutralise any strategies to address the issue.

I did not allow the matter to rest there. After sending the letter I personally discussed the matter with the deputy president who understood my concerns and said that he would discuss the matter with the president. He was of the view that besides efforts to excise the cancer from government there needed to be a focus on the party and its members from which most of the political leaders were drawn.

That was as far as I could take it as a civil servant. But as part of the liberation movement I could take my concerns further in informal discussions. A year later or so I was elected as a member of the NEC of the ruling party, which gave me better scope to raise such matters. But there were still limitations, as I could only engage within the party rather than in the public arena.

Efforts were made though by the leadership in the cabinet and within the party to sensitise people about the dangers and risks of corruption. A battery of laws to curb it was championed. Unfortunately, the cancer overtook our efforts and by the end of the first ten years of the ANC in government the festering sore burst open and splashed over all of us, turning a glorious liberation movement into a movement that fed on its own.

History will show that what wrecked the people's movement was corruption. The struggle for power for its own sake has become a life-and-death issue as it means that if one is not in power you cannot enrich yourself or ensure that you never go to jail, regardless of how corrupt you are. For some, particularly those whites who never accepted the change from a racist apartheid system to an open democracy, they saw the corruption as typical of a 'black government'. For them, and from a distinctly racist perspective, South Africa was becoming 'like the rest of Africa'. Lately, I have also heard this view, not from a racist perspective, but from an African perspective. One of our ambassadors told me that it was tough these days to represent the country as some of our African colleagues were saying, 'You are now just like us', based on what they see, hear and read.

I was told that the comments came from a place not of gloating, but of disappointment, at the fall South Africa had suffered from its iconic level in the days of the Mandela presidency. I was told that these countries had been striving to 'follow in our footsteps', that they were now concerned that the foolproof model they had hoped for was threatened by the same challenges that had drowned them.

For those of us who are still defined as black, what is happening in our country is like a 'wake-up call' and a reminder that we did not engage in the liberation struggle to seize power and then just be like 'them' – in other words, just like whites, except within the context of a non-racial and non-sexist, democratic society. In such a democracy - in which we are 'just like them' – all we would have achieved is the democratisation of pain.

For the ANC the warning lights concerning the status of the movement and its cadres came on during the 2000 General Council where it was recognised that the character of the cadres of the movement was changing and this threatened the movement's future. The agreement was that we needed a 'new' cadre to save the movement. In this regard it was agreed that we needed to strengthen political education programmes so that the 'new' cadre would still remain focused on changing the conditions of life of the people, especially the poor and not to enrich themselves at the expense of the people.

All this talk notwithstanding, risks and challenges kept on growing.

I became increasingly concerned, especially because from where I was located – at the helm of the government – I had the privilege of seeing beyond what the ordinary eye could see. Being in both the government and party leadership was an advantage. But I was also moved by my commitment to my faith, which defines justice in terms of the 'common good' of all humanity.

To deal with the challenge as I saw it I conceived a written analytical discussion paper for the president, who was then Mbeki. Although I treated it as confidential I did not classify the document because I thought the president may choose to use it within the party to help to change the course of the movement and the country. The paper was produced during 2001 under the title, 'Threats and Potential Threats to the Achievement of the National Democratic Revolution: A Discussion Paper'.

Having re-read this paper it pains me to be reminded that the signs were there, that we understood them, yet we missed them. Some would say that we did not miss them, but they could not do much about it. Yet others, like me, would say we tried to raise an alarm without much success. If we had dealt with these warning signs adequately, we would not be where we are today.

Because of the seriousness of the matter I have decided to present the paper in its entirety in the hope that we can retrace our steps to save the movement for which many sacrificed their lives.

Threats and Potential Threats to the Achievement of the National Democratic Revolution

A Discussion Paper

Introduction

1. For many years our people made enormous sacrifices, including the ultimate sacrifice of death. Many were brutally tortured and imprisoned and some were forced into exile. All this was done to:

    1.1 Free our country from the evil, racist system of apartheid, and
    1.2 Establish a just, non-racial, non-sexist and prosperous democratic society.

2. In 1994, we achieved, in part, this objective of the National Democratic Revolution (NDR). To this end, we owe those who made the sacrifices to achieve these objectives a 'permanent debt'. The only way to fully pay this debt is by ensuring that the objectives of the NDR are fully realised.

Advancing the National Democratic Revolution

3. The challenge today is for us to intensify the struggle to achieve all aspects of the NDR to ensure a better life for all South Africans, especially those who were historically disadvantaged by the racist apartheid system.

4. Knowing where we come from, extra-ordinary achievements have been made since 1994. But given the extent of the damage of the apartheid system, much more still needs to be done to alleviate the conditions of abject poverty for many of our people.

The Balance of Forces and Accelerating the NDR

5.   The pace at which this revolution is conducted depends on the balance of forces at any moment of this struggle.

6.   To determine the extent to which the pace of change (revolutionary transformation of the South African society) can be accelerated, the African National Congress (ANC), as the only custodian of this NDR and the agent of change, assesses (from time to time) the balance of forces between the forces of change and those of reaction. This enables the ANC to determine the strategic focus of the revolution to achieve maximum impact as well as create more space to win more ground for the NDR.

7.   The last assessment of the balance of forces showed that the NDR had reached a stage where it was no more possible to reverse the gains made by the party of the revolution (the ANC), the people of South Africa and their allies.

Targeting the ANC (the Agent of Revolution)

8.   It is for this reason that the enemies of the revolution have turned on the ANC (the agent of this revolution) itself as the only way to achieve their objective of stopping the course of this revolution or reversing its gains. Their objective is to erode the revolutionary character of the movement to an extent that it will not be able to carry out its revolutionary mandate.

9.   The greatest challenge, which faces the ANC, now is the identification of the threats and/or potential threats to the ANC (the agent of the revolution), which have the possibility of threatening and/or destabilising the very course of the NDR.

10. There are internal and external factors, which threaten or have

the potential to threaten the very being of the ANC as an agent of change.

Internal Threats

11. The **internal factors** (threats and potential threats) can be categorized as follows:

    11.1 Criminal elements within the ANC,

    11.2 Agents of the Old Order within the ANC or those compromised by the Old Order,

    11.3 Corrupt or Corrupted elements within the ANC,

    11.4 The new Culture of Greed and Pursuit of Self Interest at the expense of the Agent of Revolution itself,

    11.5 The new Culture of Ambitions for Leadership Positions in the movement (for personal gain) even at the risk of destroying the very organisation of revolution (the agent of the revolution).

12. Given the above, any enemy or hostile intelligence agency would be foolish not to use these old and new tendencies, which are a fertile ground for counter-revolutionary activity. As a result, the trend now is to use ANC cadres to assist the ANC to destroy itself or to self-destruct. In this regard, *the major threat to the ANC is the ANC itself or its cadres.*

Combating Internal Threats

13. To deal with threats 11.1 and 11.3, the party of revolution needs to commission an extensive investigation, using both party and state resources to root out criminal and corrupt elements within the organisation. This should include those who are compromised to an extent that poses a threat to the integrity and life of the organisation.

14. As regards threat 11.2, the ANC and its Alliance partners must

institute their own 'truth commission' to give those who were compromised by the Old Order (or used by the Old Order to infiltrate the organisation) an opportunity to disclose their circumstances to the leadership. The objective is to ensure that the old negative forces do not use these comrades' compromised status to destroy the organisation.

15. A special dispensation for cases 11.1 – 11.3 could be provided (for those who are affected) to declare the extent to which they have been compromised and not wait until they are found out later. The leadership of the organisation can then determine as to how they handle these particular cases of voluntary disclosure. Any one who does not disclose voluntarily should be subjected to disciplinary measures and/or prosecuted accordingly if they were found to have been involved in criminal acts.

16. As regards 11.4 and 11.5, it is important to note that radical changes in the nature and being of the cadreship of the movement have occurred in the light of the nature and form of the environment in which the NDR has to be executed. The ANC cadre now develops and executes his/her responsibilities in conditions where personal interest, self-development, positions (office) and personal gain are becoming the major motive force. This is in the place of the dedicated cadres who were ready to sacrifice themselves and even die for the ideal and course of the NDR (and for the ANC).

17. As a result of 16 above, the new transformed cadre has become an 'ordinary human' who is susceptible to corruption and vulnerable to forces which are fundamentally opposed to the ideals of the NDR. Accordingly, some are ready to 'sell' the struggle for a morsel of bread, and others are open to 'recruitment' by forces opposed to the NDR.

18. In this regard, the ANC has already started a campaign to rid itself of these tendencies. The 2000 and 2001 January statements of the ANC show its commitment in this regard. The campaign was demonstrated more by the main thrust of the National General Council of the ANC held in Port Elizabeth last year. The major theme for this Council was the creation of a new cadre of the ANC to ensure that the course of the NDR is not sacrificed on the altar of self-interest, greed and the negative pursuit of self-ambition at the expense of the course of the revolution.

19. The party of revolution needs to be extremely vigilant as the matters referred to in 11.1 – 11.5 are a classical breeding ground for external and/or foreign agents and interests. Members of the movement who are affected in one way or another in this regard are easy targets of external or foreign interests, which are opposed to our national interests and/or security.

External Threats

20. The **external factors** (threats and potential threats) include amongst others:

    20.1 The use of the internal factors by external and/or foreign entities to try to discredit the ANC (the agent of NDR), as indicated earlier.

    20.2 The campaign to delegitimise the ANC (the agent of change) by presenting its majority support base as a threat to democracy when this is the democratic will of the people of South Africa.

    20.3 The attack on the capacity of the ANC Government to deliver against the vast needs occasioned by the legacy of apartheid. Interestingly, the issue of delivery is used not because the forces concerned would deliver better. It is used for the purposes of discrediting the ANC Government with the view of taking over and reversing the gains already made.

20.4 The sustained vicious attacks on the person of the President of the ANC as a strategy to erode the credibility of the ANC as well as weaken its capacity to pursue the objectives of the NDR.

20.5 The effort to break the Tripartite Alliance (ANC/SACP/COSATU) to weaken the effectiveness of the ANC in pursuance of the NDR.

21. The matter raised in 20.1 has been dealt with already under 'internal threats'. Three problem areas need to be highlighted here:

21.1 The new challenge of tenders and bids with South Africans (and at times ANC members) on opposing sides as part of foreign partners. The risk here is the possibility of luring the South African players into collaborating with foreign intelligence agencies, which might be hostile to the national interests of the country. In this case the losers are always more vulnerable than the winners.

21.2 The second challenge has to do with the interests of foreign entities to promote specific members of the ANC into leadership positions to advance their interests. In this regard, the foreign entity is likely to use all means available to it to promote and fund the said candidates, including personal offers as well as compromising them to guarantee their compliance. This is clearly a threat to the national security of the country as the said leadership is bound to sacrifice the national interests of the country to serve those of a foreign entity.

21.3 The third is the threat of some ANC members becoming part of syndicated crimes, including corrupt or compromised elements, which again would threaten the national security and interests of the country.

Combating External Threats

22. On these three challenges, the intelligence community will need to be more vigilant to ensure that no foreign entity threatens the national interest and security of the country.

23. Vigilance requires as well that all intelligence entities critically evaluate intelligence information to ensure that such information is not used to advance the interests of those who are hostile to our country or those who are opposed to the NDR.

24. On 20.2, the ANC needs to expose the fallacy of liberal democratic traditions which allow democratic processes only if they are able to manipulate them to serve the interests of the privileged classes in society. The ANC needs to assert its democratic right to use its majority to deliver quality services to all South Africans, particularly the historically disadvantaged.

25. Secondly, the ANC needs to mobilise the masses of our people to participate directly in the processes of transformation and in the delivery mechanisms. The ANC must ensure that the masses of our people are well informed on the ground to beat the propaganda war aimed at distorting reality and turning a lie into a truth!

26. To achieve this the ANC Government will have to intensify its programme of interacting with various sectors of our society (political, religious, unions, business, etc) as well as engage in Imbizos to keep the people on board.

27. On 20.3, the ANC Government needs to review some of the policies of the Government as well as the implementation strategies to ensure accelerated delivery of quality services, particularly to the poor. In this regard, the target of the mid-term of the second term of the ANC Government, and the psychological mark of ten years in government by 2004 become very crucial and strategic.

28. Accordingly, the ANC and the Government need urgently to launch a campaign to accelerate delivery in the next three years leading to the next elections. In this regard, two critical actions must be taken:

28.1 A mid-term audit of performance of government should be undertaken and results made available by the Cabinet Lekgotla of January 2002. The audit to be carried out by all government entities and Clusters of Directors General will generate more enthusiasm to meet the required targets by the year 2004.

28.2 On the basis of the audit and the deliberation of the January 2002 Lekgotla, the President should consider announcing the campaign to accelerate delivery of quality services as part of the preparations for the celebration of the 10th Anniversary of the new non-racial, non-sexist democratic South Africa.

29. Furthermore, the ANC Government must ensure that the masses of our people understand the fiscal constraints, which limit the scope and extent of delivery within specific timeframes.

30. On both 20.3 and 20.4 the Government Communications and Information Systems (GCIS) and the Presidency must sharpen and intensify their communications strategies to ensure that the people of South Africa are not short-changed with information they need to

be able to pass an intelligent judgement on the performance of the party of revolution.

A Uniting Leadership for a United ANC

31. The best defence against external attacks on the ANC is a uniting leadership around which the membership rallies in defence of them.

32. Accordingly, we need to guard against leadership which advances or entrenches itself by taking sides with specific factions within the movement to enhance their chances of success in the leadership stakes.

33. The leadership needs also to resist and rebuke those members who thrive on endearing themselves to the leadership by running down other comrades to improve their chances of success or of being appointed into positions of influence.

34. Ultimately, the leadership of the ANC must strive to make its President the President of the rest of the organisation rather than for a specific section or faction of the movement. This can be achieved only if the leadership in its totality is a uniting leadership of the movement.

Conclusion

A threat to the ANC (the agent of the revolution) is a threat on the National Democratic Revolution. A divided ANC is a threat to the National Democratic Revolution.

Having read this 'Discussion Paper' we might well ask what happened between 2001 and today? Where are we in relation to the issues raised? Did we survive the 'threats and potential threats' referred to here? I prefer to leave the answering of these questions to members of the ANC as they are better placed to answer these questions through their own 'Organisational Renewal' processes, and then judge for themselves. There is no doubt, though, that many people are worried and concerned about where we are and where we are going.

In terms of strategies to combat these 'threats and potential threats', in my opinion, the proposals in the 'Discussion Paper' are still as valid today as they were in 2001.

CHAPTER 9

The Pikoli and Selebi Matters

Vusi Pikoli and Jackie Selebi are my dear comrades in the struggle for liberation and were my close colleagues in government for a period of almost thirteen years. Moreover their spouses are also comrades in their own right and whenever we met we did so as a family, in the way in which comrades in arms might.

The first time I met Selebi was in the trenches of the struggle before he was forced into exile. He was as energetic, boisterous and dramatic then as he was when he returned from exile many years later. On his return he became responsible for the welfare services for members of the ANC, together with Comrade Winnie Madikizela-Mandela. My particular point of contact with him was in relation to 'returnees' or 'returned exiles' (as they were called then) as I was the chairperson of the National Coordination Committee for the Repatriation of South African Exiles and as the general secretary of the SACC.

It is during this period of his work as a welfare officer that he

met many of the donors who lined up to assist the liberation movement and its members on their return. Many of them were ordinary business people and old friends, but some were the usual corrupt crowd that home in on anyone who is in power or is about to
assume positions of influence in order to secure their own future
and interests.

There were others who presented themselves as dignified business people when in fact they were on a mission to corrupt and
compromise the new leadership before they even assumed power.
Some were just downright criminals from the underworld who
needed relationships to cover up their criminal activities.

This is the period during which Jackie Selebi met people like
Glenn Agliotti and others, then as 'good Samaritans'. They befriended the leadership of the liberation movement as they returned
from exile. I think it explains the roots of the statement Selebi made
when confronted by the media about his relationship with Agliotti.
'Algliotti is my friend, finish and *klaar*', said Selebi. The statement
was indeed unfortunate and unwise but it reflects the historical
connections and relationships they had built up at the time when
people came to 'assist' the ANC as its cadres returned from exile.

Unfortunately, this apparently 'innocent' relationship proved to
be fatal for Selebi, causing enormous and unbearable pain for his
family, friends and those who cared about him.

Those of us who were engaged in the struggle from inside
the country worked on the basis that our revolutionary movement had an effective intelligence service with capacity to monitor and screen these relationships. The aim of such intelligence
was to ensure that the people's revolutionary movement was
not compromised or infiltrated by counter-revolutionary elements with the intention of destroying the organisation from
inside or by elements that were downright corrupt and criminal
whose interests were to use the organisation to get rich as well as

compromise it to a level where it would not be able to deal with these criminals.

Looking back, it appeared to me that the liberation movement's intelligence arm (as it returned home) was not as effective as it should have been, and many fraudsters and corrupt counter-revolutionary elements managed to embed themselves within the organisation. To be fair to those operatives, however, we must accept that transitional politics is very complex and difficult, especially during the period of integration between apartheid-era intelligence services and those of the liberation movement.

Some comrades told me that it was a real challenge to monitor all meetings conducted by the leadership of the movement, and the reasons for such meetings. In this regard many of these activities happened outside their purview. Yet others felt that my critical view on the matter was unfair as the leaders themselves (as leaders of the liberation movement) were expected to understand personally the dangers and risks involved in meeting some of these characters. If they did not know about the intentions of such characters they should have been able to work it out during their interactions. We must accept that some of the leaders who were either already compromised, or corrupt or corruptible, participated in these discussions being aware of the ultimate objective.

However, I remain of the view that this failure or inability to detect the intentions of some characters who interacted with the leadership of the ANC from the time of preparation to return home and on landing is partly responsible for the ANC bleeding from inside today and struggling to survive! There are of course other reasons for this bleeding that involve just corrupt and criminal elements.

The mysterious 'Browse Mole Report', which, following an extensive investigation, was found to have been produced by elements within the Directorate of Special Operations (DSO), popularly known as the Scorpions, was one of the wake-up calls for the country that many failed to heed. Firstly, the fact that a politically loaded document that was clearly meant to create division between comrades who were in government and those outside government on the one hand, and between various countries (like Angola and Libya) and South Africa, on the other, showed that there were indeed individuals within organs of the state (in this case the DSO) who were bent on fuelling tensions and conflicts within the ruling party, the government, and between South Africa and other governments. It was not surprising that whoever was responsible for this strategy planned to have the document land mysteriously in the hands of the Congress of South African Trade Unions (COSATU), to be released from the union in an angry press conference. To date the public does not know how this document landed in the hands of the trade union federation.

The key finding from the Browse Mole investigation was that there was a web of agents or players from within the security establishment and outside government, including foreign intelligence elements, former security intelligence officers, and moles within various organisations and the media who were consciously or unconsciously part of a strategy to destabilise the ANC and the government and create opportunities for criminal activities or secure control of key people within government, or the insertion of corrupt elements within government, to achieve their criminal interests. As part of this strategy the leadership and potential leaders of the ANC (in and out of government) were targeted by a particular set of individuals who came mainly from the business world or in the guise of business people (both national and international) with the intention of compromising them as a form of insurance for the future. The strategy was to befriend the leaders and offer them all sorts of solicited and unsolicited forms of assistance.

Of greater concern was that some of them were simply

information peddlers, mainly from former intelligence officers from both the apartheid government and the liberation movement, who were out to bedevil relationships within government and the ANC and create suspicions and confusion amongst comrades. A warning about these overtures was issued by government agencies to their leaders. Selebi was part of this process and was well aware of the strategies and tactics of those bent on destabilising the ruling party.

In the ANC government Selebi was first deployed as an ambassador to the UN in Geneva, Switzerland. Back home he was appointed director-general of foreign affairs and he ended his career as the national commissioner of police. Being in foreign affairs and the police he worked closely with me in my capacity as director-general in the presidency and in the justice and security cluster system of government. His dear wife was always there as a fellow comrade and she supported him as she still does today notwithstanding the challenges they are facing. Whatever the merits and demerits of the corruption case against him, it was painful for some of us as comrades to watch Selebi's illustrious career end in the way it did. One could not even imagine the pain his wife, children and the extended family have suffered. It was difficult for everyone who cared to accept that his career could end the way it did.

Pikoli's fate affected me in the same way. As far as I can remember my first encounter with Vusi Pikoli was when he was in exile. My recollection is that we met in Zimbabwe on one of my visits during apartheid. When he returned he was deployed as a special adviser to the then Minister of Justice, Dullah Omar, while his wife was deployed within the intelligence services. Later he was appointed director-general of the Department of Justice and then the National Director for Public Prosecutions (NDPP). In all three roles, particularly the last two, he worked closely with me in the presidency and within the justice and security cluster. His wife remained in intelligence until she moved into the private sector. In both her roles I had an opportunity to interact or work with her.

Again, given our relationship, it was painful to sit on the opposite side in the Ginwala Inquiry and in parliamentary hearings to deal with Pikoli's suspension. We looked each other in the face and we had to live with the reality that the system and history had placed us where it had and we had to act in those capacities and do so faithfully.

My relationship with Selebi and Pikoli in government spanned a period of about thirteen years and it mainly concerned state security, the combating of crime, particularly organised crime and ensuring that the justice system served the people of South Africa, especially the poor and the marginalised. Throughout the years I have worked with them I had no doubt about their sincerity and commitment to serve the people and the democratic government of the day. The two worked together in the justice, safety and security cluster as co-chairs of the cluster and up to then, the cluster worked as effectively and coherently as it could. One could say that they worked like hands in gloves and there was no indication of any relationship problems between them.

Under these circumstances, it was difficult to understand their estrangement over the last two years of their service in government. To me, they began to see each other as enemies or adversaries although they would deny this. Some attributed this to their locations and roles within government, but this is simplistic. In time the relationship deteriorated, unfortunately, to the point where the battles were carried out through the state agencies they led, including the intelligence and investigating arms of the entities under their command. The entities came close to a direct armed conflict when the NDPP made a decision to get the DSO to raid the headquarters of the police's crime intelligence service. This was one of the key reasons for the suspension of the NDPP. The other major

reason was the intention of the NDPP to arrest the national commissioner of police without giving the president enough time to
prepare the top command of the police for the move and appoint
an acting national commissioner.

As I had to interact with them, individually and collectively,
throughout this period I could not miss the sincerity and passion
with which each one of them executed his responsibilities, including that of acting against each other.

It is still a shock to me how when it went wrong, it went wrong
so badly. There were reports for instance about them monitoring
each other to find out what the 'other' was doing, firstly, to defend
themselves and, secondly, because they believed that the 'other' was
involved either in criminal activities or was compromised or simply
caught in a web of intrigue, with rogue national and international
intelligence entities and criminal syndicates from the underworld.

As fate would have it, after the suspension of Pikoli as NDPP, I
was given the responsibility of dealing with the matter and making
representations on behalf of the presidency at the Ginwala Inquiry,
parliamentary hearings, and in encounters with the media.

The question everyone asked was: why has President Mbeki suspended Pikoli? Pikoli's perspective was that he was suspended to
stop him from executing the warrant of arrest for Selebi and the
search and seizure warrants. This is the position the media supported, irrespective of what the presidency said.

The first point I need to clarify is that although there were delays
in the processes leading to the charges against Selebi the president
never at any stage said that Selebi could not or should not be arrested for corruption if there was evidence that he had committed
such an offence. This was a national commissioner of the police and
the president wanted to be satisfied that indeed there was a case
against him that warranted such action.

In response, the NDPP prepared a short memorandum for the

president to use to assess the seriousness of the matter and apply his powers as the head of state to intervene and enable the NDPP to carry out his constitutional responsibilities. The memorandum offered plea bargain arrangements that would see an entire syndicate of criminals and/or people accused of murder, drug trafficking and asset stripping go free in exchange for Selebi's conviction based on evidence from his former 'friend' Agliotti.

The president was shocked by the plea bargain and questioned its validity in law.

Pikoli insisted that that was the decision of the prosecuting authority and they had the powers to do so. The president left us in the sitting room and went to his office, clearly incredulous and angry. But this anger was not about Selebi, as the popular view would have us believe. It was about the fact that a criminal gang accused of heinous crimes would be left of the hook, simply to secure a charge against the national commissioner for a matter unrelated to the activities of the syndicate.

Left alone with the NDPP and the head of the DSO we had further discussions about the matter for my own clarity. I did not understand why the National Prosecuting Authority (NPA) could not simply charge members of the syndicate and still get Agliotti to be a witness against Selebi without letting all of them off the hook. I was told I did not understand.

The president returned and said that although the situation did not make sense to him and it seemed as if there was going to be a great miscarriage of justice, he was not going to interfere with the work and responsibilities of the DSO and NDPP. He then asked the NDPP to give him two weeks to interact with the national command of the police and the commissioner himself, and take specific actions to ensure that if and when the commissioner was charged, there would be no instability created within the criminal justice system.

The NDPP refused to grant the president that length of time. As far as Mbeki was concerned, there was no risk to their case if they waited two weeks for him to complete whatever processes he had to take care of before the commissioner was charged. Besides, he did not think that one even needed to arrest the commissioner in a dramatic manner as Selebi could simply be asked to hand himself over for prosecution, which he did later when he had to.

The second point that needs to be emphasised relating to Pikoli's suspension was the intention of the DSO to raid the headquarters of the police crime intelligence, which was even more risky and would have brought us closer to a physical confrontation between the forces under their command. The reality is that we came very close to an armed confrontation between the Scorpions and the crime intelligence service of the police when the Scorpions planned to raid the intelligence headquarters to search and seize intelligence 'source files' they said they needed for the case against Selebi. A process had been set up to facilitate access to the 'source files' and the police did not understand why the Scorpions wanted to raid the intelligence headquarters.

At one stage I was commissioned by the president to mediate between the two agencies as well as facilitate access by the Scorpions to the crime intelligence headquarters to peruse and work through the files. The intelligence officials were not going to allow the source files to be taken away because of their sensitivity, the risk involved to the 'sources', and the fact that 'source files', by their very nature, contain information that is not yet tested or corroborated.

There was also concern from the police that not all the Scorpions' investigation officers had been vetted and the police felt that they could not allow such individuals to gain access to sensitive intelligence information. Earlier, before the waters became so muddied, I was commissioned by the president to assess whether or not DSO members were vetted before they were appointed and it was found

THE THINGS THAT COULD NOT BE SAID

that the majority of them were engaged in haste and without any form of vetting. Some had been vetted for other purposes but not for the sensitive operations in which they were now involved. For the intelligence headquarters a raid by some of the DSO member who they 'knew' were not 'clean' was like placing a red rag before a bull. The language was bellicose. It was like, 'Let them come, *ba tla bona sepoko*'. Now, this is very difficult to translate into English as it is a deep expression that is more than just saying, 'They will see a ghost!'

On the other hand, Pikoli felt he was doing his job perfectly within the law and the police were obliged to comply. In our discussions without the president, I went through the process I was tasked to undertake as a 'facilitator' or 'mediator' between the crime intelligence services and the DSO and indicated that we had not exhausted all the processes to warrant so dramatic a raid on the intelligence headquarters, which carried great risks.

However, the NDPP argued that he had a warrant and needed to execute it. I remember asking: 'What if they do not comply?' He said this would amount to the crime of obstructing the course of justice. My view was that by the time this verdict was reached many of the officers would be dead and buried.

Finally, I suggested to him that the only way to deal with the matter would be to involve the commander in chief to whom all the armed forces reported to enable the DSO to do its job.

Strangely enough, this position was considered as interference in the independence of the NDPP. People forget that for the justice system to operate independently and do its work effectively one does not only need the laws of the country but one also needs the armed forces to make sure that the laws are upheld. If one policeman or woman did not comply with the law, other police would have to act accordingly, failing which the army would be called in. And for this, one would need the commander-in-chief of the armed forces to ensure that all entities of the state complied with the law.

The NDPP did not seem to think that this was necessary. His expectation was that law enforcement agencies had to abide by the law. The 'what if?' question still remained, however, but the NDPP felt they were going to do it anyway.

The next logical question was: If he did not need the commander-in-chief to raid the intelligence headquarters, did he have enough strong-armed men and women to use force to invade? This was a rhetorical question as it was known that the DSO had less than 500 personnel and no capacity to force itself in an armed way against the police. When the NDPP insisted that he would go ahead, I reached the conclusion that there was some 'madness' about the matter I did not understand.

Given this situation, the reality dawned on us that with the warrants in the hands of the NDPP and the DSO (Scorpions) and given the irrational way the NDPP was arguing the matter, a raid on the intelligence headquarters was possible without notice. In fact, there was a concern that some of the elements within the DSO were ready to act without any consideration of the consequences of their actions. Some were clearly ready to create a crisis for interests other than those of justice and that is why the presidency had to intervene to avoid the unimaginable – a bloodbath amongst national security agencies, a massacre that might have been far worse than the Marikana tragedy.

Questions would have been asked about how the president could not have foreseen the incident and why he did not act to avoid it – just as people are asking now about Marikana. The world would have called us a 'banana republic', incapable of governing itself.

With all the information at our disposal – given that the president of the country is the primary client of all information, including intelligence information – the president had to act to prevent the execution of the warrants in a manner that was irrational and insensitive, and which could lead to bloodshed. The objective, which was clearly defined, was not to stop the NDPP from charging the national commissioner or to stop the DSO from arresting Selebi or gaining access to documents they needed for the case. The objective was simply to eliminate the real risk of irrational action and manage the situation in a manner that would allow the prosecuting authority to carry out its function without any interference. The intention was to allow this to happen in a context where there was no risk of the loss of life or of violent confrontation between divisions of the armed forces or investigation entities.

I remember the pain with which Mbeki took the decision to suspend Pikoli. He talked to him like a comrade or a member of the family and expressed a concern that Pikoli was forcing him to contemplate action that he did not want to take, action that might jeopardise his future and his career. Mbeki even asked him how he thought he should act on this matter. Pikoli's response was that the president could act in whatever way he saw fit but he was not going to delay his action as contemplated notwithstanding the risk of a possible bloodbath at the intelligence headquarters.

At this stage I remember Mbeki retreating to his office to give Pikoli time to think about this matter and perhaps to find an amicable way of dealing with it. However, on his return there was no change in Pikoli's position. Reluctantly, the president had to act by suspending him. If my memory serves me correctly, this interaction with Pikoli took place over two to three days. I could not open the heart of Mbeki to determine how deep the hurt was but from his demeanour and external expressions I can say that he acted as if it was bleeding. It was not the action he wished for, as the public discourse suggests; he was forced to do it.

Mbeki understood the risks of being misunderstood, especially because of the positions the media had already taken on this matter, but he had to take the interests of the country into consideration. Furthermore, he understood that the public would not have the information he had as president and were likely to misunderstand his action. He understood that as the president one is bound to act in a manner that is open to being misunderstood.

One of the most painful parts of this saga was Mbeki's sensitivity towards and intention not to impact negatively on the person and character of Pikoli as a 'child' of the ANC. He did not want us to say anything in public that was likely to produce this effect. In this regard he advised us not to give details about the reasons for the suspension. He instructed us to leave the matter at the level of a breakdown in relationships between the NDPP and the Minister of Justice, which was fact. He felt that the details should only be presented at the inquiry, should it go ahead. Interestingly the president still believed that Pikoli would rethink the situation and accept an amicable resolution of the crisis, which would make the inquiry unnecessary.

But Mbeki paid dearly for his consideration of Pikoli's personal position. The media argued that we were not telling the truth about the suspension. They did not believe that the breakdown in the relationship between the minister and the NDPP would be a sufficient reason for the suspension and they chose to believe what Pikoli was saying – that he was suspended to stop him arresting or charging Selebi.

In hindsight it is clear that we lost the battle with the media because of the president's consideration of Pikoli's person and the fact that the media had an *a priori* position on the matter, which was unaffected by what the presidency said.

By the time the charges against Pikoli were formulated and covered all the reasons for the suspension, it was too late. Some even suggested that the charges were 'afterthoughts', rather than facts, to justify the suspension. No explanation was acceptable to the media.

Again, in hindsight, I believe we should have fully disclosed the details of what happened between the president and Pikoli, which could have put his suspension into context. Even our reluctance to create a panicked response by sharing all the details of the risks attendant on the manner in which the NDPP intended handling the matter might have been incorrect. We should have taken the nation into our confidence and told the story as it was. In Sesotho they would say, *buwa puo pha!*

From our evidence at the Ginwala Inquiry and submissions in parliament it is clear to me that Pikoli and I saw things from different vantage points. From his point of view the questions the president kept on asking – about convincing evidence against the commissioner, the plea bargaining arrangements that suggested that they were going to let murderers and drug traffickers off the hook, the manner in which they wanted to access information from the police, the warrants of arrest and so forth – reached him as resistance from the president to the intended arrest of and charges against Selebi.

But these were not only the concerns of the president. Minister of Justice Brigitte Mabandla and her deputy, Johnny de Lange, were concerned about his intention to give indemnity to 'murderers' and 'drug traffickers' in exchange for the prosecution of the national commissioner. They were worried about a potential misuse of the new plea bargaining provisions that normally applied to witnesses in the same case to nail kingpins of organised crime. In this case, the plea bargaining would achieve just the opposite: release the kingpins of organised crime. More so the plea bargaining plan involved criminals in a case unrelated to that of Selebi. There were also comrades who believed the charges against Selebi were trumped up by syndicates that saw him as an obstacle to their interests. It seemed to me, however, that the syndicate used the plea bargain system to hand over the commissioner and make sure that they were never brought to book for their own misdemeanours.

At the same time, we were dealing with broader issues relating to the national security of the country and the people of South Africa. Amongst these was the way in which syndicates or organised criminals had compromised or infiltrated the criminal justice system to the extent that they were able to determine who was arrested and charged, who the prosecutor would be, and even the choice of judge or magistrate. In the Brett Kebble murder case it was clear that a criminal gang was involved and that its players were also involved in other organised criminal activities. There were underworld bouncers who operated in the night clubs of Johannesburg, there were hired killing machines, drug lords, shadowy business people, specific lawyers who were always available to deal with the mess, and prosecutors ready to be part of the deals to let criminals get away in exchange for others.

In the Kebble case the actual killers who pulled the trigger, Mikey Schultz, Nigel McGurk and Fiazal 'Kappie' Smith, took refuge under the witness protection facilities of the DSO in order to avoid arrest by the police. At a critical moment when the police were about to pounce on them an experienced lawyer was at their disposal to assist them and negotiate an agreement to turn them into state witnesses against those who paid them to kill Kebble. The other person involved was Clinton Nassif who also entered into a plea bargaining arrangement to nail Glenn Agliotti. Arrangements were then made for Agliotti to nail Selebi. This completed the game. Kebble's killers and those who were responsible for planning it walked free at the expense of Selebi. More disturbing is that criminal charges relating to other cases they were implicated in were either withdrawn or the cases were left to collapse when the big fish was caught.

In the suspension of Pikoli, the most critical and immediate concern was the intention to raid the police headquarters and the headquarters of the crime intelligence services. To avoid the risks attendant on such a raid Pikoli had to be suspended.

After the suspension of Pikoli the president then had the two weeks he required, firstly to talk to Selebi who chose to ask for leave as national commissioner while the case was being dealt with. Mbeki then met with the national command of the police and the intelligence services, informed them about the pending charges against the national commissioner, and announced who would act in his place. That opened the way for the prosecuting authority to proceed with the case.

The preparation the president undertook to make sure that by the time Selebi was charged there was stability within the police is *the missing link* in the history of the debates about the Pikoli/Selebi matter. The media has chosen to ignore this part of our history as it negates the popular line of thinking that Pikoli was suspended to stop him arresting and charging Selebi. Once this piece of history is factored in, the story changes completely.

There is a second reason why many South Africans missed this point. They came to the subject with preconceived ideas about Selebi as a corrupt person and Pikoli as a hero taking on a powerful national police figure.

Following the Ginwala Inquiry and the parliamentary hearings I have personally accepted that Pikoli and I have different understandings about this matter. But through all these events we have maintained our comradeship and even belong to the same branch of the ANC.

On the surface, the Pikoli/Selebi affair might appear to be a case of two comrades holding positions that dictated what they should do, irrespective of their comradeship. Pikoli was head of a prosecuting authority and had to do his job even if one of his own was affected. Selebi on the other hand believed that an organised criminal syndicate was using the Scorpions or the prosecuting authority to cover their activities. Beyond Selebi, the crime intelligence officers wanted to protect their sensitive intelligence sources and information, which could risk people's lives if it fell into the wrong hands.

But this matter was much more complex than meets the eye. If one can use the language of war I would say that there was a war that was raging on many fronts involving various players for multiple reasons. In most cases some parties were even ready to collaborate with their enemies if it would enable them to escape responsibility for what they had done. At least four fronts became identifiable to me as we were dealing with this matter.

The first was the case of Kebble's murder, which involved a chain of people who were individually or collectively implicated. Amongst these were Agliotti, Nassif, Schultz, Smith and McGurk. Some of them were being investigated or implicated in a number of other cases involving drugs and criminal activity. In this case the police and the Scorpions blatantly worked against each other and played into the hands of the criminals. This drama is graphically presented in Mandy Wiener's 2011 book *Killing Kebble: An Underworld Exposed*. There is no better way of explaining it than to say that the enmity between the two agencies reached levels that can only be described as warlike.

The second front was opened at the O.R. Tambo International Airport. Post the 9/11 attacks in the US, security controls in airports were tightened. At O.R. Tambo Airport there was a scramble amongst foreign intelligence entities to monitor or control the airport to make sure that their nationals who land at the airport were safe. Paul O'Sullivan took charge of airport security around this time as the group executive of security at Airport Company of South Africa (ACSA). The problem started when he decided to terminate the contract of Khuseleni Security and Risk Management. His view was that they were incompetent and unreliable but others felt that O'Sullivan may have had interests other than just crime at the airport. Some were of the view that he was victimising a black company or a black-empowered company.

According to O'Sullivan he had a meeting with Selebi about Khuseleni and Selebi was of the view that terminating the contract was not a 'good idea'. Indeed Selebi had his own concerns about O'Sullivan, especially because he was known to have worked for a British counter-intelligence agency and only came to South Africa around the time of the transition from apartheid to democracy. He was of the view that this was a takeover of airport security by foreign interests, which, from his point of view, was a major security threat to the country. This matter created enormous tensions within ACSA, particularly between O'Sullivan and the ACSA Managing Director, Monhla Hlahla, on the one hand, and the police on the other.

Ultimately, O'Sullivan lost the job and he blamed Selebi for it. As a result he set himself on a crusade to make Selebi pay for it, and pay dearly as he believed that Selebi was corrupt. His view was that his removal was part of a cover-up for criminal gangs at the airport and in the country. Part of his crusade involved 'investigating' the underworld of crime syndicates in the country and he collaborated with some members of the Scorpions with the sole purpose of 'nailing' Jackie Selebi.

On the third count, the Scorpions were under siege on various fronts. There were corruption and fraud charges preferred against the deputy president of the ANC, then Comrade Jacob Zuma, who later became ANC president. A huge campaign was launched within the ANC against the Scorpions over a period of about two years. The line of attack was that the Scorpions were victimising or persecuting their deputy president; that the government was using state institutions to frustrate the deputy president's ambitions to become president of the ANC and the country; and that there were reactionary forces within the Scorpions who were involved in a counter-revolutionary agenda. The campaign culminated in a resolution from the ANC Conference in Polokwane in December 2007 to close down the Scorpions and transfer its cases to the police.

The police arrived at this matter from a different perspective based on the tensions that had built up between themselves and the Scorpions. The Scorpions considered themselves an elite investigation unit that dealt with more sophisticated cases than the police who were said to be dealing with ordinary cases. Part of the challenge was that the Scorpions worked with prosecutors to deal with cases while the police did not have that privilege. There was a feeling that the Scorpions were making choices about the cases they would deal with, which gave them a high profile, while leaving the rest for the police to pick up.

The Scorpions and the police services also stepped on each other's toes. For some matters, however, the issues were so serious that it bedevilled their relationship. For me, the obvious example was the case of the killing of Kebble: the police were investigating the case and were close to arresting Schultz, Smith and McGurk. Just before their arrest, and with the help of their lawyer, Ian Small-Smith, Schultz, Smith and McGurk entered into an indemnity deal with the Scorpions in terms of Section 204 of the Criminal Procedures Act to avoid arrest by the police, as discussed earlier.

As a result of these tensions the police also wanted the Scorpions closed down or subsumed into the police force. Strangely enough, this position coincided with that of the Polokwane Conference of the ANC. Selebi as the national commissioner of the police presented himself as the leader of this campaign, thereby intensifying the tensions between him and the NDPP. The investigations of the DSO against him were conducted with a vengeance intended to make sure he was put behind bars.

The fourth front was that of old-order elements within and outside the security establishment of the government that always act in cahoots with compromised elements in the liberation movement.

All controversial cases that were meant to destabilise the country or strengthen the rogue elements in their objective to take over and control the country have both old-order and new-order elements. Examples are the 1998 Meiring Report about alleged murder plots and a coup produced during Mandela's time; the 2001 coup plot falsely attributed to Mathews Phosa, Cyril Ramaphosa and Tokyo Sexwale; the 2006 hoax e-mails that implicated ANC leaders in a plot to endorse one faction in the ANC succession bid; and the Browse Mole document which I have referred to earlier.

The Pikoli/Selebi matter for me demonstrates beyond any doubt that organised crime, involving criminal syndicates both at national and international levels, is engaged in a major battle to corrupt and compromise our leadership to an extent that they will be able to control who becomes president and whose interests he or she will serve. In the case of Pikoli and Selebi they fought hard against each other, to the extent of involving the state agencies under their command to a level that corrupted the criminal justice system and left the country vulnerable.

In fact when all is said and done Pikoli and Selebi can be seen as victims and casualties of the underworld of criminals and former intelligence agents who achieved their objective – freedom – at the expense of Pikoli and Selebi, while the underworld of criminals went on unabated. Its modus operandi is that of compromising the leadership by specifically corrupting them, including drawing in the leadership into shadowy business deals or through gifts and offers that would compromise them. It is a modus operandi that was repeatedly used.

Now, most major cases that arise or are investigated come with politically connected individuals that ensure that the case dies before it sees the light of the day or it gets withdrawn from the court register. The challenge is that people can commit crimes with total impunity.

CHAPTER 10

A Solitary Journey

The journey to discover exactly who poisoned me in April 1989 was long and tortuous. But in August 2007 – more than eighteen years later – I arrived at my destination.

Adriaan Johannes Vlok (former Minister of Police), Johannes Velde van der Merwe (former commissioner of police) and three former police officers, namely, Christoffel Lodewikus Smith, Gert Jacobus Louis Hosea Otto and Hermanus Johannes van Staden, disclosed in a plea bargain agreement in the High Court in Pretoria, Tshwane, that they were responsible.

As in all marathons, as you get closer to the winning post, unforeseen challenges can crop up, but I did not expect them to originate in my own democratic government and its institutions and organs of justice; or, to be more correct, individuals within those institutions and departments. This unfortunate experience increased my pain and sapped the little energy I had left and which I needed to push on through this difficult and emotional period. There were times when I felt very alone, caught in silly battles of the Titans. But these were not the stories of Greek mythology. These were real games, played with my real feelings.

From the beginning it was clear to those of us involved in the apartheid struggle that we were drawn into a titanic battle with the apartheid system, which was prepared to use every weapon in its arsenal that it had at its disposal against us, including chemical and biological weapons. Instructions were given to the apartheid security forces to 'neutralise', or eliminate anti-apartheid leaders and I was put on the list for such action. By this stage the regime had graduated to a criminal state that was ready to kill those it could not deal with legally. To use biological and chemical weapons to kill anybody, let alone your own citizens, can only mean that you have reached rock bottom in the human depravity and immorality stakes.

The first attack happened when I was on my way to Namibia in April 1989. Although I had an order from the apartheid government not to enter Namibia, once the UN took over responsibility of running an election in that country in terms of Resolution 435, I thought that banning order would not apply. I went there as the general secretary of the SACC, together with the council president, Bishop Manas Buthelezi, to support the Namibian Council of Churches in exercising their ministry at what was a critical moment in the life of Namibia.

But the apartheid regime would have none of it, and the takeover of the transitional processes by the UN did not matter for them. I had to be stopped and if they could not do it legally (as they had before by issuing a banning order) they had the option of extra-legal methods, which were sanctioned by the highest levels of the government. But they also knew that on my return from Namibia I was proceeding to the US to meet President George H.W. Bush, together with Archbishop Desmond Tutu, Beyers Naude and Alan

Boesak, to urge him and the US to apply comprehensive sanctions against the apartheid government. And, again, this had to be stopped and I believe that the plan was to have me die when we were in the far north of Namibia to confuse issues and make sure that the apartheid government was not fingered.

Comrades would have sung the popular struggle song at our funerals, 'Hamba Kahle Mkhonto', and I would be gone!

As we drove northwards to examine conditions in Namibia in preparation for the first democratic elections I lost energy, started sweating and then shivering. I asked the driver to stop the car, climbed out staggering and started vomiting. I was struggling for breath. My colleagues helped me to stay on my feet and led me back into the car. The pain throughout my body was excruciating and I was groaning. Fortunately, we were about twenty minutes away from the Onandjokwe Lutheran Hospital in Oshikoto, north-west of Namibia, about 750 kilometres from Windhoek and 60 kilometres from the Angolan border. I was driven straight to the hospital.

Two German doctors at the hospital battled to keep me alive for about five hours until I was flown to the Florence Nightingale Clinic in Johannesburg as an emergency case. The irony is that the SACC arranged for the private jet to land at a South African military base in Oshikoto to pick me up. Arrangements were also made for a nurse to accompany me on the flight so as to continue the emergency medical procedures and manage the emergency equipment on board. Notwithstanding their efforts, neither the Namibian nor South African doctors could establish the cause of my mysterious but debilitating ailment. Various theories were advanced but proved to be way off the mark.

Three successive attacks within as many weeks occurred in May 1989 while I was in Wisconsin in the US, on my way to Washington to meet President Bush. In the first of the attacks, that is, on 13 May,

I lost consciousness for twelve hours. When I opened my eyes at 2 a.m. I saw a bishop of the Anglican Church next to my bed. He had come to say the last prayers as everyone thought I was dying. Archbishop Tutu made this urgent arrangement according to the request of Hlophe Bam who was my deputy general secretary in the SACC at the time. But by the grace of God I defied death in a way that can only be called a miracle. In this regard I am living testimony of 'a miracle'.

On 20 May I was discharged from the hospital, but I did not last for more than 24 hours before I was back in the intensive care unit. The second attack happened within two days after I was discharged from the hospital, that is, on 27 May.

The extensive medical investigation at Wisconsin Hospital, which also involved the Federal Bureau of Investigation (FBI), identified p-Nitrophenol in my urine. The report concluded that 'the presence of p-Nitrophenol in body fluids or urine along with specific symptoms (such as reduced cholinesterase activity, etc.) *is consistent with organophosphate poisoning*' (emphasis added). P-Nitrophenol is known as a rapidly biodegradable metabolite of Parathion, of which Paraoxon – a lethal toxic substance – is an active ingredient. The results of this investigation convinced everyone that I was a victim of a sophisticated operation, the intention of which was to kill.

As God would have it (and some will call this 'fate') I had to be dispatched in advance of the delegation heading for Washington. Because of my ailment I was sent to stay with Kagiso, who was then a master's student at Wisconsin University. Some people thought that I was simply overworked and needed time to rest. It was a good call, not only because I could be with my wife, who had been very worried about me, but I also received specialised attention from a team of experts and specific laboratories that had dealt with biological and chemical weapons substances before. A high-level investigation was undertaken to unravel the mystery of my poisoning.

The irony, of course, is that the US, like other key Western countries, participated in one way or another, particularly in a covert manner, in assisting the apartheid regime develop its high-level capacity to produce weapons of mass destruction (WMD), which included nuclear arsenals and biological and chemical weapons. This was done in the name of combating communism during the Cold War. Interestingly, our delegation was going to meet President Bush precisely to persuade the administration in Washington to stop any form of support for the apartheid regime and apply comprehensive sanctions.

At that stage no one knew how the poisoning operation could have been carried out, but a decision was made that everything I had been in contact with, from Namibia to Wisconsin, including my clothes, had to be removed for examination. A special FBI unit arrived at the place I was staying with Kagiso to take them away.

While I was in hospital new clothes were bought for me by Kagiso and the former Secretary for Health, Donna Shalala, who was then president of the University of Wisconsin. Donna took us to her house after the second attack in the US as everyone thought that her house was the safest. There was now some suspicion that the South Africa apartheid security police were involved. The US police were called in to ensure my safety even while I was in the hospital.

Once I was discharged and in my new clothes I was monitored and there was no recurrence of the attacks. The conclusion was that *lefu le* (the poison or the 'killer') was in my baggage. The FBI sent the baggage for testing as part of their investigation.

A long and solitary journey

After that near-deadly experience, from April to June 1989, which thanks to God I survived, I set out on a long tortuous journey to find out exactly who had carried out the operation, under whose command it was conducted and how it was carried out. The US continued with its own investigations.

On my return to South Africa from Wisconsin I appealed to the apartheid government and the public in general to trace and identify the perpetrators of the dastardly act. By that time we also had some information that there were two to three laboratories in South Africa where these chemicals were produced and demanded that these be disclosed. Following media reports in this regard the police took a statement from me but nothing happened.

During the negotiations in the early 1990s the matter of how to deal with crimes of the past came to the table and debates on some form of a 'truth and reconciliation' commission to help us cross the bridge from a violent apartheid society to a just and democratic society were started. The consensus was that we would never know what had happened to those who were assassinated, killed or who simply disappeared without the cooperation of the perpetrators of such acts, because most of these acts were done covertly.

A major compromise had to be made by offering amnesty to the perpetrators in return for the information or 'truth'. The sacrifice that had to be made was that we could not bring the perpetrators to 'justice' once they had volunteered to tell the 'truth'. That is why the commission was ultimately called the Truth and Reconciliation Commission (TRC).

Based on this logic we began to talk about giving an opportunity to the perpetrators of gross violations of human rights to come clean and disclose everything they did or knew in return for amnesty. Anyone who failed to disclose or to take advantage of this opportunity would face potential prosecution once evidence became available. We thought that in this way we would motivate the perpetrators to come out of the woodwork. We also expected that once one individual did so, the others would be compelled to follow suit as information from their colleagues could implicate them or make them witnesses. We anticipated that the strategy would have a domino effect and the approach became a key element of the TRC Act.

Given my poisoning case I seized the opportunity to call on and encourage those who were involved in or had information about my poisoning to take a bold step and make a disclosure. I indicated that I had no interest in having them prosecuted. What was important for me was the truth about who carried out the operation. I took the matter further based on my Christian faith: if they were willing to confess their deeds I was prepared to forgive them.

But no one came forward except a certain Paul Erasmus, a former member of the security branch who revealed in an article in the *Weekly Mail* newspaper that he was responsible for putting me on the death list of the police, as per instructions from his seniors. He said that he was about eighteen when he joined the police force and believed everything he was told about us (blacks), especially the view that we were either communists or influenced by communists. He was made to feel and believe that blacks were dangerous and that whites had to do everything possible to suppress them. He expressed regrets about what he had done now that he was better informed and said he was a child of his time. Arrangements were made for me to talk to him by telephone and I assured him that I had forgiven him and that I was prepared to meet with him personally.

Paul Erasmus also disclosed that he had certain knowledge about my poisoning and about the persons responsible for it. Unfortunately, we never met and it seems that he was then put in a witness protection programme as a result of whatever information he had given to the police or prosecuting authority. This matter was part of the issues I raised with the then Minister of Safety and Security in the new democratic government. In a letter to me dated 5 November 1996 the minister referred to a report of the commissioner of the South Africa Police Services that said that Paul Erasmus had 'been under the witness protection programme of the Department of Justice and had not been available to the investigating officer' until then. The letter went on:

> The matter was discussed with Dr Pretorius, deputy attorney-general: Transvaal, who said that he has contact with Erasmus, but he doubts whether Mr Erasmus would speak to the police without the intervention of his office. He also stated that, subsequent to the recent evidence by ex-Colonel Eugene de Kock in his own trial in the Pretoria Supreme Court, they have now become aware of more names of possible witnesses and/or perpetrators, who could assist in this investigation.

Since then I have not heard about Paul Erasmus and what became of him and the information he said he had. I imagine that part of the information I got through the prosecuting authority would have come from him as well.

When the TRC Act was passed, providing a legal framework for perpetrators to apply for amnesty based on voluntary disclosure, I repeated my call, but no one responded. Those who appeared before the TRC to apply for amnesty, for one reason or another, chose to deny any knowledge of my poisoning, apparently because it would implicate many people at the top echelons of the apartheid security establishment and the political leadership. Nevertheless some bits and pieces of information helped to strengthen my suspicion that the apartheid security forces were involved in my poisoning.

It was the Eugene de Kock and Wouter Basson cases that shed more light on my poisoning and helped me to zero in on specific individuals to ask them to either declare their knowledge about my poisoning or assist me with information.

At this stage, that is, 1995 to 1996, I was already a special adviser to Deputy President Thabo Mbeki and later the director-general in his office. One might have thought that in these positions I would have received lots of support in my quest for the truth, more so because we then had a new, democratic order. To my surprise there was not much enthusiasm to help. Every one of my comrades had new responsibilities to worry about, particularly regarding the transformation of the apartheid state and its institutions and structures. As a result there was not much appetite for looking back. Others felt that the best way to deal with the matter of the gross violations of human rights was to let sleeping dogs lie.

But I could not let it rest. I wrote letters to former president F.W. de Klerk, former Minister of Police Adriaan Vlok, former commissioner of police Johann van der Merwe, former Deputy Minister of Defence Roelf Meyer, former surgeon-general Niels Knobel and former army chief General Georg Meiring. All denied any knowledge about my poisoning. I also directed letters to the new members of the government asking for help in this regard. Some of the ministers I directed letters to were Minister of Safety and Security Sydney Mufamadi, Minister of Justice Dullah Omar, Minister of Defence Joe Modise, and Deputy Minister of Defence Ronnie Kasrils. All efforts relating to this investigation ended up in the office of the attorney-general of the Transvaal at the time, with an offer from the chief of the South African National Defence Force to allow technical staff from the South African Medical Services to 'help with the investigation or with the evaluation of the information, if required'.[14]

Throughout these processes I gathered enough information to

lead me to the police officers who were involved in the actual operation to poison me. Initially I received the code name, 'Smith Otto van Staden', which I initially thought was the name of one person but later I understood that this was a combination of the surnames of the three police operatives who constituted the unit that was responsible for my poisoning. Ultimately, I came to have their full names, which were: Christopher Lodewikus Smith, Gert Jacobus Louis Hosea Otto and Hermanus Johannes van Staden.

In the meantime the scientists who were responsible for producing the lethal toxic chemicals and biological substances responded to my invitation to disclose their involvement in this case. The team was led by Dr A. Immelman who featured in the 'Vlok and Others' case. They visited me at the Union Buildings and expressed regret for participating in the production of the lethal toxic substances that were used against me and most probably against others as well. One of them said something very chilling before he had even sat down. 'Reverend', he said, 'you are so damn lucky to be alive. That stuff was meant to kill!' What could I do except go cold?

Since that meeting this 'damn lucky' expression – which by my standards was 'bad language' has lingered. In search of its meaning I came across the Dave Matthews Band's song, entitled, 'So Damn Lucky'. 'Oh my God', it goes: 'So damn lucky, that you went ahead. You say, you say, I will see you later.'

Yes, maybe, using this 'bad language', I am indeed 'damn lucky'. But is it just 'damn luck'? No, I think my God was just 'damn good'. I believe that I am a 'living miracle'. It is by the Grace of God that I am still alive!

The conversation with the scientists showed me that, like Paul Erasmus, they were children of their times. They believed in what they were told and did their work earnestly. But now they realised it was like fiction. They indicated that although they did not know how these substances were going to be used, the manner in which they were prepared should have concerned them as it was clearly for offensive purposes. Together, they asked for forgiveness from me. I responded by saying that for my own spiritual health, I had forgiven them before they had even arrived.

Later I interacted with them about making our encounter public as the media had got wind of it. Unfortunately, one of them expressed a sense of discomfort as he felt that a public disclosure could jeopardise his career as a pharmacist. But the others were willing to go public. So I made the meeting known through the media without mentioning some of the names of those involved. The idea was that this story might encourage others to come forward and disclose what they knew or had done.

Having met these scientists and following the window of opportunity opened up by a statement of the president in parliament about post-TRC matters, which asked the NDPP to 'negotiate indemnity from prosecution in terms of existing laws for those who make complete disclosure to the NDPP', I believed I had an opportune moment to communicate directly with those who were involved in my poisoning and appeal to them to disclose their involvement. With all the information I had at my disposal at that time it became clear that the evidence was building up against the perpetrators of this callous act, which could lead to their arrest and charges preferred against them.

With the help of the NPA I addressed letters directly to the three police officers, asking them to disclose what they knew. I had to use the NPA, firstly, because it was in contact with the perpetrators' lawyers, and, secondly, because I did not want them to say that I had threatened them. My letters did not use emotive or judgemental language. They were also written in a manner that would not open me up to the possibility of being sued.

But first, I published an open letter in about mid-May 2003 through the media 'to fellow South Africans' in which I stated my view that 'telling the truth and giving information about what happened to victims and those who disappeared or died during the days of the apartheid system is critical to the process of reconciliation, healing and transition to a democratic society'. I also made the point that those who were 'still imprisoned by their past deeds should come forward with information so that we may proceed with the building of a new, more humane and peaceful South Africa for all South Africans'. I made public my offer to 'waive my rights to sue for damages or seek prosecution' to make it easier for perpetrators who had 'failed to take advantage of the TRC process to acknowledge culpability or involvement in apartheid inspired attacks on me'.

The first set of letters, addressed directly to Chris Smith, Gert Otto and Manie van Staden, were sent in May 2003, a week after the open letter was published. Besides the preliminaries, which I have referred to above, I wrote:

> I am aware that you have information about the attempts to murder me with toxic chemicals and biological substances. I ask you, as a fellow South African, to take up my offer by disclosing your knowledge or your involvement in such acts.

I also wrote: 'I believe that telling the truth about the past will free you from that past and make you part of a free South Africa characterised by justice and peace for all South Africans, black and white.'

I further stated that the maxim, 'the truth shall set you free', could not be more applicable at that time. I indicated that should they choose to take up the offer, I had 'no interest in taking legal action' against them or suing them for any damages. I wrote:

> I believe that the new South Africa will be better off with people who have come clean rather than with people who live in fear that one day, they may be found out and prosecuted.

That spectre has haunted other societies where past acts of in-justice have led to unrest and court process many, many years after the events.

I then made a passionate appeal to each of them, 'in the spirit of absolute sincerity, to make use of this opportunity to build a new South Africa, one that our children and generations to come will be proud of, and one that will be safe to live in'.

I received no response or even an acknowledgement. Ten months later I sent them another letter and expressed my disappointment that they had not 'even taken the trouble to just acknowledge my letter', not even through their lawyers who I had asked to pass over my letters to them. I reproduce part of the next letter I sent to them:

> Mine, as you would notice from my letter, was a friendly ges-ture that we make use of the opportunity the president had created 'to build a new South Africa, one that our children and generations to come will be proud of and one that will be safe to live in'.
>
> If your view is that this is not the best way to cross this bridge I will be happy to hear from you.
>
> If you choose not to respond, which is your right in terms of our new constitution, I shall accept that. In this case I would have to wash my hands of this matter.

Again, there was no response.

But as more and more evidence was coming to the fore the NPA prepared to arrest the three police operatives. It was the imminence of their arrest in the latter part of 2004 that sparked a flurry of ac-tivity. Vlok and Van der Merwe entered the fray as they believed in taking responsibility for those who worked under their authority or command. They interacted directly with the NPA on behalf of the three, and when they realised that they were not making progress and time was of the essence, they started a line of communication with me based on my letters and my offer.

My position was simple and deeply personal: just disclose – tell me the story, then use the channel the president announced by presenting the disclosure to the NPA, which would be expected to facilitate a plea bargaining arrangement to close the matter. Their concern was that there was no legal provision or framework for what the president had announced and that it left the perpetrators vulnerable as there was no guarantee that the arrangements with the NPA would not result in their imprisonment. Besides, a plea bargaining agreement had to go to court, which exposed them to the risk that a court could make a different ruling that could also result in their imprisonment.

For these reasons they preferred their original position, which they had presented to the NPA and the political leadership, particularly F.W. de Klerk and Thabo Mbeki, namely, a general amnesty. They acknowledged, however, that this was a non-starter as it had been rejected even before the TRC processes.

Another concern they had was that any disclosure by one person about a particular case was likely to implicate others and one could then become forced to be a witness in other cases that might be brought to court. They were worried about exposing or giving evidence against any one of their own. One could not miss the point that there must have been a pact between the operatives that they would not sell out any of their own or expose them to risk. This illustrated to me the multiple levels of lying and denial in place.

To date I do not understand how the surgeon-general, for instance, could be unaware of a huge operation to produce offensive chemical and biological substances within his own establishment by officers under his command. To develop and produce such chemical and biological substances there was an extensive covert international travel programme in place to gather the necessary scientific information. In any case, following my attack and publicised statements on the likely culpability of the apartheid security establishment, the surgeon-general and all security-related entities should have asked questions about what was happening and whether or not their entities were involved. This line of responsibility goes as far as the cabinet, including the president, then P.W. Botha, who chaired the National Security Council.

The reality, however, is that it is usually the 'foot soldiers' who are the first targets when information comes to light about specific gross violations of human rights as in the 'Smith, Otto, Van Staden' case. However dastardly my poisoning, I have to respect Vlok and Van der Merwe for not abandoning their foot soldiers, like some of their colleagues did. At a critical moment when Smith, Otto and Van Staden were at risk Vlok and Van der Merwe came out of the woodwork, took off the masks, and moved from their 'strategic lies' (to protect themselves and their foot soldiers), to declaring solidarity with their foot soldiers. They admitted what they had denied all along and were prepared to be charged along with their underlings. It is for this reason that they started the negotiations with the NPA, failing which, with myself. This was in stark contrast with the command of the apartheid South African Defence Force, who were directly and primarily responsible for this project.

Caught in between

My discussions with Adriaan Vlok and Johannes van der Merwe turned into a kind of negotiation process about how Smith, Otto and Van Staden could respond to my call without opening themselves to prosecution. Their lawyer, Jan Wagener, was also involved.

Parallel to this discussion was an ongoing dialogue between Vlok, Van der Merwe and Wagener on the one hand, and the NPA, particularly Advocate Anton Ackermann who was responsible for the case, on the other. There was also a raging debate between government and the NDPP about a prosecution policy (Principles for Prosecution of TRC Related Matters) to deal with the unfinished business of the TRC cases in line with the speech of President Mbeki in parliament.

I had the advantage of having a window into all of these processes, firstly, as part of government and, secondly, as a victim who had to be consulted about what was going to happen with Smith, Otto and Van Staden. I came to understand the complex and emotive issues involved better than most.

Some within government and the ruling party felt that we should close the post-TRC matters and do nothing further as the continuation thereof had the possibility and potential of destabilising the country. There was fear among the perpetrators of gross violations of human rights on the side of those who were part of the repressive machinery of the apartheid system and they were preparing to arrange for those on the side of the liberation movement who commanded or were involved in MK operations to be charged as well. On this issue there was agreement between both those from the old order and the new who wanted us to let sleeping dogs lie.

The problem with this position was that there were many South Africans who still saw themselves as victims or wanted to know what had happened to their next of kin who had either disappeared or died mysteriously. There were still people looking for bodies of their loved ones or graves where they might have been buried or dumped. And I was one of those who wanted to know about my poisoning. I could not be dispassionate. The reality is there was unfinished business of the TRC that could not just be swept under the carpet.

Some feared that the enthusiasm and urgency with which certain members of the prosecuting authority wanted to arrest and charge Smith, Otto and Van Staden was part of the strategy to precipitate action against some of the leaders of the new government, especially the 37 whose application for amnesty was turned down. This would be done in the name of 'equality' by balancing people to be charged between the perpetrators of gross violations of human rights on the side of the apartheid regime and ANC leaders who were involved or who commanded the war of resistance against the apartheid regime. In fact, there was a heated debate between some NPA officials and the command of the police about this matter as there was an indication that some within the NPA were planning to arrange for the arrest of the 37 ANC leaders who had applied in general terms for amnesty and took responsibility for those who acted under their leadership or command. But this did not fall within the TRC framework and the application was not accepted. One of those they were allegedly intending to arrest was the president, Thabo Mbeki, for being part of the NEC of the ANC in exile, which was responsible for the MK operations in the country.

Some believed that those seeking to have the 37 ANC leaders arrested wanted to create a crisis that would force the ANC leadership to back off from the post-TRC cases that fell under the category of 'unfinished business of the TRC'. Others wanted to prosecute people for the sake of it without considering the implications thereof, especially because of the special circumstances of our transition from an unjust racist system to a just and democratic system. So, there were many conspiracy theories going around.

In the midst of all these debates was my poisoning case. Often, I felt that my case was being used as a pawn, to be sacrificed at any time as in a chess game. I felt like both the old order and my comrades were turning me into a victim again, caught in between their squabbles and battles.

Interestingly, for Vlok, Van der Merwe and the three police operatives who were involved in my poisoning I was first considered a threat. But as the arrest of the three police operative became imminent, I became someone they could appeal to for help. They told me they were ready to respond to my offer, but the NPA was making it difficult for them.

In a letter dated 9 November 2004, Vlok and Van der Merwe referred, in different ways, to the imminent arrest and prosecution of Smith, Otto and Van Staden, which was scheduled for 11 November 2004 and urged me to intervene by discussing the matter with the president. They wrote:

> In view of the aforesaid we believe that you have now become a crucial part of the process and wish to urgently appeal to you to approach Advocate Ackermann SC of the said authority with the request not to proceed on 11 November 2004 as mentioned above, but to first afford you the opportunity to fully discuss the matter with the President, the Minister of Justice and the National Commissioner of SAPS.

I could not miss the irony in which the victim now became the one being asked to save the victimisers by speaking to government on their behalf. This, I imagine, is part of the miracle of our transition from a tyrannical regime to a democratic government. Someone characterised this unique South African experience by saying: 'This is South Africa!'

In any case, by the time they asked me to intervene, I was already engaged with all the players, including those referred to in their letter.

The NDPP, Advocate Vusi Pikoli, had already informed me about the intended action and told me that Ackermann would discuss the details with me. I had a number of discussions with Ackermann but his approach was a punitive one and not within the spirit of the post-TRC processes and the president's call, including the muted prosecution principles related to the unfinished business of the TRC. His was a straight-forward prosecution that would make me a witness against the perpetrators.

My response was that I was not interested in a prosecution for the sake of a prosecution but sought the truth about my poisoning. Besides, I had pronounced publicly that I had no interest in sending the perpetrators to jail and was ready to forgive them. And, at that stage, they had already disclosed much of what I needed from them through Vlok and Van der Merwe and Vlok had already asked for forgiveness from me. Later he went an extra mile and even washed my feet, on 3 August 2006, and presented me with a New Testament Bible with the following message inscribed in his own handwriting:

> DEAR REV. Chikane –
> I have sinned against THE LORD –
> AND Against you.
> PLEASE FORGIVE ME!
> (Ps. 51)
> (Acts 8:1)
> Acts 22:20)
> Adriaan Vlok.
> CENTURION.
> 1.8.2006.

My approach to Ackermann seems to have caused him to conclude that I was a hostile witness and he threatened me with Section 205 of the Criminal Procedures Act to force me not only to give evidence against the suspects but to disclose all the information Vlok and the others had given me. This is where our discussion ended.

The Section 205 threat reminded me of the old apartheid days. It was like putting salt on my wounds. I dared him to try it and see whether or not he would succeed where the apartheid regime had failed.

At this stage I knew I was just a pawn in a bigger scheme of things!

The consequences of this breakdown were dire, including factual errors in the 'Plea and Sentencing Agreement' in the matter between the State and Van der Merwe and others − views attributed to me without any supporting affidavit to ensure their accuracy.

While this struggle with the NPA was happening, a campaign was launched from other quarters of government, particularly from some of my colleagues from the Justice Cluster, to stop the case without considering my enduring need for a recorded confession, especially an official court record. Besides, there were still too many, mainly whites, who doubted that a government that claimed to be Christian, could commit such an inhuman and treacherous act. Many of those who came to confess to me and asked for forgiveness said, firstly, that they did not know that their government had committed such acts in their name. And secondly, they said that their worst sin was that even when it was made public that their government had committed such inhuman acts, they did not believe it.

At this stage I felt caught between three parties: those who had perpetrated gross human rights violations against me in the first place; the NPA officials; and government officials who held opposing views. I appealed to the Minister of Justice and the NDPP for their intervention, especially in relation to the threats made by Ackermann. I ultimately also reached out to the president.

There is a Swahili proverb which says, *wapiganapo tembo nyasi huumia*. A similar proverb is found in Gikuyu (Kenya), Kuria (Kenya/Tanzania) and Ngoreme (Tanzania). The popular form in English is,

'When elephants fight, it is the grass that suffers'. This is how I felt in my lonely and risky quest for the truth.

At issue here was a strategy to precipitate a crisis that would force the new democratic government to stop any further investigations and prosecutions of apartheid security members and politicians who had either committed gross violation of human rights or presided over such activities.

The strategy was to arrest the policemen who were involved in my poisoning to justify the parallel arrests of some of the key leaders of the ANC who appeared on the so-called list of 37 presented at the TRC and thereby create a huge crisis in the country. This would have resulted in me being used as a pawn. What was more extraordinary though is that my own comrades did not seem to appreciate the need for me to complete my fifteen-year-long journey then (in 2004) to uncover the truth about my near-fatal poisoning and get closure to the story.

On the fateful day of the court appearance of Vlok, Van der Merwe and others, I left the Union Buildings accompanied by one of our communications officials, Prince Mashele, and him alone. No one from government was there, nor was there anyone from my own liberation movement, the ANC. The courtroom was full of journalists, and members of my congregation who had come to express solidarity with me were not able to go in. As we got into the court I felt alone and forsaken. I felt as if someone was saying, 'It is your *indaba* alone'. This reminded me of the Black Consciousness expression of old: 'Black man, you are on your own!'

The accused and their lawyers and the prosecution team filed into the court and I went boldly – though awkwardly – to greet them and wished all of them, equally, good luck. The court orderly then asked all of us to stand for the judge. As we sat down I felt like I was back in the old apartheid court, except that this time the accused were apartheid police and their minister. Interestingly, all the players (the accused, their lawyers, the prosecutors and the judge) were white. As I sat there it was like I was in a white man's court in a whites-only country. Before I woke up from this dream the court proceedings had started. They were almost all in Afrikaans, which was very technical and I struggled to follow the proceedings. No one seems to have thought that the victim needed to be part of the proceedings or at least follow what was happening. It was again like, 'Frank Chikane, it is your own *indaba*'. I was, however, given a copy of the Plea and Sentencing Agreement in terms of Section 105 (A) of Act 51 of 1977 (as amended) and I kept myself busy reading it.

The disclosure and aftermath

What was important for me is that at last I had the story on record in a court of law. All the accused pleaded guilty to a charge of 'attempted murder' stated as follows:

> On or about **23 April 1989** and at or in the vicinity of **the then Jan Smuts Airport** in the district of **Kempton Park**, the accused unlawfully and intentionally, and in furtherance of a common purpose, attempted to murder the **Reverend Frank Chikane**, an adult male person, by way of **administering a poison, to wit Paraoxon, to his clothing**.

The factual summary of events in the Plea and Sentencing Agreement includes the following:
- During the period 1982–1992, the South Africa Defence Force ran a Top Secret project, namely Project Coast, to develop a defensive and limited offensive chemical and

biological warfare capacity and Dr Wouter Basson was the project officer.

- A front company called Delta G Scientific was responsible for research and manufacture of chemical substances for the project, and, Roodeplaat Research Laboratory conducted research in the biological sphere and to a lesser extent, also carried out chemical research.

- In the mid-1980s Dr Basson instructed Dr Immelman, the head of toxicological research at Roodeplaat to, *inter alia,* carry out research on the use of toxic substances against individuals, methods of application and the traceability of such substances following administration.

- During 1987 the Commanding Officer of the Security Police attended a meeting arranged by the South Africa Defence Force. He took 'cognisance of an *order to act against high profile members of the anti-apartheid liberation struggle* in order to neutralise their influence'. He also 'took note that, in extreme cases and only as a last resort, *consideration could be given to killing them*' (emphasis added).

- That the order was given from a higher authority via the Chief of the South African Defence Force (SADF). Earlier information which was not contained in the indictment followed the line of command to the highest office of the land.

- A *list* containing the names of persons identified in terms of this order was handed to senior members of the security establishment, including Johannes Van der Merwe, and Reverend Frank Chikane's name was in that list.

- The motive for the planned murder of Reverend Chikane was 'to prevent him from lobbying abroad for economic sanctions against South Africa and to deprive him of his role in promoting internal resistance against the government'. The execution of this order was discussed with then minister, Adriaan Vlok.

- A special unit consisting of Christoffel Lodewikus Smith, Gert Jacobus Louis Hosea Otto, and Hermanus Johannes Van Staden, was established within the Security Branch of the South African Police for the purposes of carrying out this order.

- At the time when the order was carried out against Reverend Frank Chikane General Sebastiaan Smit had taken over the command of the Security Police. He ordered Chris Smith to request Dr Basson to assist the special unit with chemical and biological substances which could be used 'against the enemy'. Dr Basson ordered Dr Immelman to meet clandestinely with representatives of all the branches of the Security Forces and supply them with whatever substances they needed.

- In respect of Reverend Frank Chikane, 'a substance that would specifically lead to his death was required'. A lethal toxic substance, called Paraoxon, was supplied and had to be applied to Reverend Frank Chikane's 'close-fitting clothing items, such as a shirt collar and/or underpants'.

- Annexure 'A' of the Indictment (which is included in this book as Appendix 1) shows that the substance, Paraoxon, was ordered on 4 April 1989 in volumes of 10 x 2 ml.

The indictment ends by saying that the accused 'acted in pursuance of a common purpose to murder Reverend Chikane'. Under aggravating circumstances the indictment says that 'the administration of poison in order to secretly eliminate opponents is an *egregious, reprehensible and universally abhorrent act*' (emphasis added).

Adriaan Vlok and Johannes van der Merwe were sentenced to ten years imprisonment, wholly suspended for five years, and Chris Smith, Gert Otto and Manie Van Staden were each sentenced to five years, wholly suspended for the same number of years.

Zelda Venter of the *Star* captured this moment with a headline, 'Smiles and handshakes for former enemies'. She wrote:

> A few minutes after being convicted and sentenced, it was all smiles and handshakes as the former law and order minister Adriaan Vlok and former police chief Johann Van der Merwe faced the Reverend Frank Chikane.
>
> The two walked over to Chikane where he sat in the front row of the public gallery and an exchange of pleasantries followed hearty handshakes. No grudges, it seemed, were being held.

Although I had prepared myself for this type of verdict and had already decided to forgive them mainly for my own self, health and healing, when the court adjourned and Vlok, Van der Merwe, Smith, Otto and Van Staden strolled out of court, a deep depression set upon me. It was almost like, 'Is it over, and they are going home?' *Ja*, that is tough! (*Ho boima Ntate*). This is the cost of peace, forgiveness and reconciliation. I waved them farewell!

As I left the court and moved towards the gate journalists mobbed me and shouted questions at me simultaneously. They asked about my feelings about the proceedings of the court? About Vlok and company walking out free? About whether or not they had disclosed everything they had to disclose? Whether or not all of them had asked for forgiveness? Whether or not this was the way in which government wanted to deal with such cases? Whether or not this would not open a Pandora's box or rub salt into old wounds instead of letting the country move forward into the future? And so on.

Of course it was difficult to answer all these questions under the conditions and I told them that I would write up a well considered response. A more comprehensive response was the one published in *City Press*, which was published on 18 August 2007 (included as Appendix 2).

After breaking through the mob of journalists and out into the street I was exposed to another South African reality. Two groups were protesting on the other side of the street. I had seen the groupings when I had gone into the court but now they were formally organised as protest groups with posters and placards conveying contradictory messages. One of the groups, which consisted of victims of the apartheid system, families of victims and supporters, was protesting against Vlok and his company for gross violations of human rights. In particular they were of the view that Vlok and his fellow accused had not disclosed everything they knew. The other group had come to support Vlok and his company, protesting against the government's action of prosecuting them and demanding that the same be done against the ANC.

I took note of the contradictions, went past and continued with my reflection about the costs of peace for the country, the expectation that the victims of the crude apartheid system were the ones who were expected to forgive and forget.

I returned to my office but could not shake off the feeling of depression that descended on me after the event. It was like the adrenalin that kept me going for eighteen years had left me. I decided to go home to the love of my wife Kagiso and my children, Obakeng, Otlile and Rekgotsofetse. I was reminded again that however strong one can be spiritually one still remains a human being. I had to accept that I was human like all other humans. It reminded me of the day I cried under the brutal torture of the apartheid security police at John Vorster Square Police Station. One of the policeman made fun of my pain and said he did not know that I could also cry. He said that when I speak in the stadium I look like a brave and fearless man, but now I was crying like a baby. Even then I had to accept that I was just human but I have to be ready to die for the cause of justice, whatever the costs.

After some prayers I picked myself up. '*Ja*, it is over', I said. From then on I held various interviews and made a number of appearances, at times together with Adriaan Vlok, talking about reconciliation. The first was at my church in the deep south-west end of Soweto in Naledi. Vlok drove alone to come and say 'sorry' before the congregation and to the people of Soweto. He also brought his colleagues, Van der Merwe, Smith, Otto and Van Staden, to me at the Union Buildings to say 'sorry' to me and to express their regret for this unfortunate history. After a few other appearances, including at the national conference of my church, the Apostolic Faith Mission of South Africa, I decided that this was enough. I had demonstrated my willingness to make peace with him and with myself. I had forgiven him and his colleagues for what they had done to me. I had a feeling now that I was being made to carry Vlok with me permanently. I needed to move beyond the past into the future. Otherwise I would remain a victim forever.

Missed opportunities to close the past

One of the consequences of government's hands-off approach to this ground-breaking post-TRC case was that opportunities were missed that could have started a rolling action to close the past and move into the future.

The manner in which the Vlok and Others case was left to NPA officials who had no interest in addressing the unfinished business of the TRC cost the country dearly. The breakdown that occurred between the principal prosecutor and myself meant that the Plea Arrangements documents were not passed through me as the 'victim' and went to court containing a misrepresentation of my feelings and views.

It still boggles my mind that there could be a submission in court that referred to me without a 'confirmatory affidavit'.

The second missed opportunity was the chance to take the following points into account and to act on them where appropriate:

- For the first time there was a confession about the decision of the apartheid regime to use extra-legal methods to deal with opponents of the apartheid system, including killing them.
- This decision was made at the highest level of government, that is, at the level of the National Security Council, which was chaired by the president of the country who was then P.W. Botha.
- The primary party responsible for this project was the South African Defence Force, which was at that time commanded by General Johannes Geldenhuys.
- There was an official commission to produce lethal chemical and biological substances within the surgeon general's establishment to be used against opponents of the apartheid system.
- A list of the commission's targets was produced; the military would deal with external targets and the police with internal targets. I know that I was on the list but we do not know how many other people were on the list.
- A 'Verkope' (purchases) record of chemical and biological substances was tabled in court as 'Aanhangsel A' and shows that 47 orders for various chemical and biological substances were made between 19 March 1989 and 21 October 1989. The question should have been asked against whom these substances were used?
- In the plea agreement the accused agreed to give evidence

against those who had participated in similar gross violations of human rights but this was not followed up, particularly not the specific names mentioned who were party to the plan and execution thereof in using chemical and biological substances to eliminate opponents of the apartheid system.

This is where my government lost it. We lost an opportunity to encourage everyone who was ever involved to come out and tell the truth so that all of us could be free from the pain of the past and move into the future as one people ready to build a new nation. The approach was not punitive. Instead, it freed people of their fears that these matters might come up in the future.

There is a definition of 'sin' that is apt in this sense; it is 'missing the point'. We missed the opportunity.

The pain of the Ginwala Inquiry

One of the pains I had to endure after this case was the Ginwala Inquiry on the fitness of Advocate V.P. Pikoli to hold the office of the NDPP. I had to appear there as the director-general in the presidency and secretary of cabinet to give evidence about how the presidency handled the Pikoli matter. The lawyers for Pikoli, like all defence lawyers, tried to rob my evidence of credibility.

Of all the things they could have used they picked up two perspectives on the 'Adriaan Vlok and Others' matter pertaining to the Plea and Sentence Agreement which was accepted by the Pretoria High Court. One was my article that was published by the *City Press* (on 18 August 2007) in which I presented the case as a success story concerning the first post-TRC case handled on the basis of the new guidelines. The headline the newspaper chose was 'NPA

Role in Vlok Matter Offers a Lesson for our Country'. Indeed, in all the interviews I fielded after the case I propagated the same view, which I also believed: I expected other perpetrators to take advantage of this success.

There was an *empa* (but) here that was not meant for the public but for the government, to indicate the weakness in the handling of the matter and some of the challenges to make sure that future cases were handled differently. In a sense I was like a guinea pig. For that reason I felt that I needed to raise specific issues with the Minister of Justice and the rest of the government. This was expressed in my letter of 22 October 2007 addressed to Brigitte Mbandla, the Minister of Justice and Constitutional Affairs. Because of the importance of this matter I have decided to present its contents here in their totality. The heading is 'STATE V VAN DER MERWE AND OTHERS' and it reads as follows:

22 October 2007

Ms Brigitte Mbandla, MP
Minister of Justice and Constitutional Affairs
Private Bag X276
PRETORIA
0001

Dear Minister:

STATE V VAN DER MERWE AND OTHERS

As you would know, the case of those who were involved in
my poisoning, namely, Johannes Velde VAN DER MERWE,
Adriaan Johannes VLOK, Christoffel Lodewikus SMITH,
Gert Jacobus Louis Hosea OTTO and Hermanus Johannes

VAN STADEN was disposed of at the Pretoria High
Court on the 17th August 2007 through a Plea Bargaining
arrangement between the accused and the State.

Although I am pleased that we have concluded this matter,
I am concerned about a number of issues, which I would
like to raise with you and, hereby, the Government of the
Republic of South Africa. I hope you will find it necessary to
share my concerns with Cabinet as I believe that this will be
helpful in handling other matters of a similar nature.

The first point I would like to raise is the handling of this
matter by the National Prosecuting Authority (NPA). From
my interaction with the relevant officials within the NPA,
it is clear to me that the said officials are simply the wrong
people to deal with the 'post-TRC' matters. My experience
of them is that they will not be able to relate to victims of
gross violation of human rights or their next of kin with
the sensitivity that is required. In fact, they did not seem to
understand the nature of the challenge we were facing. Firstly,
my court case was used to fight battles between the NPA and
the Government about the 'Guidelines' for dealing with post-
TRC cases. Throughout this process I was left with a feeling
that no one in fact cared about me – as a 'victim'. What
mattered were the politics around the handling of the post-
TRC cases and how people would win their battles.

As part of the consultative processes relating to the case
of the *State v Van der Merwe and Others*, Adv. Ackerman, the
Special Director in the Priority Crimes Litigation Unit,
and his assistant visited me (as the 'victim'). Instead of just
consulting me as 'the victim', he entered into an acrimonious
argument with me about the approach of the Government
on 'post-TRC' matters and the Guidelines. From this
interaction, it was clear that he was radically opposed to the

Guidelines as agreed upon by Cabinet and the Parliament of the Republic of South Africa. In fact, he seemed to be more interested in prosecution for the sake of it rather than the management of this difficult 'post-TRC' process.

What I detested most was that my case was being used to fight their battles with the Government. In pursuit of this objective, a draft letter which was constructed in a manner that would enhance their position in the prescribed forum with other departments was presented to me for my signature. What was more disgusting for me was that when I refused to sign the draft letter, Adv. Ackerman then threatened to use Section 205 of the Criminal Procedures Act against me to force me to surrender all the information he claimed I had received from Mr. Vlok on my poisoning. I dared him to do so, and reminded him that this was tried against me during the apartheid days and it did not work and that there is no reason why it would work now. He backed off and left. His colleague who was with him is my witness in this regard.

Secondly, I was not consulted about the details of the Plea Bargaining Agreement. The NDPP informed me in writing about the arrangements for suspended sentences for the accused. My views were not solicited in this regard. In fact, I was not informed about the basis for the Plea Bargaining Arrangements. I only saw the Plea Bargaining Agreement during the proceedings in Court. I was particularly distressed by the submission in Section E, paragraph 6.3 of the 'plea agreement' which claims that I was consulted about it and that I was 'satisfied with the plea agreement' and that I did 'not wish to make any further representation in connection with the matter'. The reality is that I could not be satisfied with something I had not seen. Having now considered it, there are naturally a number of issues I have concerns about which I had no opportunity to deal with. This leads me to the second matter I would like to raise.

Failure to consult me before the Plea Bargaining Arrangements were made resulted in the presentation of documents in Court which did not only have factual errors, but were politically and philosophically problematic to me as a 'victim'. Firstly, my background is presented as if I was both General-Secretary of the SACC and Vice President of the UDF when, in fact, I held these positions at different times (see paragraph 28). Secondly, the Plea Agreement falsely argues that it was the stated policy of the UDF 'to propagate and support ... *violence* for the ... purpose of rendering the country ungovernable' (own emphasis).

There are three issues I would like to raise on matters of substance. Firstly, Count 2 was withdrawn as part of the plea arrangements, and by so doing, the collaboration between the Security Police Special Unit and Wouter Basson and his team in producing and or procuring the lethal chemicals used was not probed further when it is clear from the plea bargain document that more information could have been extracted. Secondly, there is a reference in the plea arrangement document to a 'list' containing the names of 'high profile' members of the anti-apartheid liberation struggle who were to be acted against, and in 'extreme cases' be killed (paragraph 37). There is no indication that this matter was probed further. The State should be interested, for instance, in a copy of such a list to determine as to who else was on the list and what happened to them. Thirdly, there is no indication as to what discussions the NPA had with General Basie Smit and Dr. Basson to source more information about their operations and what the NPA is planning to do about them. Fourthly, there is no indication that there has been a process to probe the involvement of the SADF on these matters and what happened to their list of external targets.

The Guidelines for the 'post-TRC' cases make it clear that our objective is not just prosecution but the need to solicit more information about what happened to victims of gross violation of human rights, especially those who died or disappeared. Moreover, it is to get a better understanding of how the old national security management system functioned to make sure it does not happen again. Although the Van der Merwe and Others case assisted me to know more about what happened to me, failure to follow the Guidelines (and thereby collaborate with other entities of the State, like intelligence services, the Police and the Defence Force) made us miss opportunities to learn more about what befell other people who might have been affected in the same way.

Lastly, I found the Court itself completely 'foreign' and insensitive to me as a 'victim'. Firstly, the Court was completely white, from the Judge to the Prosecutors, defence lawyers and the accused. But worse, the proceedings were conducted in Afrikaans without due regard to the 'victim', especially where technical, legal and court processes are involved. As a result, I missed the greater part of the proceedings in the court. I am sure that we can make the court friendlier to victims than what I experienced that day.

On the side of Government, I felt that the handling of the State v Van der Merwe and Others case was left to me, as a 'victim', to explain to the public instead of the State or the Government. No effort was made by Government to manage this process or deal with public perceptions about it. No one got involved to make sure that the process achieved the objectives Government had agreed upon. Clearly, once the NPA acted unilaterally the Government apparently walked away from the matter. I do not think that this hands-off approach assisted us in any way to achieve the objectives set out in the Guidelines.

I shall be pleased, Minister, if the Government could deal with all the matters I have raised as well as remedy the situation before another case is dealt with.

Sincerely Yours,
FRANK CHIKANE
DIRECTOR-GENERAL

The Pikoli lawyers sought to find a contradiction between my views about the state and the 'Van der Merwe and Others' case and my internal critique of government in terms of the handling of the matter. I tried to say to the lawyers that two documents were like backstage and onstage scenes. But there is also an evaluation scene after the performance that is more critical to help the performers to do better next time. So, my letter to the minister was like an after-the-performance analysis to help the government to improve the handling of these cases.

But in an adversarial justice system the facts, reality and truth at times do not matter. What matters is how I can destabilise the witness to achieve my objectives. The problem with it is that the media picks it up and leaves the public out there with skewed perspectives and understanding.

The tragedy about all this is that the fundamental issues I raised got lost in the battle to win arguments about the Pikoli matter. No one followed up as to what happened with my letter to the minister and whether or not the issues I raised were dealt with. The response to my letter came a year later and it did not address all the issues I had raised.

But what was more painful for me at the Ginwala Inquiry was that I had gone through the 'Van der Merwe and Others' case to find out about my poisoning without much support from government and my own comrades, and now my pain was being used again to win other battles that are unrelated to my poisoning. In fact my poisoning was not even as important as a pawn. This act that was described as 'egregious, reprehensible and universally abhorrent' was turned into a game to win other battles.

This, unfortunately, has influenced my views about assisting with the unfinished work of the TRC. Sometime in 2012 I was requested by the human rights lawyers who are dealing with the Pardons cases to make a statement to affirm the contention of the victims that the perpetrators had not disclosed everything they knew. From the pain of the Ginwala Inquiry I felt that I would not want to be subjected to the pain of court processes again. For this reason I refused to assist with the Pardons Applications Case as I did not want to go to a court or commission of inquiry that does not care about the pain I suffered. I will not participate in any action that is likely to turn my pain into a game.

CHAPTER 11

The Scourge of Corruption

Harvard University, where I spent a few months on a fellowship prior to taking up a position in the office of Deputy President Mbeki during the Mandela presidency, is known for its case study method of teaching and learning. One of the cases my group was asked to analyse in preparation for a class discussion was about corruption. Upon engaging with the material, I discovered that the case study focused on a set of African countries. I was furious. I paced aimlessly about my small apartment. 'Here it goes again,' I said to myself. Whenever there is talk about corruption it must be about Africa. It seemed everything about Africa was negative. I went to the kitchen to make some coffee as a way of distracting myself from the disturbing case study.

After some time I had to convince myself that I was in the US to study and could not walk away from the subject at hand. In any case, I was thousands of kilometres from home. The best way to deal with the matter, I told myself, was to study the case critically, compare cases from other parts of the world, particularly North America and Europe, and be ready for a critical encounter in class the following day. After all, that was where one's views could be expressed in an intelligent way, rather than as a mere outburst of emotions. I returned to my desk and forced myself to go through the case study in detail.

I was hit by a second bout of anger, this time, at my African brothers and sisters who were involved in corruption at the expense of their own people. The case study showed that we had African presidents who lived like kings, with millions of dollars stashed in foreign accounts, while their people were dying of hunger or struggling for a morsel of bread. Except for a few rich people, expatriates and foreign non-governmental organisation (NGO) employees who were able to provide for themselves in some of those countries, nothing worked. Telephones were down, post offices were dysfunctional, the roads were in a state of disrepair, conditions in hospitals and schools were shocking and drinking water was at risk, foreign aid for the poor ended up in the pockets of the leaders and the elite, donations in kind were sold and the money pocketed. And so on.

In one of the countries covered by the case studies the leader had been at the helm of government for many years and lived like a king. Over time, he made the state his own property and the state began to work for him, his family and friends, rather than the people. In fact, it went beyond just family and friends. He selected whomever he wanted to empower and gave him or her 'a share' in the state. This was patronage at its best. Those he empowered were in turn expected to support him politically. He also secured commitments from them to protect him against anyone who might try to threaten his regime. The military, the police and the intelligent services were given their own stakes (individually and collectively) in the national corruption project.

Any dissention – in the form of outright disagreement, or simply different viewpoints or opinions – was dealt with harshly. If you do not die or disappear, or your family was not harmed, you were served a different type of dessert. The corruption brigade would exclude you from the organs of state, in the same way blacks were excluded from the racist apartheid state institutions. This exclusion served as a lesson to others: either conform, or you are out. In addition to being punished for dissent, you would also be seen as a risk because you understood how things worked. In Sesotho they say '*o tlo ba bonela*', that is, literally, 'you will see their nakedness'. That is a dangerous place to be. This exclusion extended beyond the state to the private sector – if there was any 'private sector' to talk about.

In some African countries the only employment opportunities are in government or in government-related institutions as the private sector has not developed to a level that could serve as an alternative employer to the government. So once you are excluded from government, exile is your reward.

This state of affairs reminds me of a case later in my life where the registration of my church (like others) was cancelled and all of us were asked to reapply. The official on the other side of the counter asked for a huge amount of money to be paid to him before the re-registration was processed. The local leadership of the church asked the headquarters of the church to assist them with that money. Everyone knew that it was a bribe but it was accepted that that was the way of life. We said no, we are prepared to pay the normal regulated registration fees and not less or more. 'How could we bribe our way to get the church registered? What message will that church preach after that?' But, no one knew about the exact regulated amount for this purpose. The amount asked for depended on the official one found at the counter. If you were less known in the community or did not know how to play the game properly you were made to pay more.

Despite my instinctive aversion to its apparent anti-African stance, my Harvard case study reminded me of a visit I made to one of the countries covered by the study. I was a guest speaker at a conference in the 1980s. I had to change my travel schedule but I could not find a functional telephone with which to call the travel agent or the airline. Eventually, I was sent to the Central Post Office, but even they did not have a working telephone. I was told the last option was the president's palace.

'The only working telephone is at the president's house?' I was disgusted, more so because I could not go there as the palace was barricaded like a fortress and no ordinary people like me were allowed in there. Eventually, I had to travel several kilometres to the periphery of the city where a foreign NGO had a working telephone.

Yes, corruption exists in Africa, but what was not said in any of the Harvard case study material was that the leadership of these countries usually acted as a proxy to some powerful country that is ready at any cost to secure the position of the leader and thereby the national interests of that country.

Some of the leaders and bureaucrats had agreements with some of the (mainly foreign) suppliers of basic goods to mark up the prices and then share the difference. People were indeed desperately in need of these goods for survival but the goods were acquired at a price that robbed them of other desperately needed services or goods. The worst cases were about those who sold supplies of medicines meant for the sick and pocketed the money. For one to do business in some of these countries one had to have bags of money to bribe one's way through. The competition for business is about who is able to pay more in terms of bribes to secure the business or tender. There are many case studies I could cite on these matters but I prefer not to go into details here.

In addition, public servants who were not paid for many months or years paid themselves on the job by taking bribes or selling the government services they were supposed to render free of charge. In this regard they do not see anything wrong with their actions. Given that they had not been paid for a long time they rationalise what they are doing and accept it as a way of life.

There is a critical point at which levels of corruption become so normal that it becomes a way of life rather than an exception. In such a situation, the cost of living escalates and the majority of the people (in the main, the poor) drop-off the system or the system drops them off to die because of hunger and need.

Once bribes have to be paid for almost everything, they become part of the normal business of the country. Decent people pay bribes without blinking as it becomes a way of life.

Thus, it was that I attended my Harvard class the next day with a bundle of mixed emotions that were about to burst and a brain that was working in overdrive, racing from one thought to another.

During the discussions I expressed my disgust about what was happening in the continent of my birth and indicated that there was no excuse that could justify this behaviour. At the same time I argued that the legacy of colonialism should not be forgotten in the midst of this challenge. Colonial systems and neo-colonial systems were by their nature and design corrupt, wicked and rotten to the core. Apartheid South Africa was a classic example of this. In fact, it was known as 'colonialism of a special type' as the white colonial ruling class and the oppressed majority are located within a single country. And, those who inherited the systems at independence became just like their colonial masters – good students of oppressive, exploitative *and corrupt* colonial regimes. The difference is that they were oppressing their own people whereas the colonial and neo-colonial regimes were oppressing 'the other'. I argued we had to take this into consideration as we dealt with corruption on the African continent.

At some stage I forced the discussion towards a comparative

analysis and expressed my concern about making Africa the sole embodiment of corruption. The facilitating lecturer was quick to answer this question as he had heard it before. No, Africa is not the only corrupt continent. Corruption, he agreed, was a universal problem. In fact, he said, there could be more corruption in the US than in Africa. The difference is that corruption has a more devastating impact on poor people or countries than it has on the rich. It is for this reason, he argued, that he chose a case study set in Africa rather than Europe or the US.

And when corruption happens in government or the public sphere, it affects the poor even more. Better endowed people need less help from their government than poor people. That is why better-off people argue for 'privatisation' and 'less' government in a neo-liberal sense. Even 'public goods' like security become redundant for the wealthy because they create their own 'secure spaces' in a sea of insecurity. If other 'public goods' such as roads are not provided by or maintained by government, rich people can buy a 4x4 vehicle. Those who can manage it even go to the extent of creating private landing strips at their huge private plots. If the educational system does not deliver quality, rich people simply create private schools to ensure the best education for their children. Even just owning a generator when electric supply systems fail makes a vast difference. If government fails to deliver these basic services, poor people suffer most.

Corrupt governments are like systems that leak. Even when you put public money into service provision, the money leaks out to benefit the better endowed first before the poor. In most instances the privileged participate in creating the leaks to benefit themselves. But even when they are not responsible for the leak, they have the means and capacity to design systems that enable them to benefit from it.

* * *

The discussion got me thinking deeply about life and I concluded that things naturally seemed to work against the poor or vulnerable in favour of the rich or powerful.

I argued this case in a seminar at the Kennedy School of Government where some 'naturalists' protested. To them, nature was perfect until humanity intervenes. They argued that 'natural conditions of living' were better than the mess humanity had created. My response was that for the poor what they are experiencing feels like a 'natural phenomenon' that works against them all the time and from all angles. If you are poor you pay higher rates of interest for loans. The rich will talk about 'prime plus one or two' while the poor will be repaying at the highest rates of interest. Poor people are seen as a 'risk' in our economies. As a result, the poorer you are, the more interest you pay.

It does not matter how 'people friendly' the justice system is, the poor are always worse off than the rich. For the same crime the rich accused will pay for bail immediately and go home while the poor accused will sit in jail. When one is well-off one is likely to find the best lawyers to ensure their acquittal, while the poor, without adequate legal representation, are sent to jail, even if they are innocent.

One could go on and on. The reality is that things seem to naturally work against the poor, underprivileged and powerless in favour of the rich, privileged and powerful.

★ ★ ★

On my return home I joined the University of Cape Town as a senior research officer with the intention of using my time to study this phenomenon further. I picked on the Reconstruction and Development Programme (RDP) housing project as one of my case studies. In this regard, the intentions of the ruling party were clear. It wanted to help the historically disadvantaged and the poor to acquire houses precisely because they did not have money. Many were unemployed. Some had disabilities that made it impossible for them to fend for themselves. Others were of advanced age without resources. The policy clearly intended to defy the natural trends – call it the system. The established building industry was unhappy about this policy and banks felt left out as the policy covered an area considered too risky for them. In any event, the government was to pay for the programme. The black-empowerment part of the policy was also meant to benefit the poor and disadvantaged.

My intention was to track the process from the time the policy was debated in parliament until the final product was delivered to the intended beneficiary (the poor and vulnerable). I wanted to establish whether or not 'the system' would negate this 'good intention' and benefit the rich rather than the poor.

Unfortunately, I was never given a chance to complete this study as I was deployed into the presidency. But by that time I had already presented a Ph.D. research proposal to the university, and as part of my research, had visited parliament and had met the ministers or directors-general or senior officials from the relevant departments who were primed to deal with this project. I chose Gauteng as the focal province and met the relevant members of the executive council (MECs) and officials who were going to be involved in the project. I met the mayor of Johannesburg. In Soweto I met the sub-regional mayors and officials of the council. I also had interactions with some of the interested industry players in order to understand their perspectives.

Although I did not take the study as far as I would have liked, preliminary results showed that as the policy was processed through parliament, it was the privileged who had the means to follow the debates, study the relevant documents, consult people in high places and plan how to access the funds available. Some of them set up housing consultancies to assist the government in implementing the policy. Some formed new building companies to meet the requirements of the law to be able to play in this space. Others used black faces to lobby for deals. Yet others simply used the blackness and political influence to secure contracts, regardless of expertise. The worst of them were ready to simply bribe their way through.

After my research was put on hold, I continued to observe developments from the presidency, and as a member of my community in Soweto and a citizen of the country. Many houses were built and some of them were of good quality. But many soon started to fall apart. Some of the houses such as those in Orange Farm, a district about 45 kilometres outside of Johannesburg, were built on flood plains while others were built in the middle of nowhere, far from people's work places. The worst cases were houses that had been paid for, but did not exit. Some simply pocketed the money, declared bankruptcy, and walked away.

Even without having completed the study it is clear that corruption played an important role in the failure to deliver what the policy intended. Again, the victims were the poor rather than the rich. At Orange Farm where I was called to see the damage caused by floods I was accompanied by the local councillors. Not only were the houses inhabitable, but the sewerage system had collapsed, spewing excrement all over the settlement.

Some of the houses were so flooded that the occupants had to take off their shoes and pull up their dresses and trousers to get into and simply live in their houses. Others had lifted up their beds with bricks (if they had any beds) to be able to sleep. In some of the houses water was damming up in the houses so that it made more sense to open holes at the other end of the house to allow the water to flow through. In one of the houses they complained about snakes from the river that came through the holes they had made.

When I asked how long the sewerage system had been

non-functional, the response was three months. I could not believe it! In Sandton, one of Johannesburg's richest suburbs, it would have been fixed within 24 hours.

I reported the matter to the relevant officials, the mayor and the relevant MEC, and indicated my outrage. For me, this was an emergency that required immediate attention. The MEC for local government visited the area and in our discussions later I was informed that the group that put in the sewerage system had gone bust or were not able to fix it. In any event, the system seemed to be beyond any repair. It needed to be rooted out and redone. While the community lived in squalor, those tasked with the job had pocketed millions of rands and were living in luxury elsewhere.

★ ★ ★

As indicated earlier, within my first two years or so in the presidency I started to pick up worrying signs that ordinary comrades who had been ready to die for the liberation of our people were being sucked into corrupt practices. The assumption that comrades were immune to corruption was unravelling. Over the years of our struggle, they had resisted the bribes offered to be bought out of the struggle. No amount of patronage from the apartheid government could lure them away from their demand for the total liberation of the people. Comrades declared then that however poor or hungry they might be, 'they were not for sale'.

But now, it seemed, they were ready to be bought for a song. They were not only easy targets for bribes but were ready to rob their own people, particularly the vulnerable by stealing their pensions and grants through fraudulent and corrupt schemes. Some civil servants within the Department of Social Development have been arrested and charged for this. As time went by what remained of the 'comrade' was empty radical slogans. In the place of militancy against the evil apartheid system came militancy against one's own comrades and the intimidation of those with different views. In place of military camouflage was the concealment of corrupt intentions.

What really troubled me was that some of those who were corrupt in the old order (apartheid system) were beginning to corrupt or lure the new 'comrade' civil servant into corruption. It was almost like a decoy to make sure that they were not caught. Even if they were found out there would be a 'comrade' of a significant political weight involved who would make it difficult for the new order to prosecute. Corrupted comrades began to do the same: draw in others who were strategically placed to make sure that they could never be touched. The private sector players were always ready with bags of money to compromise one or other of the bureaucrats or political office bearers if it served their interests. The more they got of them the easier it was for them to secure their interests.

At a political level there was another worrying trend: there were old-order people and business people who were visiting political office bearers and making all sorts of offers to do one thing or another which could compromise them. In fact, it was found that there were a set of wealthy, highly placed international and national business people who targeted the leadership or potential future leaders of the movement to befriend them, make offers to help them in one form or another, and in some cases corrupt them in preparation for future deals. These characters had no ideological interests or preferences for one party or another. What they were interested in was influence over leaders who were either strategically placed to serve their interest or may be strategically placed in future to do so. An analysis of these high flying people shows that some of them were active during the time of the apartheid government. When it became clear that the apartheid regime's life was limited, they began to visit Lusaka and other centres to reach out to the leadership of the ANC. They also did the same internally.

Corruption, it seemed, was a highly contagious disease. What worried me was the extent to which new public servants were drawn into corruption networks by more experienced people. The involvement of strategically placed senior comrades gave members of the network a sense of invincibility, and the practice, a certain credibility.

When the exiles returned in the early 1990s some of these high flyers hovered around the offices of the liberation movement or homes of leaders to make offers to assist in one way or another. These offers looked innocent and were indeed very helpful in a situation of great need. The first prize for a high flyer was to be able to reach the leader directly without going through secretaries and private offices. The second prize was to be able to call a secretary and the secretary would know that this was a person who should be given unrestricted access to the principal. The third prize was to be able to reach out to the leadership through third parties. During the 2005 to 2007 period, when it became clear that there might be changes in the leadership of government, this activity intensified again.

Within two years of joining the presidency I wrote to then President Nelson Mandela and copied to his deputy at the time, Mbeki, to raise my concerns about corruption of ANC members. It was unusual for a highly placed official in the presidency to communicate with the principals by letter. One could have used other opportunities one had to raise the concern. But I took this matter so seriously that I felt that if the leadership received my written letter in advance it would help to make the discussion more serious and considered. The letter was delivered by hand and it was treated as 'highly confidential' at that time.

I wrote the letter in my personal capacity as one of the leaders of the NDR. My concern was that if the people's organisation was compromised to a level where it would not be able to carry out the project of the NDR it would mean that our comrades who died during the struggle for liberation and those who suffered dearly in the course of this struggle would have done so in vain. In a sense I was raising an alarm; an early warning signal to say that this emerging trend was so dangerous that it could compromise what we had struggled for and what our people suffered and died for. There were also foreign players in this space who could threaten the national security of the state and what the ANC and the NDR stood for.

In the letter, I suggested to the leadership that this trend should be nipped in the bud before it spread like cancer in our body politic. Later, I had further discussions with the deputy president, Mbeki, about the matter. My expectation was that a public campaign would be launched to warn the new public servants and political office bearers of the trend, which was a threat to our national strategic objectives. I expected that they would urge the leadership and members of the liberation movement to be alert and ensure that no one compromised them in any form. The leadership chose a different route, which I accepted as a more strategic approach given the circumstances at the time. The starting point had to be the ruling party, that is, the ANC. Given the democratic culture of the ANC the conversation had to start from the NEC and feed down through to the provincial and regional structures, the branches of the party and then back to the NEC.

I was not part of the NEC at the time and I was not privy to all the processes then. But what I know is that the leadership used every opportunity to talk about this matter within the ruling party, government and in parliament. During the 1997 to 2007 period when I served in the NEC of the ANC, the matter was raised from time to time and members were urged to help deal with this scourge of corruption. It was also acknowledged that this scourge was a risk to the future of the liberation movement. My view is that not much was done practically to root out corruption where it manifested itself.

We even struggled with the concept of 'morality', which was a difficult construct for those who did not want to make this issue a religious matter. Others had problems with the popular under-standing of the concept of morality as they viewed it as 'personal morality', which they felt intruded into individuals' private lives. But generally everyone understood that it was immoral to steal from pensioners or vulnerable groups like children and people with disabilities. Everyone understood that there was 'right' and 'wrong'.

Later, the debate went to a higher level of what we called 'revo-lutionary morality', which pushed the debate beyond religion and personal morality, nationalities, cultures, traditions, customs, group interests, etc. to the 'common good'. The argument was that if your private conduct affected others negatively it could not be accept-able. A literature search on 'revolutionary morality' usually sends one in the direction of Cuba as the Cubans had grappled with related issues.

Revolutionary morality for me also helped us to distinguish be-tween activities considered 'revolutionary' but that were, in fact, counter-revolutionary. One may have the right to protest as a revo-lutionary but there is nothing revolutionary in stoning innocent motorists on the N1 or N12 motorways during protests. There is nothing revolutionary in looting shops or destroying the goods of ordinary street traders who have nothing to do with the issues peo-ple are protesting about. This type of behaviour is counter-revolu-tionary as it alienates the people from the noble cause of the revo-lutionary project: transforming South African society. The debate on revolutionary morality also reminded us of our revolutionary task to defend our revolution by combating counter-revolutionary tendencies such as corruption.

As part of the effort to deal with corruption government also arranged workshops and seminars, after which a regulatory framework to stop corruption within the public service was developed. Accordingly, the following legal instruments were passed through parliament and implemented accordingly: the Prevention and Combating of Corrupt Activities Act (Act No. 12 of 2004); Protected Disclosures Act (Act No. 26 of 2000); Promotion of Administrative Justice Act (Act No. 3 of 2000); Promotion of Access to Information Act (Act No. 2 of 2000); the Public Finance and Management Act (Act No. 1 of 1999) and the Local Government: Municipal Finance Management Act (Act No. 56 of 2003). The Public Service Act of 1994 and the Executive Ethics Act were also part of the effort to combat corruption. More recently, government enacted laws like the Financial Centre Intelligence Act (FICA), which is aimed at reducing access of criminals to financial services for money laundering. There were also policies and campaigns like 'Batho Pele' to encourage public servants to focus on the people they served before they thought of themselves.

Notwithstanding these measures, the cancer continued slowly but surely to spread and destroy the healthy tissues and organs of the body of our comrades. Corruption corrodes. It eats its way steadily with destructive persistency. Corruption is not just about petty bribery issues like paying for a favour you want from someone in authority in the public or private sectors. It is also not just about paying a traffic cop to let you go without given you a ticket. Corruption goes deeper than that. It involves the awarding of tenders, contracts, etc. At even higher levels it includes the use of power to dish out goodies for themselves, family or friends. Today it even goes beyond family and friends to political factions. This is what I have called the demon of the 'triple F', that is family, friends and factions. The worst part of these tendencies of corruption is involvement with or playing in the terrain of organised crime. This involves syndicates and criminal gangs that operate both in the country and beyond our borders. Here, the risk for the security of the state balloons beyond manageable proportions. A compromised leader who is compromised because of one act of corruption is vulnerable and could be forced to offer other services on a corrupt basis. But getting involved with syndicates that operate beyond our borders is a risk to the security of the state. It is known that intelligence services or agencies, especially foreign intelligence agencies, work through criminal gangs and syndicates.

During the height of apartheid, P.W. Botha said that the ANC terrorists would not succeed in South Africa as there was no 'bush' to hide in. But he made an exception of Soweto, which he said was the only bush in which they could round up and flush out the terrorists. This is where my struggle training took place. Part of our training involved understanding the strategies and tactics of the apartheid regime, how oppressive regimes could compromise or neutralise comrades, turn them against their own and then use them for their own purposes. There were three things the system could use to turn you: money, love affairs and personal weakness.

To start with money, there is a famous maxim that says: 'The love of money is the root of all evil.' All of us need money and there is nothing wrong with that. The real problem is the 'love' thereof. When they say that somebody *uthand'mali* (loves money), that suggests that there is something negative about it. You do not just need money to meet your needs but you love it so much that you are prepared to do anything legal or illegal to get to it. My first-year course in economics taught me that money is never enough, not even for multi-billionaires. If you start off poor, you would probably be happy with a bicycle to get around on. Once you have got a bicycle you would want to get a scooter, then a small car. Once you have a car, then the talk is about five or seven series luxury cars. Once you have a house, you want a holiday home. Then one on the beach with a boat of your own. Then your own private executive jet. Once you have it you probably want to go to the moon for a holiday. And after all this, you probably still do not have peace of mind.

The temptations of money do not only affect the poor as some would have us believe. The more affluent people are, the more they face temptation, except that they pay their way out of trouble once they are caught. This is not the only problem. The love of money often goes with living above one's means. This keeps one permanently in debt. In this state one is an easy target. You are on sale, ready to be bought.

When my boys were younger they used to ask: 'Why don't we have the things that other people at your level have, Dad? Look at what their children have?' My answer always was, 'If you do not know where they get the money from to live at that standard, then do not try it yourself.' My motto, which I told my boys, is, 'Work hard and live within your means.'

At times a financial crisis has nothing to do with living above one's means. It could be totally beyond one's control and might involve the loss of a job, the failure of a business, a global financial crisis, or a death in the family. It is when one is in a state of crisis that the enemy agents visit and made offers to help. But remember, there is no free lunch. In the old days of struggle we used to say that we would rather die than sell our souls.

One has to be wary of unsolicited offers that could ruin your life forever. One high-level 'armour-bearer' who accompanied a special visitor to meet the deputy president during the first decade of our democracy got stuck with me while the principals were having their meeting. When he heard that I was still staying in Soweto and working in Pretoria he was shocked. 'Why can't you just get a house in Pretoria and move with the family?' he asked.

I told him that would cost me money I did not have. The reality was that apartheid forced me to build my house in a place where I could not put it on the market and use the money to purchase another. I indicated that many of our comrades got into trouble by taking a second bond to have another house in Cape Town once they were elected as members of parliament.

My companion then offered to assist me by buying my house in Soweto so I could purchase another closer to work. I thought he was joking and I teasingly told him that my house would be worth R2 million if it were in Sandton. In Soweto it could only sell at about R300 000 to R400 000. If he bought it, I said, he would have to make up for the injustice caused by the apartheid system.

He then seriously offered to pay the R2 million. I asked him what he would do with the house, and he said he would give it away to be used for community services. He was dead serious.

'No, thank you. I can't do it,' I said. 'How will I justify the costs of acquiring the new house?'

'It's easy,' he replied. 'Just say that it was a donation as they needed the house for community services.'

I refused. From where I sat, that was a bribe. I said I would rather drive daily to Pretoria until I was able to buy or build a house within my means. He was shocked, and gave up on me.

The way in which personal relationships could be used against operatives has been highlighted in spy films, especially those about the US and Russia. Unfortunately, and in most cases, it is a woman who is used against the weakness of the men and it feels sexist. Samson and Delilah is a classic example of a case in which a woman – Delilah – was used by the Philistines to entice Samson to give away his secret, which led to his capture. I also know of a real case where a man was used against a woman comrade. An undercover security policeman befriended a woman comrade, fell in love with her, and assisted her in her underground assignment to move comrades who were at risk through the borders into our neighbouring countries. When he was bust by the liberation movement, he triggered action by the security police to arrest her and all those who worked with her.

The point is: all of us have weaknesses. The enemy forces always looked at our weaknesses with a view to using them against us. If you had an inability to manage your finances properly this could be used against you. If you had a problem of complex 'love affairs' the enemy could use it against you. You may think that these are personal and private matters, but they can be national security matters. If you have a weakness for alcohol, it could be used against you. In fact that is how foreign intelligence agencies collected information from an unsuspecting target.

★ ★ ★

It is important, however, to understand that corruption is not only what is called bureaucratic corruption, that is, corruption by public servants or political office bearers in government. The trail goes back to the political parties themselves. Since the new democratic order was established we missed this critical area, which became an incubator for uncontrollable forms of corruption or corrupt activities. When the ANC won the elections with an overwhelming majority in 1994 we went into government as those cadres of the movement who were there simply to serve the people and advance the NDR. We believed that we could build a unique society that would meet the needs of the people. This is what we fought for and many died for. The RDP was our guide. We were idealistic but also realistic. We understood that we had a major task of achieving tough objectives. We also knew that there were global forces that would mark us and make sure we did not set a bad example to the many who were involved in similar projects.

Because the stakes were high, we used to have regular sessions on what we called 'the balance of forces'. A critical analysis would help us to decide whether to pursue a particular struggle at a particular time. This was about strategic timing. We also had policy instruments like 'Ready to Govern', which were supposed to prepare us for this task.

The last thing we expected (or at least the last thing I expected) was that our comrades could be such easy targets of corruption. There were critical shifts that we failed to pay adequate attention to. We missed the fact that what had produced the extraordinary cadres of the movement – leaders such as Albert Luthuli, Oliver Tambo, Nelson Mandela, Govan Mbeki, Walter Sisulu and others – were the conditions of the struggle that required us to risk our lives for a cause. For many, the rewards for being involved in the struggle were either detention without trial, torture, jail, exile or death. The cadre of that time was ready to die for others. And once you are ready to die for others your personal interests cease to be an issue. In the early stages there was no money to wage the struggle. We had to go out there and resist the system whatever it cost. But once we went into government the conditions on the ground changed dramatically. Money became the centre of everything we did.

The second factor we missed was that the comrade who was in exile or underground was taken care of by the liberation movement. This covered just the basic necessities like clothes, food, accommodation and travel costs. Luxury was not part of the package. Once the liberation movement was unbanned, exiles returned home and those who were underground emerged, a system was needed to take care of all of them. At one stage there was a system of equal salaries for comrades who worked at 'Shell House', the headquarters of the ANC. Others relied on returnees' grants while some got jobs. I imagine that the transition for comrades to move from a system that met their basic needs (however inadequate) to one in which you had to fend for yourself was a major challenge. Yesterday you were a collective that shared whatever you had. The following day you were on your own.

The third factor we neglected was that after many years of sacrifice comrades would want to now live normal lives. The younger ones were better off here than the older comrades. If you were 40 or 50 years old you had very little chance to return to a normal life. The truth was that our comrades were human. Their extraordinariness was a product of the conditions of struggle rather than some intrinsic element contained within them. In recognition of these issues, the 2000 Port Elizabeth National General Council of the ANC dedicated much of its time to discussions about 'the cadre of the movement'. Ten years after the unbanning of the ANC and the South African Communist Party (SACP), followed by the establishment of a non-racial, non-sexist, democratic government in 1994, the 'cadre of the movement' was failing the movement! But no amount of resolutions taken at that National General Council could turn the tide. The comrade had become an ordinary human being who was susceptible to corruption like any other.

The language of bo 'phuma singene' (time to go so we can come in) has become prevalent. For some, government has become an 'eating place'. They go there to 'eat' (baya Mmusong go ja) rather than to serve the people. We were in danger of becoming like a country whose president, I was told, had a high turnover in his cabinet to give as many of his people a chance to enrich themselves and their families. If you did not do so it was your fault. You had no one to blame. This made corruption part of the lives of the people.

This 'phuma singene' phenomenon has translated itself to the politics of the organisation. If I want to be a member of the executive of the local council I campaign for the person in the party who is likely to appoint me into that position. At times the person involved is paid in advance to produce that result. If I want to be a MEC of a provincial government I mobilise and vote for the chairperson of the party who will make sure that I am appointed to that position. The same would happen as well at a national level. But it does not stop there. It also goes to tenders, contracts and other deals. Candidates are not promoted because they are the best amongst the leaders available at the time. They are promoted to facilitate lucrative deals. Private sector entities have entered the fray. They buy people or bribe them to campaign for specific candidates who will make sure that tenders and deals are reserved for them without any consideration of the legal framework that governs these processes.

At one place where I was deployed as an NEC member I dealt with a situation where comrades were at odds with each other. One regional council was voted out of power. And when the other group got its chance, it also voted them out. For me each one of these two groups – call then factions – operated like a party within a party. Each group had its own leadership, its own caucus meetings before official meetings and its own structures. It also seemed like they had their own troopers some of them in military gear to look like Umkhonto we Sizwe or assume the legitimacy of Umkhonto we Sizwe. Apparently the military gear was meant to present them as radical revolutionaries. Their job was to disrupt meetings violently. It also seemed that there was a budget to finance their disruptive activities, including drowning them with strong drinks (liquor) and in some cases drugs to enable them to do the dirty work for the leaders in a bold way without any conscience. In one of the meetings there were NEC members in attendance. The NEC members were insulted and ruffled up. The atmosphere was so threatening that some of the regional and provincial leaders had to help the NEC members to leave by using a side door.

In one of the meetings where I was present these drunkards comrades arrived in an open *bakkie* at the stadium with bottles of strong liquor in their hands and music at its highest volume to make sure that members of the ANC who had come to the meeting were not able to hear each other, even with a public address system. Once the *bakkie* had stopped next to the stage they began to swear at the leadership. They paced up and down in front of the stage before they went up the terraces of the stadium. Once at the highest point of the stadium they smashed their bottles, sending pieces of glass flying and splashing liquor on the people. I remember old women and men running down the stairs, some tripping and others holding on to each other, afraid of comrades who had turned into beasts because of tenders and business interests. The police were called but did not intervene as they felt it was a party matter. I reported formally to the leadership and directed a written letter to the NEC to warn them about this new trend that was threatening to destroy the ANC. I urged that it be nipped on the bud before it got out of control.

The conflict was not ideological. It was not about a vision for the future of the region. It was not about whether or not one of the groups (call it a faction) would deliver services better than the other. It was all about tenders and benefits for themselves and not about the people. When one group (call it a faction) takes power it victimises the other, including any person who would have been associated with the other. Here, losing power means total exclusion and the loss of jobs (civil service jobs). It also means exclusion from private sector activities, which have nothing to do with government. In this situation people resort to violence to stay in power or gain power. The recent killings of mayors and deputy mayors suggest that we might be on a dangerous road that does not bode well for the future of the country. This, I submit, is the stuff that breeds dictatorships.

This emerging trend I have described shows very clearly that the seeds of the most toxic forms of corruption do not lie in a traditional understanding of bureaucratic corruption. The most toxic forms of corruption start with corruption in our party politics. If our party political activity or practice is corrupted, that corrupt culture will be carried over into government. If the self or self-interest is the driving force in our party political practice then self or self-interest will be the determining factor in our management of government. If a comrade is elected to advance the interests of 'self' and his or her group (clique/faction) we should then not be surprised when they do the same in government.

This is what is called 'political corruption' as opposed to 'bureaucratic corruption'. I want to submit that political corruption leads to the worst forms of bureaucratic corruption. It is intense and can break the system. Corruption causes leaders to define themselves as being above or beyond the law. They easily throw away the regulatory framework when it comes to self-interest. At this highest level of corruption no stone is left unturned until the corrupt elements control all the organs of state to ensure that they serve their interests. This involves influencing judges, prosecutors and the police. The cases involving allegations against the NDPP, the Scorpions, Judge Hlophe and the Constitutional Court judges, the release of classified intelligence information to the public, etc., are indicators of how close we came to making the institutions of the state part of the corruption project. In fact the worst situation in the corruption stakes is when the judges, prosecutors and the police are bought to produce particular outcomes. At this stage the country gets turned into an overt mafia and corruption is in your face.

Having worked in government, I have learnt that as one deals with corruption one needs to remember that at the highest levels of corruption involving syndicated forms of organised crime and mafia-style criminal activity, systems and institutions of law enforcement agencies can be captured by a syndicate and manipulated in a way that serves their interests. In this regard innocent people can be sent to jail while the real criminals maintain their freedom to continue with their criminal activities without hindrance. I have also learnt that where there are competitors in a bid for a tender the losers always run a campaign to discredit the winners in the hope of the tender being re-opened to give them a second bite.

The Arms Procurement Programme or so-called Arms Deal is the highest profile case on corruption that needs to be documented in the form of a case study for students of politics, law and public administration. It has all the elements that can help such students to understand the complexities of corruption and the challenges of ending it.

Like all multibillion rand government projects the offer for companies to tender attracts both national and international entities that compete against each other. Each of these companies sets up systems to conduct commercial intelligence against each and some are assisted by their governments or private intelligence entities. This is done not just to be able to present the best bid but also to run campaigns to discredit their competitors. Corruption stories then get written, which are in the main decoys to cover the real story that might be happening at other levels. In many instances bribes in all disguises are paid to influence the decision-making process. The bribes are at times like a shot in the dark. They start from the decision makers to the peripheral players who are believed to be able to influence the decision makers.

There are number of challenges that make an investigation of this type of corruption very difficult. First, one has to cut through the machinations of the interested parties, including a possible disinformation campaign. In this regard the state has to use all the information and intelligence capacity that it has to isolate truth from falsehood. The challenge here is that where there is doubt about the credibility of the state this approach gets rubbished. Secondly, opposition parties in parliament tend to focus more intently on discrediting the ruling party rather than getting to the bottom of cases. In response the ruling party simply digs its feet in and fight back rather than focuses on how to root out corruption. The third challenge is about dynamics within the ruling party that could constrain the pursuance of cases that affect senior members of the party. The fourth is that the corrupted and the corruptor have a common interest: to ensure that none of them gets caught unless the police have overwhelming information about one or the other. The fifth is the media, which tend to focus more on controversy than the substance of the case.

I would argue that the best way to deal with corruption is to de-politicise the cases and focus on the evidence available to prepare a case that can stand the scrutiny of our courts. We need to engage one another about how we can turn the tide of corruption to ensure that the country does not slide further into a situation in which corruption becomes an intractable part of our lives.

PART FOUR

CHAPTER 12

Drugs, Pharmaceutical Companies
and the Poor

South Africa is well known for its world–class medical facilities
and the services of its medical specialists. The problem with
these facilities and services is that they were developed during the
time of the apartheid system and were in the main meant for the
white minority, which constituted less than twenty per cent of the
population. This percentage has decreased over the years to about
twelve per cent of the population. The black majority, which accounted for the balance of this percentage, was excluded from these
high–level services. Access was limited to basic services at segre-
gated hospitals and clinics.

Thus while whites received 'first world' medical facilities and services, blacks had to contend with the basic and inadequate facilities
and services associated with poor developing countries. This was
not simply a case of having the raw end of the stick; it was a case
of not being able to grasp the stick at all in a sea of white privilege.

The demise of apartheid opened the way for us to correct this gross injustice and to ensure that the black majority had full access to quality health facilities and services. This was one of the key strategic objectives of the democratic South Africa.

Pursuing this key objective in a world of gross inequalities and privileges was difficult. Firstly, the new government had to make services accessible to the majority without lowering the quality of the existing world-class facilities and services. It was seen that opening up facilities designed to meet the needs of a few would stretch the capacity of these facilities to breaking point within a short space of time. On the other hand, increasing their capacity would require enormous additional resources that the country did not have.

Racists had an easy explanation for what was perceived as an attendant decline in standards: 'Once blacks take over, the quality of everything deteriorates.' But it is not rocket science: opening up services meant for whites only and stretching them by a factor of at least five, which was unsustainable.

Expansion of facilities to meet the needs of the (largely poor) majority required a dramatic increase in the budget for health services. Taking loans to do so and increasing the budget deficit as some suggested would have elevated our indebtedness to unsustainable levels that might have invited the IMF.

In general the government agreed that taking loans to pay for social services was not advisable. Loans had to be part of an investment to multiply the resources of the country to meet the needs of the people rather than only for consumption.

This challenge was compounded by the policy decision to offer free medical services to children under six years old and to all pregnant women who could not afford proper medical services. For the democratic government this was a critical intervention to meet the needs of the most vulnerable sectors of society. It was in line with the pro-poor policies of the ruling party, that is, the ANC.

Accordingly, ways and means had to be found to deliver these services, despite resource constraints.

Of all the strategies that were developed and implemented during this time, trying to reduce the costs of medicines to competitive levels became the most controversial part of the reform process in the health sector.

Ways and means had to be found to reduce the high costs of drugs in order to make them available to the majority of South Africans. As the then Minister of Health, Dr Nkosazana Dlamini-Zuma, argued, South Africa had some of the highest drug prices in the world.

In their defence, pharmaceutical companies argued that South Africa could not procure drugs at more competitive prices because the country had entered into agreements with the pharmaceutical companies over their intellectual property rights. These rights did not allow South Africa to procure the drugs outside its borders. Parallel importation, they said, violated World Trade Organisation rules.

A plan to introduce generic medicines, a practice in many other countries, was soundly resisted by the pharmaceutical companies, as it substituted the patented drugs.

But the fact remained that if South Africa was to meet the needs of its people, it had to be able to acquire medicines at cheaper prices. To achieve this objective, government introduced a set of legislation, one of which was the Medicines and Related Substances Control Amendment Bill.

The objectives of the legislation were to open up the country to cheap imports, encourage the use of generic substitution and to curb the mark-up by pharmacists. All this was done in the interest of the poor and the most vulnerable in society.

Despite its noble intentions, the legislation unleashed a vicious reaction from the powerful global pharmaceutical industry, which shook the new democracy to its foundations. Although the heat was on Dlamini-Zuma as health minister, the president's office was under intense pressure to intervene.

One thing that established Western democracies failed to understand about South Africa was that the country took its democratic system more seriously than others. There could be no decision or policy from a minister that was not approved by the national cabinet. By the time bills are tabled in parliament cabinet would have acted on them already. Nothing goes from government to parliament without the approval of cabinet. Accordingly, policies pursued by ministers are not policies of those individuals but those of government.

At the time Mandela was the president and he was fully in support of efforts to make drugs accessible to all South Africans, especially the poor. While Dlamini-Zuma was the driver of the policy to improve access, she was not acting alone. Her policy was also that of the South African government and the ANC. Challenging policy was thus tantamount to challenging the policies of the ruling party, which were based on a commitment to better the lives of all South Africans, irrespective of race, colour, class or creed. The ringing slogan was 'A Better Life for All!'

Deputy President Mbeki, who was in the engine room of President Mandela's government, had the unenviable task of providing leadership in this regard. He was responsible for the transformation processes of all the facets of government and our society and took responsibility to work with Dlamini-Zuma to realise these objectives, against all the odds. As director-general in Mbeki's office, I also became involved as part of my responsibility to enable him to carry out his responsibilities.

There were also advisers in Mbeki's office who were involved, namely, Advocate Mojanku Gumbi (legal adviser); Mr Moss Ngoasheng (economic adviser); Mr Vusi Mavimbela (political adviser); and Dr Essop Pahad (parliamentary counsellor and later deputy minister in the presidency; but he remained integrally as part of the advisory services machinery in the presidency).

There were also senior staff involved from President Mandela's office, including Professor Jakes Gerwel (director-general in the president's office), Joel Netshitenzhe (the communications chief), Nicholas Haysom (legal adviser) and his parliamentary counsellor, Ahmed Kathrada.

The Minister of Health also had an extraordinary team that assisted her in dealing with this difficult challenge, including Dr Ayanda Ntsaluba (director-general of health) and Dr Ian Roberts (special assistant to the minister). Except for Roberts all of them were longstanding and experienced cadres of the liberation movement. All of them understood well what the end game was: a better life for all!

The presidency as a whole supported Dlamini-Zuma and her team in this regard. Having failed to divide the cabinet, the powerful pharmaceutical lobby turned its heat on the country as a whole. For them South Africa looked like a 'delinquent' little country that needed to be stopped in its tracks before it ruined their interests. They saw the stance of South Africa as 'arrogant' and 'cheeky'.

We needed to be disciplined as we would set a 'bad example' and set a precedent. If South Africa was allowed to succeed in challenging the system that, in their view, sustained the pharmaceutical industry, including maintaining its large profit margins, the rest of the world would follow. This would cripple the industry. A deeper but related fear was that tampering with the international intellectual property and patents regime would threaten industries unrelated to the pharmaceutical industry, such as the music industry, arts and so forth.

Thus, South Africa's intentions were threatening an industry and the logic of the global economic system that favoured the rich and powerful at the expense of the poor and vulnerable. The morality of South Africa's cause did not matter. The companies did not even consider alternative ways of addressing the country's need. The response was just 'No', 'No', 'No'.

Their attack was fierce and fast. It was like '*re tlhotlhile motshitshi wa dinotshi*'. We shook the bee hive and the bees came out, stinging like mad. Everyone who was close to the action was a target.

The international and the South Africa Pharmaceutical Research and Manufacturers Association coordinated their response in a way that showed that they meant business.

The industry threatened to withdraw from South Africa, an act that could have destabilised the entire health system. They suspended their investment plans and threatened to disinvest in South Africa and close all manufacturing plants in the country. These actions would have resulted in significant job losses and drugs would have been unavailable to patients who needed them desperately.

They did not stop here. They mobilised other industries and investors to take a stand and threatened to withdraw from South Africa. Furthermore they lobbied the US administration to pressure us, starting with the US ambassador in South Africa, followed by the secretary for commerce and industry, vice-president Al Gore, right up to the president Bill Clinton. Although Clinton and Gore were friends of the new South Africa they could not do otherwise but represent the interests of the US on this matter. The national interests of the US took precedence over other interests, including the interests of the poor in South Africa. These were mainly American companies and they had to be protected. Here, the moral weight of Nelson Mandela did not seem to matter.

When this issue was raised at one of the one-on-one meetings between Deputy President Mbeki and Vice-President Gore during the Bi-National Commission the atmosphere would abruptly change. It was friendly but tense. Mbeki and Gore had by then developed a close relationship through the Bi-National Commission but this matter threatened this relationship. It was expected that Mbeki would back off. But this was a life-and-death matter for Mbeki and for South Africa. It was about the lives of our people, particularly the poor. And to backtrack would spell disaster for the most vulnerable.

This standoff with the pharmaceutical companies forced us to arm ourselves with information about their history and their oper-ations in other countries. Unfortunately, understanding the power of these pharmaceutical entities did not help us much. It simply made us more alive to the level of risk the country and the leader-ship were facing. A study of the history of the powerful pharmaceu-tical industry showed that a threat to their interests was dealt with mercilessly, and that caused us to worry about a security threat to the leadership of the country, especially those who were involved in the campaign. The levels of the security threat did not require a threat analysis and assessment by our intelligence services. It was written on the wall. This in fact is one of the few moments of my thirteen-and-a-half years in government when I felt that both the deputy president and Minister Nkosazana Zuma might possibly be in physical danger.

Although there were salient comments from some bold journal-ists, the greater part of the South African media did not help much. They simply delivered the views of the pharmaceutical companies and the US administration as if they were the obvious truth – the generally accepted way of life. The tone was the same, if not more vicious. For them it was not possible that the pharmaceutical in-dustry and the US could be wrong. It had to be South Africa that was wrong.

The fact that the economy of South Africa, including the phar-maceutical companies and pharmaceutical outlets, was almost wholly white-owned did not help the situation either. It divided us on racial lines. The main opposition parties followed suit, and along the same lines. It made sense for them to do so. Again, as for some of the media, white business could not be wrong. This was like an *a priori* position that made more sense for the media as well. One could say that in all this we reverted to the old racially based South Africa, far removed from the rainbow nation we wanted to be.

Again, the moral authority of Mandela was ignored. In fact, on controversial matters of this nature the media tended to discount Mandela's position by separating him from his own troops (the ANC and government) and treated him as if he were different from them.

Our domestic politics, particularly perceptions relating to the ANC, the support for the controversial Virodine HIV and AIDS drug research, the controversy around the Sarafina production intended to educate the public about HIV and AIDS and other media pet stories about the health minister and the ANC clouded the views of the South African media to the extent that it missed one of the most ideologically significant moments in history: a relatively powerless country was taking on one of the worlds' most powerful industries that was backed by the only superpower at the time on a critical matter of justice for the poor. The issue had the potential to change the way in which the whole industry functioned globally in the interests of the poor.

This little 'upstart', as some would say, was taking a stand, against the odds, that would benefit millions of poor people not only in South Africa but in the whole world. In fact, many countries in the developing world nicodemously expressed their support for South Africa's stand and urged us to press on as the outcomes would be of great benefit to them. They indicated though that they were too vulnerable to raise their heads in this regard.

This was again like a David and Goliath type of struggle. It was so unequal and unfair. We had just come out of a racist apartheid situation where the majority of the people, particularly the poor, were excluded from world class health care because of their colour. Our policy was 'access', 'access', 'access' for all. And suddenly we discovered that breaking down the walls did not help as there were other layers that still excluded the poor or limited their access to resources they so desperately needed.

At this point it became clear that the mask of crude racism that operated in South Africa during apartheid was covering other deeper forms of racism and global economic injustice. Despite democracy, the drugs were still inaccessible to the majority of our people, this time because of price determination and legal constraints that outlawed choices. We understood the rules of intellectual property rights and patents and why they needed to be respected. But we also believed that these could be applied differently to make it possible for the poor to have access to medication. In fact we were of the view that all that we wanted could be achieved within the stringent rules of intellectual property rights and patents. We wanted this to be a subject for negotiations but some of the pharmaceuticals would have none of it.

Credit must be given to Minister Dlamini-Zuma for not relenting, notwithstanding the personal attacks and abuse she had to endure. On the other hand the pharmaceuticals had too much at stake to capitulate. They squared up for a vicious battle with South Africa just for trying to do the best for its people, particularly the poor.

When South Africa insisted that it would proceed with the bills, the pharmaceutical companies went to court. From here on the discourse went beyond politics and justice to legal technicalities about the World Trade Organisation's regulatory framework. The Department of Trade and Industry was drawn in to advise on the international rules of trade, including the issues of intellectual property rights and patents. As usual lawyers differed about the interpretation of these rules. After extensive debates, including

FRANK CHIKANE

parliamentary processes, the Medicines and Related Substances Control Amendment Bill was passed with some amendments.

The pharmaceutical companies ultimately withdrew the court challenge. But the next battle was just around the corner: at the dispensing level.

This case shows beyond any doubt that the global community is not concerned about finding solutions to end poverty, diseases and pain. It is concerned about money, power and control. But the story also suggests that if we persevere and strategically target grossly unjust systems and practices we can slowly chip away pieces of the unjust global economic system.

This story also illustrates that, in the midst of all the challenges in our country and our internal ideological debates and debilitating politics, we often miss some of the most significant achievements of the new South Africa. The risk here is that our gains could be reversed if we are not alive to the importance of such gains. We cannot wait for history to tell these stories. They need to be told now because the achievements we make, however insignificant, help to build our confidence for the next front of the struggle. *Aluta Continua!*

CHAPTER 13

Mbeki and the HIV and AIDS Controversy

One of the most controversial issues of the Mbeki presidency and his legacy is the HIV and AIDS matter. From the time I decided to write about 'the things that could not be said' I determined that I could not avoid writing about this controversy. In fact, it would be strange if I did not.

The next question was, are there no risks in writing about such a controversial matter? The answer was emphatically, 'Yes', huge risks. This was followed by another question about whether or not it would help if someone who was in the office of Mbeki during this controversy wrote or spoke about it. The answers here were, 'Yes' and 'No'. Yes, because those who were close to the matter could help the national and international public to understand the story better.

The 'No' has to do with the perception that if you were close to Mbeki or worked with him you were unlikely to be objective about the matter – the 'proximity issue'. In this regard it is interesting that all those who have written books about this matter never took the trouble to talk to those of us who were close to the developments. In my view, the exclusion of these perspectives robbed the public of information that could have thrown light on some developments relating to the matter. The public has the right to hear all the perspectives and make up their own mind.

My intention here is not to write an objective critique about Mbeki's views about HIV and AIDS. Mine is to write about my personal experience and knowledge about the development of government's programme on HIV and AIDS and the related controversies. In a sense I am one of the living witnesses of some of the developments of the time.

In any story there are historical bits and gaps that can only be filled or completed by those who witnessed or had a direct experience of it. In the case of HIV and AIDS the verdict has been passed and one is either on the side of Mbeki or not. No one is allowed to think differently or take the middle ground. Besides, the debate was so emotive that no intelligent discourse was possible. In this war of words, of personalities, of conflicting interests, of people's lives, and of money, historical facts did not matter.

In a war the first casualty is the truth. The tragedy is that the issues have become so confused that those who were not part of or affected directly by this controversy cannot any longer access the 'truth' about it.

Can one write about this story without becoming part of the controversy? Well, I doubt it. In fact, writing about it is one of the surest ways of becoming part of the controversy. The best way to avoid it would be not to write or talk about it at all. But this would be a cop-out. Those of us who were close to the controversy have a responsibility to tell the story and leave it to the listeners or readers to judge.

I intend here to tell the story as I encountered it and the way I understood it. Indeed there will be different perspectives and views about this story depending on different positions and starting points. As a starting point, one needs to understand that although the matter of HIV and AIDS was a government-wide issue the department driving the programme was the Department of Health. Accordingly most of the activity related to this programme would have been within that department. The presidency only became directly involved as a leader within government, especially when difficult and controversial matters had to be dealt with. I must also state that as a director-general (in the office of the Deputy President and later for the integrated presidency) I was not intimately involved in the day-to-day activities related to this matter. I had a panoramic view of it as directors-general would on many matters their departments were dealing with. What follows is my perspective from the vantage point as a director-general in the presidency during the time when the policies on HIV and AIDS were developed and when this controversy was raging.

There is a book I consider to be Albert Nolan's classic work. The book is entitled *Jesus before Christianity*. When I first heard the title I wondered what Albert Nolan meant. In the book, Nolan managed to make the point that many of us remember the historical man called Jesus from the perspective of the Crucifixion but not the man before the Crucifixion. His view is that Jesus' crucifixion became such a dominant factor in his life that it became difficult to know his life before or outside this event.

I consider Mbeki's HIV and AIDS story such an event. It loomed so large that some cannot see anything else that Mbeki ever did before or during his presidency. Mention the name 'Mbeki' anywhere in the world and it is associated with the HIV and AIDS matter. Even when the discussion is about matters unrelated to HIV and AIDS, the discussion almost always ends up with a discussion about HIV and AIDS.

Since the controversy about 'HIV and AIDS and Mbeki' erupted many have no recollection of what Mbeki's views about HIV and AIDS were before his first salvo in October 1999, which changed the discourse. This is where I would like to start as it will help us to understand how Mbeki ended up where he was during his presidency. Again, my intention is to tell the story that I know and as I understand it. Because it is told from my perspective I accept that it cannot be complete or account for other perspectives. If it has to be judged it should be judged from that perspective.

Mbeki's pre-1999 views on HIV and AIDS

When I joined the deputy president's office in 1995 the issues of Human Immunodeficiency Virus (HIV) and Acquired Immune Deficiency Syndrome (AIDS) were not as prominent in my mind as the reconstruction and development of the country. In fact the level of consciousness about HIV and AIDS issues was very low amongst many in the country. Knowledge of HIV and AIDS started to emerge during the 1980s, which was at the height of our struggle for liberation. During this time the struggle preoccupied us so much that we could not focus on HIV and AIDS. I imagine that many of us who lived with the reality that we could be killed by apartheid security forces and their agents at any time would have missed details of some of the pressing issues that affected people at the time. Some of us were daily on death's door, not because of illness, but because of the risk of being taken out by the system.

There is evidence that the apartheid government did initiate programmes to deal with HIV in the 1980s and early 1990s but it was mainly aimed at whites, particularly amongst gay communities. In any case this was a time when the struggle against the apartheid system had reached its height. As a result there was little chance that such a government programme would have impacted on or even reached black communities.

Interestingly, those who returned from exile had a better sense of the challenge of HIV and AIDS than those of us who were in the country. Their level of awareness was based on their exposure to the international concerns raised about what was understood as a 'new disease' in the early 1980s. Their awareness was also based on their experiences in the countries in which they had sought refuge. They also had some experience of dealing with cases of HIV and AIDS amongst themselves during the time of their exile.

The 1990 Maputo Statement on HIV and AIDS in Southern Africa is an indication that the region had started to deal with this challenge. It is also worth noting that the Networking HIV/AIDS Community of South Africa at times referred to as the National AIDS Coordinating Committee of South Africa was established as early as 1992, following a conference held in 1991. This coincided with political negotiations for a democratic South Africa.

When I was roped into the deputy president's office, firstly as a special adviser and later as director-general, the new democratic South Africa had already launched its AIDS programme. In fact South Africa adopted a National AIDS Plan within months of the country's first democratic elections in 1994. The first meeting I attended on HIV and AIDS was at Tuynhuys (the president's offices in Cape Town) shortly after joining the presidency. The meeting was facilitated by the Minister of Health Nkosazana Dlamini-Zuma and was chaired by Deputy President Mbeki. The role of Mbeki in this matter was clarified later to me. An agreement was reached that Mbeki as the deputy state president would take responsibility for government-wide oversight functions relating to the campaign to combat the scourge of HIV and AIDS. This was to make sure that there was leadership at a presidential level and full participation of all organs of the state. A number of ministers and deputy ministers who were dealing with areas relating to the issue attended the meeting. Senior officials from various departments were also in attendance.

The presentations at this meeting helped me to understand better what HIV and AIDS was about, it's scope internationally and the challenge that faced South Africa at the time. An inter-departmental committee on HIV and AIDS was formed to develop strategies to deal with the challenge. One of these strategies was to raise the levels of consciousness about HIV and AIDS. The emphasis initially was on prevention. The campaign strategy was taken to cabinet for its approval.

From there on Mbeki became a champion of the HIV and AIDS campaign while the Minister of Health ensured that the campaign strategies were executed accordingly. It is important to note that at this stage there was no inkling that there would ever be any controversy about HIV and AIDS. The urgency here was how to combat the spread of HIV and AIDS and how to take care of those who were already infected or affected. One would say that this was a period of 'innocence', a time when we simply wanted to meet our responsibilities as a nation.

I remember well Mbeki's enthusiasm to ensure that all public servants were not only conscious of the challenge but were part of the campaign to raise consciousness about it within government and beyond. He expected all public servants, including members of the executive, to be part of this campaign. He started from his own office and made sure that all staff wore the red ribbon used to promote awareness about HIV and AIDS. All his senior staff and cabinet members were expected to wear the promotional material as he believed they would be the best vehicles for raising awareness of the scourge as they interacted with the masses of our people.

I generally did not like putting on labels of any nature and initially resisted wearing the ribbons. But Mbeki checked daily or whenever we met to ensure that we complied. I felt quite harassed as he made sure of it. In the beginning many of us kept this material in our pockets or bags in case we had to meet Mbeki for one reason or another. Ultimately we had to comply by wearing it all the time.

Thus we became advocates of this campaign in the communities from which we came. Some of us extended it to the institutions we belonged to, such as churches, social clubs and sports organisations. Besides the Minister of Health Mbeki became the public face of the campaign. Almost every speech he gave made reference to the challenge of HIV and AIDS in one form or another. Meetings in all the three spheres of government and intergovernmental fora were used to raise consciousness about the scourge of HIV and AIDS.

The simplified message to deal with this scourge at a public level was threefold: Abstain; Be Faithfull; and Condomise. That was the 'ABC' message. Some religious groups that had some difficulty about the 'C' part of the campaign rather chose to emphasise the 'AB' aspects of the campaign. Various groups were contracted to promote the campaign. Some groups were set up by communities or interest groups. Many did it of their own volition. Amongst these groups and organisations were Khomanani, Love Life, Soul City, Soul Buddz and so forth.

As I have indicated earlier, the campaign at the beginning was about awareness and prevention. The next step sought to address attitudes and stigma and the need to test for HIV so that one could know one's status. More and more people who were affected by or infected with HIV and AIDS began to speak publicly and some chose to declare their status as part of this campaign. Instead of a negative attitude towards people living with HIV and AIDS and imposing a stigma on them, the public was urged to change its attitude. The country was also urged to offer support to those who were infected and affected as well as participate in care programmes for those who needed care.

Again, up to this stage (awareness, prevention, changing attitudes, helping and supporting each other and so forth) there was no controversy about HIV and AIDS. All of us, including Mbeki, understood that we had a national challenge on our hands that needed the whole of our society to help deal with it.

A review of history shows that the controversy relating to HIV and AIDS was never about prevention, education and care, except where prevention involved drugs like Azidothymidine (AZT) and drugs for the prevention of mother-to-child transmission (MTCT). The controversy was about treatment, drugs, diet and the science of HIV and AIDS. There was also some controversy relating to HIV testing methods, which ended up being a debate about the science of it as well.

There were five critical issues we had to face in dealing with HIV and AIDS. Some of these questions were interrelated. The first was about how we could prevent the transmission of HIV from pregnant mothers to their children. The second was about treatment for those who were infected with HIV and those who had AIDS or were affected by opportunistic diseases. The third was about the impact of HIV and AIDS on the poor − the need for nutritious food to be able to use drugs and how this affected poor people. This also involved the issue of diet to help boost the immune systems of those who were infected. The fourth was about the scientific search for a vaccine to prevent infection by HIV or to treat those infected with it. This led to the fifth question about the science of HIV and AIDS, which became the pinnacle of the controversy about HIV and AIDS in South Africa.

Interestingly, the debate about the science of HIV and AIDs took place over a short period of time (2000 to 2002) in the history of the controversies about HIV and AIDS in South Africa. But it felt like a decade-long controversy. In fact, many analysts and commentators still think of Mbeki and the HIV and AIDS issue as a story of denialism and dissidence from beginning to end.

THE THINGS THAT COULD NOT BE SAID

The reality is that Mbeki started dealing with HIV and AIDS like all of us – totally faithful to the orthodox approach and without any question. Even the controversy about the use of drugs like AZT and Nevirapine to prevent mother-to-child transmission was a debate about the efficacy of the drugs within the orthodox approach of dealing with HIV and AIDS.

The controversy

The speech that really raised eyebrows was the one that Mbeki made at the National Council of Provinces in October 1999. This was a whole five years into the programme to deal with HIV and AIDS. In this speech Mbeki raised concerns about accepting conventional wisdom without question. For him questioning conventional wisdom was part of an intellectual enquiry that would assist in finding answers to questions that were not yet answered about HIV and AIDS. But for those who were incensed by government's delay in using drugs to deal with HIV and AIDS, questioning conventional wisdom about HIV and AIDS was part of government's prevarication about treatment. Later, this speech by Mbeki was recast as the speech that sounded the beginning of Mbeki's 'denialism'. The reality, however, is that at that stage Mbeki was still supporting the research on an HIV vaccine. Such research was based on the existence of a virus, the destruction of which required a vaccine.

One could say that at this stage the questions Mbeki asked were not about the science of HIV and AIDS but about the toxicity of the drugs, the politics of their use in developing countries as opposed to developed countries and the costs thereof. It was only in 2000, six years into the national campaign that he began to raise questions about the relationship between HIV and AIDS. Even then, these were research questions aimed at understanding the nature of HIV and how it is related to AIDS.

To understand the controversy about HIV and AIDS in South Africa better let us start from where it began – the drug AZT or Zidovuline as it is sometimes called. The first issue that occasioned controversy was the use of AZT to prevent mother–to–child transmission. AZT was approved by the US Food and Drug Administration in 1987 as it was found to prolong the life of patients with AIDS under specific conditions. Later in 1990 it was approved as a preventative treatment to reduce the risk of infection in cases where people (particularly medical staff) were exposed to infected blood or in the case of pregnant women to prevent MTCT.

The challenge here was the cost of AZT and its toxicity, not the science of HIV and AIDS as many of the popular legends suggest. AZT was costly and unsustainable given the huge numbers of affected people and the limited health budget of the country. Extra funding would have to be found to cover these costs. The controversy, as one would expect, was an ethical one. Can you leave people to die arguing that you do not have money to save their lives? Where else do you spend your money and why would you not divert these funds to prevent people from dying? What are your priorities?

The toxicity of the drug was the most controversial part of the policy discourse. No one who had read about the levels of toxicity of the drug AZT as stated by its manufacturers would disagree about its high levels of toxicity. This in fact is where Mbeki got into trouble. He read about these drugs from the literature supplied by the drug's manufacturers, GlaxoSmithKline's. He also read about the conditions under which the drug was approved for use by medicines control organs of the countries where the drug was used. The trouble started when he articulated his concerns publicly as the deputy president of the country.

I often felt that Mbeki's problem was his intellectualism. If he had read about or researched these drugs in the capacity of an academic or a professor at a university, and pronounced on them publicly, it would have been acceptable. Even if it was controversial it would not have mattered much. But he was the deputy president and later president of the country and that is what exposed him to such high levels of criticism. Generally, presidents do not read such literature and express their views publicly.

Another problem was that he was president of a continental economic powerhouse and was seen as a leader of the vision of an African Renaissance and the developmental struggle of the rest of the developing world. At one stage during this period (1996-2003) South Africa was chair of the Non-Aligned Movement, chair of the AU and chair of the SADC. Accordingly, an expression of an opinion of this nature had consequences for the use of the drugs in much of the developing world, impacting negatively on the profit margins of the pharmaceutical companies.

There could be no disagreement about the toxicity of the drug AZT amongst those in the know. If there was any disagreement it was at the level of uninformed public debate or where emotions ran high owing to concerns about the rapid spread of HIV and AIDS. Those who were better informed knew that the real challenge was not about whether or not the drug was toxic. It was the fact that there was no other alternative drug on the market to deal with HIV and AIDS. The unavailability of alternatives affected the 'risk and benefit' ratio of the assessment of the drug. For many (the popular view), the toxicity of HIV infection at the time outweighed the risk of drug toxicity. Indeed if one was at death's door a debate about the toxicity of the drug would be like an insensitive academic exercise. For people who found themselves in this situation, as long as AZT had a possibility of prolonging their lives, they would not worry about the attendant risk involved. For them it was a choice between the possibilities of living as opposed to the certainty of dying.

For Mbeki, however, the issue was not just the 'risk and benefit' ratio of the assessment of the drug. The problem became political. His question was about whether or not the same 'risk and benefit' ratio was used in developed countries as in developing countries. In debates with those of us who thought he needed to tone down his expressions of concern, given the political pressures under which he operated, he always pointed us to two ways of testing as to whether or not our approach to this matter was correct. The first reference point was the country where the drug was manufactured. He asked us to look at the way in which that country used the drug and the conditions under which it was approved for use by its own citizens. The second reference point would be the US as it produced most of the drugs and had a reliable way in which it tested drugs produced in other countries before they were used in the US.

On AZT he had read about it and made up his mind. The drug was produced in the US but was not prescribed there as a mono-therapy (single drug treatment) drug the way it was for developing countries but as, at least, a triple combination of drugs (or more). In his reading Mbeki found that AZT was taken as part of highly active antiretroviral therapy. This was done to prevent mutation of HIV into an AZT-resistant form. In this regard the US Food and Drug Administration was his major reference point.

Mbeki's problem was that the specific conditions under which the drug would be used as approved by the Food and Drug Administration were not factored in, in the case of South Africa (read, developing countries). Secondly, in South Africa (read, developing countries), it was used not for what it was prescribed for in the US. Accordingly, he could not understand why he should risk his people against the standard accepted scientific view about the drug. Unfortunately this position – however orthodox – went against the popular views of the time. These popular views were deviating (consciously or unconsciously) from the orthodox views about the drug to desperate positions motivated by the possibility of saving lives.

At a technical level you were bound to lose the argument with Mbeki most of the times. He did his homework well on any subject he had to deal with. The issues he dealt with were not necessarily in the area of his expertise, but he was a prolific reader and a researcher *par excellence*. Those who worked with him knew that before you raised an issue with him you had to know what you were talking about. You had to do your homework before engaging him.

For Mbeki, the unequal treatment between people in developed countries and developing countries was unacceptable. He was not prepared to approve of the use of toxic drugs in a way that was not prescribed by the manufacturers of the drug. He argued that he could not in good conscience agree to this. Under normal circumstances this would be an accepted rational position, but not so with the sensitive matter of HIV and AIDS.

His resistance to the use of the drug in a way that was not prescribed by the manufacturers exposed Mbeki to a heavy critique from pharmaceutical companies and people who were affected by HIV and AIDS. To Mbeki this was an ethical issue. But for those who opposed Mbeki's approach, the matter was a life and death issue that required desperate measures. They had to use the drugs irrespective of the risks Mbeki was talking about. Delays by Mbeki to making the drugs available were considered unethical while Mbeki, on the other hand, believed that he was in fact acting ethically.

The debate about the toxicity of AZT had taken place earlier in the course of the development of policies and programmes relating to HIV and AIDS. It had started during the time of Mandela's presidency and Dr Nkosazana Dlamini-Zuma's term as Minister of

Health. It took place before Mbeki raised questions about the science of HIV and AIDS. The question of whether or not HIV is the only cause of AIDS had not yet been raised. There was at this stage no talk about 'denialism' or 'dissidents'. The question was purely that of costs and toxicity of the drug and the risk of it mutating into an AZT-resistant form for those treated with it.

There was also a political dimension to this debate. Mbeki found that South Africa was asked to do what developed countries were not doing or explicitly decided not to authorise such. To use the drug as a single drug treatment rather than as part of a combination of drugs that prevented mutation of HIV into an AZT-resistant form was not allowed.

It is a matter of record that pilot test sites were identified around the country where AZT tests were conducted on HIV-infected pregnant women. The sites were also used as training centres for those who were going to be involved in executing this programme. These were later stopped following the concerns I have referred to above. It is this stoppage of the trials that triggered the campaign against the Minister of Health and Mbeki, who was chairing the government committee established to develop responses to the HIV and AIDS challenge.

A campaign was initiated to pressurise government to use AZT to prevent infected pregnant mothers transmitting the virus to their babies. Zackie Achmat's organisation, the Treatment Action Campaign, was formed initially in response to the tragedies that affected some of their colleagues who they lost as a result of AIDS. Ultimately the Treatment Action Campaign became a leader of the campaign to force government to approve the use of the drug.

The Democratic Alliance acted in defiance of the national health department in the City of Cape Town and allowed civil society groups to run test sites where AZT was used as a preventative drug as well as treatment for those who had AIDS. The intention was to prove the efficacy of the drug and to show that it reduced the risk of infection and that it prolonged the lives of those who were infected.

Later another relatively cheaper drug was introduced to prevent mother-to-child transmission. Called Nevirapine (Viramune), the drug was manufactured in Germany by Boehringer Ingelheim. It was also prescribed as a triple combination therapy drug and not as a single therapy drug. Again the costs for triple therapy treatment were prohibitive and as a result the World Health Organisation (WHO) endorsed the use of a single dose Nevirapine prophylaxis in many developing countries. They felt that this was the most cost-effective way of reducing MTCT.

Pilot test sites were established to test its efficacy. But the drug had similar risks when used as a single-drug treatment. With his usual intellectual prowess Mbeki did some reading about the drug and found that in Germany where it was manufactured it was not used in the way it was recommended in South Africa. It was used together with other drugs to ensure that those who were treated did not develop resistance to the medication. He also found out how the US used the drug and confirmed that the Federal Drug Administration had approved its use only as a multiple drug treatment. But the WHO recommended the use of the drug as a single treatment drug in poor developing countries as the multiple combination drugs were too expensive. The argument was that developing countries could not afford it and thus had to take a higher risk than developed countries by using it as a single drug treatment.

Mbeki could not understand why a drug that was known to carry the risk of developing resistance to treatment should be approved for use by the WHO in the manner in which it did. It felt like the WHO had different standards for developed and developing countries. Poverty for him could not be the basis of risking the lives of those who were infected or at risk. But his argument, however

267

logical, was countered by those who felt that children were at risk of being infected and the drug had to be used to save them, even if the risks were high. This became a debate about degrees of risk or of comparing one risk with another and then making choices about which risk one was prepared to take.

Based on this approach, a campaign was launched to force government to increase the number of test sites to reach more people, especially where facilities were available to do so. The Minister of Health, now Dr Manto Tshabalala-Msimang, refused to extend the trials based on the risks identified. This poured fuel onto the fire, which led to the accusations that President Mbeki and the health minister were responsible for the deaths of many babies who died as a result of their resistance to and delays in allowing the use of the drugs. Achmat's TAC appealed to the courts to force government to extend the sites or the availability of the drugs. The court ruled in their favour and forced the minister to extend the pilot sites to other health facilities.

Another concern Mbeki had was about a new trend that was taking root because of the HIV and AIDS epidemic: people who suffered from known diseases, such as tuberculosis and malaria, which were similar to HIV and AIDS-related opportunistic diseases, were now treated as if they were HIV and AIDS cases. This approach caused health practitioners to treat ordinary TB cases as if they were terminal diseases. There were indications that some people were being allowed to die of curable diseases because they were thought to be beyond help.

Mbeki's view was that many medical practitioners had not sufficiently familiarised themselves with HIV and AIDS. In this regard he consulted with many specialist doctors and raised his concerns about toxic drugs and their use. I recall a time when a number of meetings were held with individuals and groups of doctors at Mahlamba Ndlhovu, the presidential residence in Pretoria, Tshwane.

Many of the doctors, even those who were specialists, admitted that they had not given the matter of HIV and AIDS serious attention as they were focused on their specialised areas of work. It did not seem like many were involved in dealing with the challenges of HIV and AIDS. Some of the doctors committed themselves to give the disease more attention. A consensus was reached though that there should be a campaign to urge medical practitioners to treat all diseases, including those that looked like HIV and AIDS-related opportunistic diseases. In any event, medical practitioners were expected to treat patients even when there was no hope that they would live.

Mbeki was also concerned that treatable sexually transmitted infections such as gonorrhoea and syphilis were being categorised as part of HIV and AIDS-related diseases and people suffering from such diseases were not receiving adequate attention. He noted that venereal diseases also affected one's immune system, which some attributed to HIV. Mbeki considered this dangerous because antiretroviral drugs (which he considered as toxic) would be administered when they were not necessary and lives would be unnecessarily at risk.

Some commentators regard the point at which Mbeki began to argue for a stricter separation between contagious venereal diseases and AIDS-related illnesses as the beginning of his 'denialism'. At this point he began to articulate his view that AIDS – Acquired Immune Deficiency Syndrome – was not caused by HIV *alone* (my emphasis).

He argued that immune deficiency could be 'acquired' or caused by various other factors such as venereal diseases and even extreme conditions of poverty, where diet was inadequate. He drew attention to the meaning of the abbreviation 'AIDS', reminding people it was not a 'disease' but a 'syndrome'. Although most of us had dealt with matters of HIV and AIDS regularly we had seldom given attention to the actual name for which AIDS was an abbreviation or the significance of the word 'syndrome'. I remember him arguing this case in parliament in a heated debate, which I think many never understood.

We were also forced to return to our dictionaries to check the meaning of the word 'syndrome'. The *Oxford Dictionary* defines it as 'concurrent symptoms in a disease'. The *World Book Dictionary* defines it as 'a group of signs and symptoms considered together as characteristic of a particular disease'. We understood that AIDS was a concurrence of symptoms of (opportunistic) diseases occasioned by an immune deficiency. It is the concept of the multiplicity or plurality of causes of immune deficiency that caused him to be accused of denying that HIV causes AIDS.

Mbeki accepted HIV – Human Immunodeficiency Virus – as part of the many other causes of AIDS. But his sin was that he dared to raise a question. But as I have argued, the fact that he was a president of a regional economic powerhouse meant that what he said was seen to impact negatively on the balance sheets of many pharmaceutical companies. It also raised anger amongst those who were at death's door.

The argument that poverty was one of the major factors responsible for human immunodeficiency and that poverty complicated the treatment of AIDS followed the debate about AIDS as a 'syndrome'. Mbeki suggested that poverty was one of the reasons for the virulent spread of HIV and AIDS. He argued that poor people who had no access to proper nutrition were generally more vulnerable to disease. He traced the history of HIV and AIDS in South Africa and the US back to the early 1980s and observed that the initial occurrence of HIV and AIDS was amongst male gay individuals or communities. Initial preventative strategies were also directed at gay communities. As time went by the virus spread to heterosexual couples, but it was not a dominant phenomenon.

In the southern African region, however, the virus spread quickly amongst heterosexual couples. This was difficult to understand. It is at this stage that promiscuity was raised as one of the possible reasons for the rapid spread of HIV and AIDS. Given South Africa's past, the debates were quickly reduced to issues about race and stereotypes. The statements of journalist and rape survivor Charlene Smith about the high incidence of rape in South Africa were perceived by Mbeki as deeply racist because there was a suggestion that blacks were promiscuous.

These and other emotive debates gave greater prominence to the role of poverty in HIV and AIDS. The speech made by Mbeki at the 13th International HIV and AIDS Conference in 2000 was premised on the logic that we needed to deal with poverty as part of strategies to combat HIV and AIDS. In this regard Mbeki made HIV and AIDS an economic 'developmental' issue. He tried to move the debate from the controversial issues of drugs to preventative strategies like dealing with poverty as a major factor in the virulent spread of HIV and AIDS.

Mbeki was also outspoken on the issue of developmental funds being diverted to popular programmes to combat HIV and AIDS. He was of the view that this worsened the situation for the poor rather than helped. Money was required to deal with HIV and AIDS challenges but this could not be done at the expense of developmental assistance to poor countries. This continued to fuel the controversy about Mbeki and HIV and AIDS and also took the debate to an international audience.

Mbeki argued that it was not possible for the drugs, which needed to be taken with food, to be used properly by patients. He argued that the lack of proper nutrition opened the door to a lack of compliance with the treatment regime, leading to other complications, including the development of resistance to the drugs. The concerns were borne out by cases of poor, HIV-infected mothers who out of desperation sold the milk formula supplied to them for free by government and breastfed their babies against the advice of medical practitioners. This led to many babies becoming infected with HIV, even after being saved by Nevirapine, which prevented the transmission from the mother to her unborn child.

The problem with the debate about poverty, food, drugs and HIV and AIDS is that it deteriorated to simplistic debates about beetroot, garlic, olive oil and lemon juice – those foodstuffs identi-fied by the then Minister of Health Manto Tshabalala–Msimang as immune boosters, instead of focusing on overall good nutrition as an important factor in building health. Tshabalala–Msimang was ac-cused of substituting drugs for beetroot and garlic, despite the fact that case studies showed that healthy diet could prolong the life of people living with HIV.

The extreme positions that developed on this matter did not help. In fact one would argue that it was this heat in this debate that moved Mbeki closer to what would be called 'denialist' positions. If one used sophisticated hearing devices to sift extreme noise from rational thinking one could see that there was common ground for all, which could save some lives. Good food prolonged the lives of those who were infected although it obviously cannot prevent some of the opportunistic infections resulting from a deficient im-mune system. It could also not kill the virus. On the other hand, some of the antiretroviral drugs also prolonged the lives of those who were infected, notwithstanding their toxicity. The drugs also could not kill the virus.

In a rational debate a middle ground could have been found, which agreed that healthy food and effective drugs in combination, and used in a proper manner, could help infected people live longer under better conditions. The challenge of the constraints of poverty would remain. Those who were better off could provide both of these elements for themselves and live longer. But those who were poor could not access these facilities and they suffered more and died earlier. For the government, the demands simply went beyond its capacity.

The struggle to find a vaccine for HIV and the Virodene research project controversy

As the controversy raged, a parallel struggle was ongoing to find a vaccine for HIV. These developments were drowned out by the noisy high-level debates about the use of drugs for prevention and treatment. The arguments were so distracting that the public was unable to follow the scientific quest to find a vaccine for HIV to save not only those infected already but generations to come. Admittedly, the research project had a lesser profile because of unresolved ethical questions that forced it to go semi-underground.

From the beginning everyone understood that there was no cure for HIV. Efforts had already been made in the US and elsewhere to find a vaccine and enormous resources were ploughed into this research but without any success. Faced with this challenge any indication of a breakthrough was likely to be warmly welcomed. This eagerness for a solution explains in part how Dlamini-Zuma, Mbeki and the new democratic government got caught up in the controversy relating to the Virodene research project.

The promise of a possible breakthrough based on the preliminary indications relating to Virodene was first reported in 1995, just a year into the new democracy and was brought to the attention of Dlamini-Zuma in early 1996. The preliminary research was undertaken by a Pretoria Hospital researcher, Olga Visser. In mid-January 1997 Olga Visser and her team reported to Dlamini-Zuma what

they saw as dramatic result that 'far exceeded' what they had anticipated. They said that their treatment was 'far superior and effective
than any known treatment to date worldwide'. There was so much
excitement about the reported results that the matter was presented
to cabinet by the third week of January 1997.

Apart from the obvious relief occasioned by the discovery of a
possible vaccine, there was also excitement about the promise of
dramatically lower costs for the drug as compared to AZT. The
figures used then were R80–R160 per month for Virodene as compared with R4 000 per month for AZT. Based on these estimates
Virodene would have been cheaper by a factor of 25 to 50. The
availability of such an affordable drug would have gone a long way
towards addressing the controversy attendant on the use of AZT.
The urgency with which this matter was dealt with by government
was based on this expectation of low prices and the prospects of
making the campaign to force government to make AZT available
irrelevant.

In addition to the obvious boost to South Africa's image in
the international arena, another reason behind the government's
excitement over the development was the possibility that Africans
had found a vaccine for an ailment affecting Africans. The promise of a breakthrough came at the time when the vision of the
African Renaissance was being widely promoted and such a discovery would certainly have improved this campaign. Visser, for
instance, used expressions like 'medicine development in Africa
for Africa'.

Some people believe that Mbeki's firm statement in April 1997
that the 'African Renaissance is upon us' was influenced by the
promise of a breakthrough relating to the HIV and AIDS vaccine. But having been closer to the development of the African
Renaissance vision and project, I can say that this extrapolation is
far from the truth. The statement had its own context within the

logic of the African Renaissance project that had nothing to do with the Virodene matter. It certainly never even occurred to me until I read about it elsewhere.

The fourth reason for me relating to the excitement about the Virodene research was the possibility that South Africa could be a leader in the development of a vaccine to cure HIV and AIDS. None of us at the time could fail to see the global implications of such a breakthrough from South Africa.

It is a matter of public record that the Medicines Control Council (MCC) resisted pressure to approve the conduct of Virodene trials on humans. In fact the MCC stopped any further human trials and rebuked Visser and her company for administering the drug to patients without approval. Given the politics surrounding the issue, the withholding of permission for trials by the MCC was seen then as part of a conspiracy to ensure that no new vaccine was found to compete with existing drugs that were not only toxic but very expensive. There was also a view circulating of a suppression of a possible breakthrough coming from Africa based on the prevailing African pessimism.

A review of these developments in hindsight suggests that Visser and her company failed to follow normal research procedures to satisfy the MCC's requirements to grant them permission to proceed with the trials on humans. In fact, those who supported Visser at the University of Pretoria were subjected to disciplinary action relating to this matter. It is also a matter of record that tests on humans were continued in London at the Gay's Drug Research Unit and within the Tanzanian military. By 2002 the Virodene researchers had failed to show that the drug in fact acted against HIV.

The protracted story about this controversial research project, which spanned a period of about seven years from 1995 to 2002, has been documented and told by various analysts and commentators. For this reason I do not intend to present the details again here. What is important about this development for those trying to understand Mbeki's perspectives about HIV, and AIDS, is that throughout this period (at least up to 2000) Mbeki still believed that there was a virus called HIV, which was related to AIDS, and that a vaccine was needed to prevent or treat this virus.

The statement Mbeki made at a press conference following the cabinet discussion on this matter in January 1997 is informative in this regard. He said he believed that the Virodene researchers, based on their presentation in cabinet, had managed to 'destroy the virus in a test tube'. Mbeki also said that he would not rest until the efficacy or otherwise of Virodene was established scientifically. This is at the time when it was believed in some quarters that the MCC was putting up unnecessary barriers to this research.

It is known that Mbeki shifted his views about HIV during the Virodene controversy. During this period he began to see HIV as one of the causes of AIDS rather than the sole cause. But even here he still believed that HIV was one of the contributors to AIDS, otherwise he would not have been so supportive of the research to the level of risking his credibility.

The shift in Mbeki's thinking was in the main a developmental process based on his own reading, research, debates, discussions and consultations with medical experts and scientists both in the country and outside the country. In my estimation this happened between mid-1999 to 2002. The most dramatic event and activity that earned him the labels 'denialist' or 'dissident' was his effort to convene a panel of experts to assess various aspects of the science of HIV and AIDS. To be fair to Mbeki, an equal number of orthodox and dissident HIV and AIDS scientists and medical practitioners were invited. Amongst those invited were known scientists who had questioned the science of HIV and AIDS like David Rasnick and Charles Gesheckter.

The opposition to this meeting by those opposed to government's approach to HIV and AIDS was loud and clear and Mbeki was called a denialist by association before the meeting even happened. This caused most of the orthodox scientists and medical practitioners to decline the invitation. Some simply did not turn up. Mbeki was disappointed about this response but went ahead with the meeting anyway.

Although I was not directly involved in the planning and convening of the meeting I was concerned about the direct involvement of the president in convening it. My view was that this meeting should have been convened by the Department of Health or at the level of the Medical Research Council or the MCC and not at a presidential level. In particular, I was concerned about invitations to scientists and medical practitioners being signed and sent by the president. Besides exposing the president to direct attacks in the highly charged context at the time, the level at which the invitations were issued fell outside any standards of protocol. By the time I raised concerns as the director-general in the presidency it was too late. The invitations had gone, the dates and venue fixed and the president was to be the host.

Last-minute efforts were made by some of us to convince the president to leave the hosting of the meeting to the Minister of Health. The president could make an appearance but did not need to stay throughout the meeting, it was argued. Mbeki reluctantly agreed but it was too late to deflect direct attacks. The meeting had already been labelled the 'Presidential AIDS Advisory Panel'.

The meeting of the panel sealed the characterisation of Mbeki as a 'denialist' and 'dissident'. His questioning of whether or not HIV caused AIDS or was the only cause of AIDS was interpreted as denial of the orthodox view that HIV causes AIDS. It is also thought that the failure of the Virodene project reinforced Mbeki's questioning of HIV as the only cause of AIDS. His letter of invitation to the scientists was not helpful either as it suggested a willingness on the part of Mbeki to take on the question of whether HIV existed at all. Some would argue strongly that Mbeki in fact denied that HIV caused AIDS, putting him squarely within the denialist group.

It is clear that Mbeki embarked on the journey to combat HIV and AIDS from conventional orthodox perspectives. On the way he hit a number of hurdles, some of which were fatal. The first was the use of double standards in prescribing toxic drugs to poor people. The second were the emotional responses to the crisis, which did not make rational sense to him. Thirdly, he believed that he was being denied the right to question conventional wisdom as well as advance the search for solutions to one of the most challenging problems facing humanity. Even the convening of the consultation of experts on HIV and AIDS was a justifiable intellectual exercise that should have assisted government in making its decisions about this vexing problem.

But the journey ended with him being firmly labelled a denialist and dissident, an enemy of the pharmaceutical companies, a detested person by those who campaigned for government to make anti-retroviral drugs available to those who needed them. The events of 2000 through to 2002 caused those of us who were close to him to believe that his security risk profile was so high that it warranted special attention.

CHAPTER 14

Intervention to End the Controversy about HIV and AIDS

The transition from the presidency of Nelson Mandela to Thabo Mbeki in June 1999 was one of the most well-prepared-for transitions. From the beginning the expectation of the world was that we would need a larger-than-life person to fill the boots of Nelson Mandela. As Mandela ascended the stage to take over the leadership of the new democratic South Africa questions were already being asked as to who would succeed him and continue with his legacy of reconciliation, nation-building, magnanimity and peacemaking. He was seen as the person who saved South Africa from a destructive racial war.

Given the challenge of succeeding a 'larger-than-life' president, Mbeki was prepared early on. From the onset Mandela delegated the larger part of his functions as president to his deputy. He made Mbeki manage and lead the transformation of society, including the transformation of the state and its organs. He gave Mbeki the responsibility of managing the restructuring of the apartheid economy to ensure it would serve the interests of the majority, especially the historically disadvantaged. He also allowed space for Mbeki to drive the African Renaissance vision of the ruling party, which he did with distinction. Throughout the period of Mandela's presidency, Mbeki chaired many cabinet meetings on behalf of and in the place of Mandela. He was also expected to attend to the day-to-day business of government while Mandela focused on broader national strategic issues to keep unity in the country. If there was ever anybody prepared to take over government from Nelson Mandela in 1999, it was Thabo Mbeki.

In a television interview reported in the *Chicago Sun-Times*, on 8 July 1996 Mandela said that 'Thabo Mbeki [is] ... very talented ... And if the party were to elect him when I step down, then I would take the view that they had made the correct decision'. In commending Mbeki as his successor after his inauguration as president in June 1999, Mandela publicly stated that he was confident that Mbeki would be able to take over from him as he was already running government. He said, 'I have no doubt that we have a capable man who will rise to the challenge.' Mbeki had effectively run government for three years before his inauguration, Mandela commented.

The actual transition from Mandela to Mbeki was also designed in such a way as to render it seamless. The formal transition process was started at the 1997 Mafikeng National Conference of the ANC where Mbeki was elected president of the ruling party to succeed Mandela. Mbeki was elected by the conference unopposed, with ululations and spontaneous approval by conference participants. The baton was being passed. The image of Mandela and Mbeki holding each others' hands and raising them high remains in the mind even today.

The elective conference was followed by the development of the ANC election manifesto, which was to be used for the upcoming national elections at which Mbeki would be presented as the next president. The manifesto was designed to make it clear to those deployed in government as to what was expected of them. The focus was on party policy with a strong emphasis on the collective rather than the individual. The collective approach has been part of the ANC's DNA, notwithstanding efforts to see Mandela as separate from the party. The media and the world had extracted Mandela from the party and made him the singular saviour of the country outside his comrades. Indeed the history of the struggle gave Mandela extraordinary influence. But Mandela himself always made it clear that the policies he was following were ANC policies. However, no amount of protestation from Mandela himself could change the fact that he was singled out. This status gave the international community cause to wonder whether or not the ANC had another Mandela to succeed him. The ANC itself knew that it had sufficient high-calibre leaders to take over from Mandela.

The 1999 national election campaign portrayed Mbeki as the visible leader of the campaign but with subtle support from Mandela. The campaign was powerful and the ANC emerged with an even higher majority than it achieved during the first democratic elections in 1994. The party celebration of the election victory was designed to present Mbeki as the undisputed successor of Nelson Mandela. He was presented as the president who was ready to govern. The language amongst the strategists of this transition was that 'Mbeki must hit the ground running' to remove any doubt about his presidency.

The inauguration ceremony and the restructuring of the presidency were executed with absolute precision and the transition in the Union Buildings was seamless. The inauguration was held on 16 June 1999 and two days later the cabinet was appointed and sworn in. By 21 June 1999 key staff in the president's office, were in place. Within the first week there was no doubt indeed that he had 'hit the ground running'. In my role as director-general in the office of the deputy president, a role transformed overnight into director-general of the presidency (incorporating the former president's office and the former office of the deputy president, also executed on day one), I had the singular honour of managing this transition and I am proud of its success.

Another area of success was the positioning of Mbeki as the visionary of African Renaissance on the continent. From the May 1996 'I am an African' speech, three years of hard work followed to prepare the ground for Mbeki to emerge as the visionary of the renewal of the African continent throughout his presidency and beyond. Even today, no one can take this legacy away from him, notwithstanding the turbulent years of 2005 to 2008 in the politics of the ANC and the country. Anyone who attended the launch of the Thabo Mbeki Foundation in October 2010 left the occasion without any doubt that the vision of the African Renaissance was still alive and well in Mbeki. In fact, a worrying vacuum following his removal as president seemed to be filled through the launch of the foundation. The former African presidents and African intellectuals who were in attendance affirmed this and urged Africa to pursue this vision.

As I look back over the Mbeki presidency it has become clearer to me that although we prepared well for the transitional processes from Mandela to Mbeki we never really prepared for the HIV and AIDS-related events that unfolded immediately after the inauguration of Mbeki as president. The more so if I compare it with the work and time spent on the African Renaissance programme. Did I anticipate that Mbeki would fire the first shot from government in the HIV and AIDS debate in October 1999, just four months into the presidency? The answer is categorically 'no'. I could not have anticipated it even if I had stretched my imagination to the limit.

At that time I was managing the challenging merger between the former offices of the president and the deputy president into one. As in all mergers, emotions and feelings of uncertainty and insecurity were running high. While I was busy with the protracted internal merger project, which continued into 2000, Mbeki dramatically entered the fray in the HIV and AIDS issue – by suggesting in a speech to the National Council of Provinces that conventional wisdom on HIV and AIDS should be challenged.

The contents of the October 1999 speech were not a shock for those of us who were alive to the issues Mbeki was grappling with. But we were not prepared for the timing of his public salvo, nor the response it elicited. His comments were made partly in response to statements made by journalist Charlene Smith, amongst others, which he believed were outrageous. I do not believe that Mbeki had planned to fire the shot at that time. It was a response to a particular event that no one could have anticipated.

At the time my concern was the sensitivity of the Smith case as it was an emotional rape-related issue. I was of the view that Mbeki could be construed as being cold and unsympathetic towards a woman who had been a victim of rape. Indeed this attack was waged against Mbeki in a more vicious manner than I anticipated, but generally, I do not think that many of us who were in that office understood the implications of that opening statement within the greater scheme of events that were to follow or unfold relating to the HIV and AIDS matter.

Could I have anticipated that within eight months of Mbeki's presidency the world would be talking about him as an AIDS 'denialist' or 'dissident'? The answer would be 'no' again. The 'denialist' and 'dissident' sparks began to fly around like ominous missiles, which suggested a larger-than-expected war ahead of us. Did we anticipate this? Again, the answer is clearly 'no'. In any event, most of us were not even aware of the 'dissidents' versus 'orthodox' debate about HIV and AIDS when we prepared for the Mbeki presidency. Could I have anticipated the hostility of the HIV and AIDS lobby that built up against Mbeki both inside and outside the country during the 2000 to 2002 period? The answer again is categorically 'no'. The developments shocked many of us. We had gone through the battle with pharmaceuticals from as early as 1996 and we had expected their reaction as this fell within our political competence. But the avalanche of responses to Mbeki as a 'denialist', its suddenness and ferocity, was not anticipated at all.

I have frequently asked myself whether Mbeki was alive to the implications of the war he started and was waging and the impact it would have on him and the country. I cannot represent Mbeki's views on this matter as I have not discussed it with him. Thus, my views presented here are based on my experiences. Whatever I write here reflects my views, which should be tested against Mbeki's views.

Having said this, I would like to try to answer this question: Was Mbeki alive to the implications of the war he was waging? My answer would be 'yes'. Mbeki was one president amongst a few who personally understood the geopolitics of the world and could anticipate what was likely to happen. Was he aware of the risks and dangers, including a risk to his own life? I would again answer 'yes'. He was so committed to the cause of combating racist attitudes – even in dealing with health issues – that he was ready to die for it, both politically and personally. He was not going to allow the historically disadvantaged, oppressed and exploited to be undermined and treated as less than human. Just the logic of the argument that one drug is not good for Europeans and Americans but good enough for poor Africans, was totally unacceptable to him, whatever the case and arguments advanced. For him this was like a red rag to a bull. It was like a continuation of the colonial and imperialist attitudes of old. It was also like a continuation of the struggle in South Africa against a racist apartheid system, but now it was at an international level. In my interactions with Mbeki at the time he expressed serious concerns about giving drugs that were sure to 'kill our people'. And he was not prepared to be party to that.

In hindsight it is clear that Mbeki's thought processes were located within a struggle against racism and underlying ideologies that hailed from the period of slavery and the colonial era. His focus was on defending the dignity of the African people (including people from developing countries) and their right to self-determination. What was critical to him was the right to think, and think independently, notwithstanding the views and perspectives of the powerful and privileged. For him Europe and the US were not going to continue dictating as to what should happen in the world. For him nothing that undermined the African people (including people in developing countries) and their intellect could be tolerable. I am of the view that those who worked with him were on the same wavelength. This was where the vision of the African Renaissance was also located.

The AIDS lobby entered the discourse from a different perspective that focused on the fact that people were at death's door and anything that could help was to be welcomed, even if different standards were used for people in developing countries compared to those in developed countries. Mbeki, on the other hand, was concerned about the lives of the people taking drugs that were stated as toxic. Those opposed to his views were more concerned about the fact that people were going to die unless they were given the drugs that had the potential of saving or prolonging lives. Their concern was about the 'risk and benefit' tolerance ratio rather than the tolerance of ideological and racist views that undermined the historically oppressed and exploited.

Would it have been possible to realign the two wavelengths to ensure that they spoke to each other as well as reconcile these seemingly disparate positions? The answer here must be 'yes', but only if we could have anticipated it and planned strategically to deal with it. Unfortunately, for this war against the HIV and AIDS scourge, we did not plan as if we were going into war. It might have happened at the level of the health department, but I do not remember it happening in the presidency. If it did, it would have been on the sidelines. We planned as if we were going to have an innocent peaceful campaign where everyone was of one mind – to combat the scourge and do it as effectively as was humanly possible.

If we had planned like we were going into war we would have also planned for the unexpected, the unlikely, the inconceivable and the unimaginable. To plan like this we would have been able to deal with both the known and unknown risks. Simple desktop research would have informed us about the dissidents and denialists debate and we would have planned better to deal with this situation than we did. But this was not done, at least not within the presidency where I was involved.

In hindsight it is clear that we should have considered the reality that people who are at death's door think differently about life than those who stand elsewhere in relation to that door. In this regard we should have listened more to those who were infected and af-fected and tried to understand the perspectives from which they viewed this challenge, even when we had different views about the toxicity of drugs and the manner in which they were used. We could also have been more empathetic despite the differences about the issues at hand.

Secondly, I believe we should have ensured that the strategists involved in planning for this campaign were alive to the 'dissident' and 'orthodox' views about HIV and AIDS and the risks that these radically different perspectives posed to our policy positions. It is possible that the team at the Department of Health may have been aware but I was not aware of it from the presidency as this was not my area of speciality. The likely reason for this would have been that the health department did not think that these views were worth considering or talking about at all. Our experience now teaches us that keeping ideas and views we do not agree with away from the people and our own strategists is not helpful, especially during this age of globalisation and the World Wide Web.

Thirdly, we should have also factored in the interests and power of the pharmaceutical companies and the support they would get from the powerful countries where they were based. Pharmaceuticals spend billion of rands to research and put drugs onto the market and anything that is likely to disturb their plans to recoup their costs and ensure large margins of profit would not be welcomed. Accordingly anyone who declared war against the pharmaceutical companies should have expected a response from the US as the sole superpower of the time.

Fourthly, we should have looked at our vulnerabilities and risks involved for the country and devised strategies to mitigate against them. Taking on powerful pharmaceutical companies and the mighty countries where these pharmaceuticals companies were based exposes one to risk. If we had done this analysis we would have understood that it would be extremely risky to put our president at the forefront of this war right from the onset. Even if he wanted to, we should have advised strongly against it.

All this was not done. Or if it was done at all the strategies would have been totally ineffective for one reason or another.

The period 2000 to 2002 felt like a war. The convening of the Presidential Advisory Panel of Experts on HIV and AIDS attracted attack from multiple fronts. The fire was like heat-seeking missiles. Everywhere were Mbeki went for any reason, his business was diverted towards the HIV and AIDS controversy. No matter what subject he was dealing with, the discussions always ended up being a discussion about HIV and AIDS. Our communicators tried their best to deflect this attack, without much success. Mbeki made a couple of trips to the US during this period (2000–2002) over and above the UN annual business. It was during these trips that it dawned on us as to how much in danger Mbeki's life was. The anger amongst business people, particularly those who were in the pharmaceutical industry and related industries, was palpable. We began to hear direct rhetorical questions, such as, 'Do you know how much we lose per annum for every day you and your government continue to refuse to use the drugs?' Some bandied about figures of two billion dollars. They considered South Africa a leader amongst developing countries and the positions taken by South Africa on drugs directly affected their business elsewhere. That is when the campaign about the number of people who were dying while South Africa 'prevaricated' was intensified. The intelligence services began to pick up worrying concerns about the president's safety.

The delegation accompanying the president returned from a trip to the US in 2002 convinced that we had to do something radical to change the course of events and save Mbeki's life as well as the country. Together with some of his special advisers, we started engaging in discussions with the president while we were still in the US, between meetings and events he was involved in. We continued these discussions on our way back home.

The discussions were sensitive and delicate. We were entering into a 'no-go' area for Mbeki as we knew how sensitive he was and how strongly he felt about the subject. We were conscious that we were going where angels feared to tread. But we also understood that only those who were close to him or worked closely with him could risk such a discussion. It had to be people he trusted and whom he knew were not part of the campaign to vilify him or stop him from pursuing a cause that was critical for the poor and vulnerable. For him, the drugs were clearly a risk, especially for the poor people in developing countries. We understood that we had a historical mission that had been thrust on us by virtue of our proximity to him and the trust he had in us. It is important to note that even this trust was shaken during these discussions.

Our initial approaches were deflected away as he felt that we were beginning to be driven by fear and ready to sacrifice the lives of the people in the name of political expediency. He felt that we were cowards. He also made it clear that he did not need to 'save' himself at the expense of the people. If he did he would have failed the people as a leader. The 'people' for him were the people of the world, particularly those in developing countries (including South Africa), who were vulnerable and likely victims of these drugs. As much as we felt that we had a historical mission to convince him to change course or to deal with this matter differently, he also believed that he had a historical mission to save lives. He was categorical about the fact that it would be irresponsible of him as a leader to agree to what the world wanted him to do if it was going to result in the deaths of people. In our discussions he began to see us as part of this 'world'.

Mbeki truly believed in his cause and was ready to die for it. For him it was a continuation of the struggle for liberation but now at a higher level. He was not worried about being labelled a 'denialist' or 'dissident' as he believed that the world was irrational and treating him like a 'heretic' who deserved to be burnt at the stake. This for him did not change the truth. As a result he was not going to participate in or be party to the authorisation of drugs that he knew for sure would kill. He believed that the unequal standards used in developing and developed countries were totally unethical.

Mbeki believed that the labels of 'denialist' or 'dissident' were meant to silence him and he refused to be silent. For him it was clear that HIV was not the only cause of AIDS and that what were understood as opportunistic diseases were not all related to HIV. He also believed that HIV was not the only cause of immune deficiency.

He argued that the issues of poverty were a reality and could not just be dismissed because of a strong lobby. He made similar arguments about nutrition and HIV and AIDS.

What outraged the world was his raising questions similar to those of the so-called HIV and AIDS 'denialists' and 'dissidents', like whether or not there was such a virus as HIV and whether or not it had ever been isolated and identified in studies conducted up to that point. But for Mbeki, asking these questions was a way of encouraging further research to deal with the crisis.

The view of the team in the presidency was that the president had made his point on the science of HIV and AIDS and that he did not need as president of the country to continue fighting this battle, especially in public. If the battle had to be continued it would have to be left to others, especially specialist researchers in this field, to do so. His response was that there was no one who was bold enough to deal with this matter and that left him with no choice but to continue addressing it. Indeed, he was right: there was no one bold enough to take on issue, outside those classified as 'dissidents'.

The irony of this is that the 'dissidents' appropriated Mbeki as their champion. Some even described him as a 'patron' of the dissidents. They began to speak of him as the only leader in the world who was prepared to debunk the conventional wisdom on HIV and AIDS, which they believed was wrong. This did not make our lives any easier. In fact, it just complicated our project. Even those who supported Mbeki within the medical fraternity found it difficult to continue supporting him because of this label of a 'dissident'. They did not want to be associated with the 'dissidents'. As a result they drifted away from Mbeki. Some even made statements to dissociate themselves from the position held by Mbeki.

Although his cabinet members supported him on his earlier positions – his resistance to the use of toxic drugs for developing countries, the need for research on a safe vaccine for HIV, the impact of poverty in the spread of HIV and AIDS; the importance of good nutrition and so on – the matter of the science of HIV and AIDS and the 'dissidents' and 'denialists' positions were difficult for them as well. Doubts began to build up amongst some of his cabinet colleagues and cracks began to emerge, except that most of this was expressed in a hush-hush way outside of formal discussions. Some raised concerns away from Mbeki's ear. The same happened at a party level, although to a lesser degree.

Mandela was brought back out of retirement to express a view about the matter in the hope that it would help to change Mbeki's perspectives and the course he was following. It was clear then that there were concerned leaders who could not face Mbeki directly on these matters and felt that drawing Mandela in might help. Utat'uMandela at that time was too old to be drawn back into a rough and risky combat area. Essentially, an appeal to Mandela was a clear indication that we had failed as leaders to deal with the challenge we were facing.

The pain of all this is that our revered Mandela was exposed to a debate in the NEC of the ANC, which was uncharacteristic of the movement and caused comrades to take positions either for or against Mandela's response. Interestingly, the debate itself gravitated from the issue about HIV and AIDS to 'protocol' issues around whether or not former presidents could engage in current debates relating to governance, especially where it could be construed to be against a sitting president. What were the protocols governing the role of retired president in terms of political engagements? Some felt that this was about the rights of any member of the ANC to engage in any debates, whether or not he or she was a former president. Whatever the issues, the debate was nasty.

I personally did not like seeing Ntate Mandela being subjected to this type of debate that seemed disrespectful. In one of the Sesotho languages it would be called a debate *e botlhaswa*. I do not have an English word to explain this expression. It is more than being insensitive or careless. It is not just being undignified. It is *botl-haswa*. For me, the debate around Madiba's involvement was totally unnecessary. He did not deserve it, and should not have been subjected to it. I took the position of defending Tata against the abuse from those who could not personally face Mbeki and those who felt he put himself on the firing line by entering a debate about a serving president. I stood 'in defence' of Ntate Mandela. I argued that we should leave Tata out of this and deal with it ourselves.

The leadership of the liberation movement had all along consciously and deliberately protected and preserved the integrity of Tata Madiba from the time he left prison to his retirement. We took on the more controversial issues in the name of the party rather than in his name for the period he was president, except where he chose to intervene. Where we used his name it concerned national unity, nation-building, peacemaking and reconciliation, given his history and magnanimity. My defence of Tata Madiba in the NEC debate remained in his memory. Whenever he meets me he relates the story over and over again. It always makes me blush.

However, the debate highlighted the fact that the matter of HIV and AIDS was beginning to affect both the party and government. The Gauteng provincial government at one stage took a unilateral position to extend testing sides and make more antiretroviral drugs available. For an ANC-controlled province to take this step was an indication of the levels of restlessness that were setting in, even amongst ANC members.

This made our discussions with Mbeki even more pertinent and urgent. We had lost the battle to save him politically or personally as he was of the view that he was not going to keep quiet just because his life was at risk. If this was the case, we would still be oppressed. The argument we stuck with was the risk to the country and the impact on his work as the president of the country, both of which went beyond his personal circumstances. Here, we argued, other people were going to be affected and he could not decide on their behalf. This logic finally seemed to move Mbeki.

On the issue of Nevirapine to prevent mother-to-child transmission (MTCT), our view, again, was that he had made his point and if anything went wrong the world would remember what he had said. His first response was that he could not risk the lives of people when he knew they were in danger. Part of the problem was that results that were coming through from the pilot trial sites on Nevirapine were already suggesting that those who used Nevirapine the way in which it was prescribed for developing countries were beginning to develop resistance to medication. Mbeki repeatedly asked why we wanted him to allow a situation in which people would get killed in the name of avoiding pressures that came from quarters that had vested interests in this matter other than the interests of the people. This was a difficult bridge to cross.

At this stage, we engaged Joel Netshitenzhe (from a political and communications perspective) and Ayanda Ntsaluba (from a scientific and health perspective) to debate these matters and develop strategies to intervene in this destructive war. The team ultimately consisted of Mojanku Gumbi, Netshitenzhe, Ntsaluba and myself. Some specialised health department officials were drawn in from time to time when needed. The Minister in the Presidency, Minister Essop Pahad, and the Minister of Health, Dr Manto Tshabalala-Msimang, were consulted from time to time as we deliberated on this matter. The two ministers formed part of a cabinet reference group on HIV and AIDS.

Part of the discussions were about the best way in which we could address the concerns of Mbeki in a way that did not make him feel he would have abdicated his responsibilities as the president of the country. Ultimately our plan was to present whatever solution we produced as a policy of government that Mbeki would articulate as such. This approach differentiated between the personal views of Mbeki and government policy. Further interaction with Mbeki on this matter resulted in him giving us the latitude to develop such a policy for the consideration of government although he was totally sceptical about it. He did not believe that we would find an amicable solution or position. But he wished us luck.

This response from Mbeki opened the door for us to think hard about the matter and develop strategies to deal with this crisis. We sifted through the existing policy and reaffirmed those areas where there were no disputes or controversies. This approach allowed us to restate the matter of prevention as the best strategy to combat the spread of HIV and AIDS. The emphasis was on the fact that there was no cure for HIV. On Nevirapine as a drug to prevent MTCT, the courts had already ruled against government and government was obliged to comply by extending the pilot sites where trials were conducted. The new emphasis here was that Nevirapine would be made available on condition that the risks to the mother and the child were clearly articulated to assist the affected people to make conscious and intelligent choices. The responsibility was transferred to the affected and or infected person.

The second matter to be repackaged was the issue of care for those who were infected or affected by HIV and AIDS. Again, there were no controversies about this matter. Strategies were elaborated to make the programme as effective as possible.

The third matter concerned testing for HIV to ensure that one knew one's status. The challenge with this was that it veered in the direction of the science of HIV and AIDS again. The question was, 'What was being tested?' Mbeki kept us on tenterhooks on this one. The fact that some of the testing methods at the time were totally unreliable did not make our position easier. Again, testing methods for developing countries were prescribed that fell short of the standards used in developing countries. We knew this would not fly with Mbeki. Health department colleagues were asked to investigate the matter further and make recommendations or suggestions. No solution was found, which was totally acceptable. Compromises were made for which Mbeki did not have to take responsibility. The responsibility rested with the cabinet.

On the use of drugs to treat HIV and AIDS infected persons a similar position was outlined as in the case of Nevirapine. The choice was to be that of the infected and or affected persons. In this regard Mbeki did not have to take direct responsibility for the consequences of the drugs.

Mbeki ultimately agreed to let go, although in a reluctant way. His parting shot was that we would have to take responsibility for any deaths that occurred as a result of the positions we were proposing. It was almost a case of washing his hands of us. He let us go ahead to secure cabinet consent.

But before stepping away completely from this discussion with Mbeki we had to persuade him not to go into combat in cabinet, but let cabinet take responsibility to make the decision. Cabinet knew his views and there was no need to repeat them there. He looked at us with eyes of disapproval and said nothing. But he ultimately consented.

How Mbeki would respond to questions on HIV and AIDS if asked in the future was another difficult issue. He felt that he could not in good conscience lie about what he knew was wrong or about what he believed in. He would have to tell the truth. Normally, politicians are ready to take any position they believe is expedient to secure their position, even if it involves lying. Mbeki would not. He was clear that he was not going to lie.

His position did not surprise us, but it did put our strategy at risk. We needed to think outside the box. In interactions with him we found a strategic angle that was acceptable to him and met his concerns and moral qualms. From the time cabinet would have made its decision, Mbeki would refuse to make any further personal statements about HIV and AIDS. Any statement on HIV and AIDS would be based on the agreed policy position of government. The cabinet memorandum was carefully crafted to explain every facet of this policy to make it easier for cabinet to adopt it as proposed. Unfortunately, cabinet business is classified and cannot be discussed here, except for the outcomes that were made public.

In 2003 the National Policy on HIV and AIDS was adopted and presented to the public as the official position of government. There was a huge sigh of relief, which I cannot describe in words. It felt as if we had just landed the ship safely following a long journey across violent and stormy waters. There was a 'wow' factor. And those who were religious thanked God for it!

The sense of relief was not only within our team and those who worked on this strategy with us or contributed to finding solutions, but it involved cabinet and permeated through all government entities and institutions.

The media was caught completely unprepared for this change in policy. It was done so quietly that they missed it. They had no opportunities to report about leaks from the team as the process of finding solutions to this challenge was managed in a highly confidential manner, and on a 'need-to-know' basis. Some reported on it with a sense of disbelief wondering how this feat could have been achieved. Many asked whether or not this meant that Mbeki had changed his position on whether or not HIV caused AIDS. Our answer was, firstly, that this was a government policy position and not an individual's position. Secondly, we made it clear that the policy was premised on the assumption that 'HIV causes AIDS'. Others doubted that Mbeki would accept it. But we made it clear that this was government policy and Mbeki was a leader of that government.

Yet others suggested that this was a slap on the wrist for Mbeki or a rebuke of Mbeki.

Those of us who crafted the policy position knew that this was far from the truth. He held his personal views, which were indeed unconventional. And, he was not about to conform to the prevailing conventional wisdom that he believed was wrong. But he had made his point and did not have to continue to talk about it any further. His was now to present the official government position rather than his personal position. This was difficult for the media to fathom and our government communicators also had an arduous time explaining it. The media wanted Mbeki to say whether or not he had changed his view that 'HIV did not cause AIDS'. He kept on saying that he had not said it, and in any case, he was representing government policy as the president rather than as an individual with personal views.

Mbeki's protestation that he had never said that 'HIV does not cause AIDS', was initially confusing, even to those who were close to him, let alone government's communicators. The media wanted Mbeki to convince them that he was not a 'dissident' by explicitly stating that that 'HIV causes AIDS'. But Mbeki was not about to sing that chorus of conventional wisdom. He kept on talking about AIDS as a 'syndrome', which may be caused by many factors other than HIV.

In hindsight, it seemed that Mbeki never in fact said that 'HIV does not cause AIDS'. He did raise questions about it, however, which caused him to be classified as a dissident. What is clear is that he argued that HIV was not the only cause of AIDS. He said that he could not understand how a single virus could cause a 'syndrome'. His argument was reduced to a simplistic 'HIV does not cause AIDS' position. The fact that he did not denounce the dissidents' views about HIV meant that he also believed that HIV did not exist. But this took us back into the science of HIV and AIDS where there was no hope of reaching an agreement. It is for this reason that we felt his point had been made and he needed to step off that subject and focus on the government programme.

This separation of Mbeki's personal views about HIV and AIDS from the policy of government was initially difficult for the media to understand. Either he had changed his mind or cabinet had made a decision against the positions he held, they argued. The truth is that neither of the two had happened. Mbeki kept his personal views and cabinet made a decision on government policy, which the president had to officially represent.

Efforts were made to provoke him into restating his personal views, which were not compatible with his government's position. But he resisted this and stuck with the official position. At one stage he had to ask whether the media wanted him to answer the question in his capacity as the head of government and president of the Republic of South Africa or at an individual level. One journalist said that they wanted to hear his views about HIV and AIDS. 'Have you changed or do you still believe that HIV does not cause AIDS?' He answered that he was there as the president of the Republic of South Africa and he was not about to answer the question at a personal level. He stated that the policy of government was premised on the assumption that 'HIV causes AIDS' and that there should not be a debate about that.

But even the use of the word 'assumption' was a problem for the AIDS lobby. Assumption meant that there was still doubt that HIV causes AIDS. They wanted him to explicitly say that it is a 'scientific fact' that HIV causes AIDS. He again referred them to the government policy document that used the language, 'HIV causes AIDS'.

From then on the media and the AIDS lobby haunted him about his views expressed in the past and refused to listen to his presidential position.

I must say that we were always on tenterhooks whenever he was provoked to speak on HIV and AIDS. This happened both in parliament and in media and public encounters. The provocation angered him and he came close to expounding on his personal views. But he always held back and stood by government policy.

During one of the visits to the US he was subjected again to this questioning, which was becoming irritating. He made a comment on his personal views but stipulated that they were personal rather than those of his government as an illustration to make them understand the difference between speaking as a president and expressing personal views. We were worried that the media would latch on to the comments and say that Mbeki had reverted to denialism. Indeed, some of the media tried but could not take it further. It was fact that Mbeki was no longer representing his personal views but that of his government.

This should have closed the story about the HIV and AIDS matter and about the controversy. But it did not. Those who hated Mbeki for whatever reason – including their anger about Mbeki's views on HIV and AIDS – continued with the campaign against him as if there was no clear policy of government. Analysts and commentators wrote and spoke as if the policy of government did not exist or as if Mbeki was not strictly representing the 2003 National Policy on HIV and AIDS. They wrote and spoke as if Mbeki had not stepped off his personal platform.

As reports about resistance to Nevirapine started to filter through, Mbeki reminded us about what he had said to us. We acknowledged that he was indeed being vindicated, but were of the view that he should leave this to history to judge. Interestingly, when the final result came through proving the drug's lack of efficacy, there was not much publicity given to the matter. For Mbeki this was an indication of the level of dishonesty of the world he had been in combat with. Two other better-researched results followed around 2005 and in 2009 that confirmed these preliminary findings.

More can be said about this subject but it should suffice for now to say that it was a pity that the controversy raised tempers to a level where rational discourse and thinking was no longer possible. The controversy ended up being a noisy debate among the deaf. We erred in allowing interested parties like pharmaceuticals to be a factor in determining our course of action on drugs to prevent or cure some of the opportunistic diseases. Abandoning an absolutely necessary scientific enquiry about HIV and AIDS, to a debate about 'dissidents' and 'denialists', was indeed unfortunate. Somehow we needed cool heads and suppressed emotions to have a meaningful dialogue. A climate needed to be created for those who do research to do so without any hindrance; for those who are engaged in campaigns to prevent the spread of HIV and AIDS to do so freely; and for those who take care of the affected and infected to do so without any constraints. In this way much more can be achieved and a common ground can be found as opposed to harping on the old discourse. This is like flogging a dead horse.

On the issue of prevention, for instance, there is no disagreement. We all accept that there is no cure or vaccine for HIV for now and the best way of dealing with the HIV and AIDS scourge is to prevent it from spreading. The public awareness expression: 'Imagine a generation without AIDS' was meant to capture this ideal. Prevention requires a change in lifestyles, a commitment to live less risky lives, high levels of awareness and care in all health facilities and homecare projects, and the extremely careful treatment of any situation in which blood is involved.

The prevention of MTCT is critical in terms of our prevention strategies. But the controversy remains. We have to accept that most antiretroviral drugs are highly toxic and the 'risk and benefit' ratio is higher than would normally be acceptable. One has to use them with caution, aware of their toxicity. This is what the 2003 National Plan on HIV and AIDS did. It sought to make affected persons aware of the risks and help them to use them, as far as possible, in the way they were prescribed. It informed people of the implications of using the drug in a way not originally prescribed. Again, this is a matter of the 'risk and benefit' ratio, which makes it an emotional issue.

On care there is less controversy. What we need is to expand the care system to reach out to as many people as possible. We need to be seen as a caring society. On treatment there should not be much controversy either, except that we have to all accept that these drugs are toxic and people need to understand the possible risks in using them. This we have already dealt with above.

The science of HIV and AIDS need more attention as it is the only way in which we can effectively deal with HIV and AIDS in the future. No stone should be left unturned to find a vaccine or cure for HIV. The attacks and counter-attacks between the so-called orthodox and dissident scientists should come to an end. We need focused and critical minds that will persist in finding a cure for HIV.

PART FIVE

CHAPTER 15

The Pain of the TRC Error

The codicil to the report of the TRC, which was presented to President Thabo Mbeki on Human Rights Day in 2003, contained an error that caused me great pain and agony. It shook my solid relationship with TRC chairman Archbishop Desmond Tutu in a way that had never happened before. In fact, if the relationship had been built on a weak foundation it would have been shattered beyond repair. But ours was a solid relationship built on a foundation of our common faith. The way in which it was shaken worried both of us and required a special meeting for us to remove the thorn in our flesh.

The celebration relating to the handover of the codicil of the final report of the TRC had not ended before the bombshell hit us. It was like the evil one was bent on robbing us of the joy of the completion of such a historic task.

The TRC has become the marvel of the world. In the words of Tutu, 'Wherever one goes, South Africa's peaceful transition to democracy, culminating in the Truth and Reconciliation Commission process, is spoken of almost in reverent tones, as a phenomenon that is unique in the annals of history, one to be commended as a new way of living for humankind.'[15] There were many truth commissions before ours and many more are following on from our example. But, as Archbishop Tutu has said in the same foreword, 'Ours is regarded as the most ambitious, *a kind of benchmark against which the rest are measured*' (emphasis added).

Indeed this is worth celebrating, and this is what the devastating error in the report tried to rob us of. It also tried to cloud a unique national achievement.

Within days after the report was released I received a number of disturbing and dramatic calls from concerned individuals who had started to read the codicil. 'The codicil says that you murdered a whole family!' said the first caller. At first, I laughed and declared it madness. Many calls followed the first: 'They say that you confessed to wiping out a whole family.' I started to worry.

In fact, the messages were a great shock to me. I did not believe what I was told, and like Thomas, I wanted to see it for myself. As one would expect, except for the president's personal copy the presidency had given all copies of the codicil away to guests and to the media. I had no copy by which to confirm the reports and I was not about to worry the president for his. Instead, I focused on what I was expected to do as the head of the presidency: ensure that the implementation plan for government was executed promptly following the handing over of the codicil. We set up the structures and systems to look at the report, identify areas that needed to be acted upon immediately and those that needed long-term strategies. When at last I did lay my hands on a copy of the codicil and had time to read it I was not only terribly shocked but was very angry. The codicil, in Volume Six, page 267, read as follows:

Some operatives expressed a wish to take responsibility for their actions, particularly towards their victims. In Pretoria on 14 June 1999, Rev. Frank Chikane told the Amnesty Committee:

'My motive for being here is to actually show that the family finally knows who actually was part of the activities of eliminating their brother, their parent, their father and for that reason, I felt motivated to come here ... I feel that because there was no [indistinct], there was no investigation, or suspicion against me, it really touched me deeply, to have to come out and expose myself, to say that I was part of that type of activity.'

My anger was derived from the fact that there was no way in which all the commissioners and staff could have missed this obvious error. If they missed it, then in my view one would rightly conclude that they had not done their work properly or were not paying attention to detail. Firstly, I had never appeared before the TRC. I had good reasons for this. One was that I was well known in the country as part of the leadership of the liberation struggle during the most challenging times of the 1970s and the 1980s. I also became general secretary of the SACC, a commissioner of the Independent Electoral Commission (IEC) and later director-general in the presidency and secretary of cabinet. My own persecution at the hands of the apartheid regime – which involved gross violations of my human rights, including arrests, detention without trial, being kept in solitary confinement for long periods, being subjected to extreme forms of torture, and poisoning with highly toxic organophosphate chemicals – received high levels of publicity nationally and internationally. Accordingly, I did not think it was necessary for me to appear before the Truth Commission to repeat a well-known story. And, this I had communicated to the commission in written form. It was a surprise therefore to learn that I was quoted as having said anything at the TRC. There could be no record like that, not by Frank Chikane in any way, and there was not the slightest room for a mistake.

Furthermore, I did not know anything about the incident about which I was alleged to have made a confession. Neither did I know the people affected. Everyone (especially the commissioners) knew that I had never engaged in any acts of violence. I understood why some of our people resorted to violent means of resistance against the brutal apartheid system -- what was then called a 'just war' against a brutally violent tyrannical regime. But I was never person-ally involved in any acts that would have resulted in the 'elimina-tion' of anybody's brother, father, mother or anyone.

This was clearly an inexplicable error! What I could not un-derstand (then) though was how all the TRC commissioners and editors of the codicil could miss such an outrageous typographical mistake, if that was what it was.

Although I knew that no one of our generation would have believed such an outrageous report about me, which Tutu called 'utterly bizarre' in his letter to me dated 6 May 2003, I was worried about those who were not informed who might believe whatever they read in the report. I was also worried about the historical re-cord and that future generations who had been part of this history would take it as fact, except, of course, for A-rated critical research-ers and analysts.

Accordingly, I raised the alarm with the TRC commissioners, notwithstanding the fact that they were dissolved as a commis-sion. I also raised the alarm with the Department of Justice and Constitutional Development, which was now responsible for all the unfinished business of the TRC. I did so because I believed that the commissioners had a direct responsibility in this regard and could resolve it speedily by simply making a public statement. I asked the Department of Justice to act on this gross misrepresentation of my person as a matter of extreme urgency. Of paramount importance at that stage for me was a need for a public statement to clear this matter, followed by the necessary corrective measures.

Fortunately, Tutu responded promptly (in just over two weeks) to this disaster. Besides pleasantries about what he described as 'a wonderfully moving service before the official handover' of the codicil and the fact that the commissioners were 'all appreciative of the splendid handover ceremony at the Union Buildings afterwards', he clearly stated that he wrote the letter (dated 7 April 2003) 'to apologise profusely for a bad mistake in Volume 6 of our report where you are erroneously named'. He said, 'The error occurred due to the hurry in preparing the volumes when your name was inserted in place of a Mr Lazarus Chikane.'

Susan de Villiers, the editor of the TRC Report, followed with a letter dated 16 April 2003 and said how 'deeply sorry' she was 'about the error'. She said the error 'occurred during the proofing stage' and was a result of the incorrect insertion of my name 'in the place of a Mr Lazarus Chikane. In other words, your title and first name were inserted whenever the name Chikane appeared.' De Villiers also explained why the commissioners would not have seen this 'technical error', which she said, happened 'during the last stages of preparation and did not appear on any prior documents'. She said the version that the commissioners saw simply read 'Mr Chikane'. She repeated her apology and said 'how sorry' they were for the 'distress' they had caused me. She further explained: 'The editorial and production team was under enormous pressure to finalise the report after the settlement with the IFP [Inkatha Freedom Party] and it was in this context that the mistake was made.'

Although it was distressing to be reflected in the way the report did I accepted the explanation, and that the insert was indeed a genuine error. I also accepted the fact that the commissioners had not seen the final copy because of the pressures the editors were working under. Above all, I appreciated the genuine apologies conveyed to me by both the Archbishop and De Villiers. What I could not understand though was why they could not make a public statement to set the record straight. The reasons given were that the commission had been dissolved and thus had no standing in law to make a statement. For me, the fact that the commission had been dissolved at that time did not mean that the erstwhile commissioners could not make statements in their personal capacities simply to say that they regretted this grievous error and that they expected the Department of Justice to take the necessary corrective measures. Publishing their letters of regret directed to me could have been sufficient, without necessarily giving themselves a particular standing in law. Unfortunately, and painfully so for me, no statement was made. Surprisingly many other statements were made by some of the commissioners about one matter or other relating to the commission and its aftermath without invoking this constraint.

My expectation was that they could have made statements as individuals just to say that a grave error in their report had been brought to their attention; that they regretted this unfortunate error that could damage my person; and that they had asked the responsible department to correct this situation as a matter of urgency. I would also have expected them to follow up with the Department of Justice to make sure they acted on this matter. However, they did not.

My appeal to the Department of Justice did not produce results either. In the nature of government (and I am better placed after thirteen-and-a-half years of service at the helm of the public service to know this) I knew very well that the relief I sought would not be forthcoming any time soon. Not because they were unwilling to help but because of sheer inefficiency or sloppy management. I also knew that when it did ultimately come it would be so late that irreparable harm would have already been done. Thus, my plea for and insistence on the quick intervention of the erstwhile commissioners in their personal capacities.

My appeals to the director-general for justice and the minister also did not produce any results.

It was for this reason that the president made a statement in parliament on 15 April 2003, to lay this matter to rest once and for all. The statement read as follows:

> Elsewhere in the same volume, the Rev. Frank Chikane, Director-General in the Presidency and former General Secretary of the SA Council of Churches, is falsely reported as having made a presentation to the Amnesty Committee, which he never did.
>
> He is then said to have told this committee that he had participated in killing people. We do not understand how this grave and insulting falsification found its way into the report of the TRC. We are pleased to report that Archbishop Tutu has written to Rev. Chikane to apologise for this inexplicable account.

It is this statement that aggrieved Tutu. He said that he was puzzled and deeply distressed as it seemed that the president and I believed that what happened 'was the result of a deliberate and calculated act of malice on the part of the commission or some members of it'. The reality is that at the point at which we exchanged letters about the matter (followed by the president's statement) it was difficult to understand how such an error could happen. I was also not convinced as to why members of the commission could not make a statement at a personal level to clarify this matter. I am still of the view that if any of the commissioners had been presented in the way I was in print they would have made public statements immediately and condemned whoever was responsible. But I did not do that because of my position in government. In my formal response to Tutu who was in the US at the time I said:

> It was unfortunate that we have to communicate in the way we are doing – via exchange of letters. The distance between us is regrettably too great for us to meet. Secondly, it pains me that this disastrous human error has led us to exchange the types of letters we have exchanged. You should know that this has never happened between the two of us for as long as I have known you. I hope that we will have an opportunity soon to discuss this matter so that it does not become a factor in our relationship which I so value.

Ultimately, we did find an opportunity at the O.R. Tambo Airport to meet and dispose of this matter and make sure that it did not affect our personal relationship. I also made sure that the tension between me and the commission was not made public lest it detracted from the valuable work the commission had done. Interestingly, it is a similar position I held on the post-TRC processes leading to the plea bargain agreement between Van der Merwe and Others and the State outlined in Chapter 10 and my position about the way in which the state treated me, which led lawyers for Vusi Pikoli to try to present me as being inconsistent as outlined in Chapter 9, where I made a distinction between the greater good institutions do and the difficulties occasioned by individuals involved or just because of a genuine error.

But this was not the end of the pain. The most serious of my concerns was that even if I understood how the error occurred and accepted the apology, the damage had already been done, at least amongst those who had seen the copies. There is an expression in Setswana that says, '*Lefoko ga le bowe go bowa monwana*' (which means that what comes from one's mouth cannot be pulled back, but a pointed finger can be). It suggests that the written word, once read, is like the spoken word. It gets stored in the memories of people unless a repudiation of the written word is made. In a written text the word also goes on and on from one reader to another and as narrated by one reader to others unless the text is pulled back. But even if it was pulled back those who had read it and those they discussed this matter with would remain with these negative impressions indefinitely. Thus, the need for a public statement!

Regarding the corrective measures, both Tutu and De Villiers made great efforts to rectify the situation although it proved to be a great challenge. In a letter dated 16 April 2003 De Villiers elaborated on the immediate steps taken. She had asked: (1) the printer to black out, 'The Reverend Frank', in all copies that the printer still held (the majority); (2) the Department of Justice to return all the copies in their possession to the printer so that the correction could be made; (3) the Government Communications and Information Systems to retrieve copies distributed to the media during the press conference and to redistribute corrected copies; and (4) the department to rectify the error on their website.

I recognised the value of all these actions, but suggested two improvements: I felt that blacking out 'The Reverend Frank' was not good enough. The page needed to be reprinted. This request was generously acceded to. On 13 August 2004, Director-General for the Department of Justice Advocate Vusi Pikoli confirmed that the incorrect page was replaced by the corrected one. A copy of Volume 6 of the report was sent to me to assure me that the page was duly corrected. My second reservation was based on the fact that some of the copies containing the error were given to individuals who attended the handover ceremony. My concern was that the corrective measures did not include this reality. The challenge was retrieving these copies and those that were already in some bookshops – some of which had unfortunately been sold already.

The great erratum chase was carried out diligently and lasted for almost eighteen months. Copies containing the error were tracked down to individuals, bookshops, the media and so forth. But, after all these efforts and time about 150 copies could still not be accounted for. This sent me back again to the critical need for a public statement. The Department of Justice undertook to publish advertisements in both the print and electronic media to inform the public about the error and to urge those who had earlier copies to return them. The statement would also be for the public record even if not all the copies were returned. I made this request through a letter directed to the Department of Justice dated 17 August 2004. In this letter I appealed to the Department of Justice 'to walk the extra mile' to assist in this regard. In response, the department assured me that its public education and communication unit was 'handling this matter'. Unfortunately, and in an inexplicable way, by January 2005, five months later, the statement had still not been made.

This added to my pain as I felt that by not making a public statement about the error, the government I had served so well and respected did not see this as a critical matter needing urgent action. If I acted like any citizen, by appealing to our courts to intervene, I could have forced the government to respond and do so timeously. But I did not go that route as I felt that it would be odd for me as the director-general in the presidency and secretary of the cabinet to take the government to court. Besides, it could have caused a great embarrassment to government, particularly the president I was working with.

It is in situations like these I felt it was a great disadvantage to work for government, especially at its helm, as it robbed me of my rights. It limited my freedom to make choices or defend my rights, and it took away my right to speak freely. The logic here is that the government does not take care of its own. Everybody was busy with their jobs and no one saw the importance of my matter.

In my letter to the director-general of the Department of Justice dated 21 January 2005 I reminded him about the promise made by his department six months ago, which had not been fulfilled. I said:

> In this regard your Department offered to put an advert on the radio, TV, and the print media to recall all the books received before the erratum [*sic*] was corrected. Regrettably, this has not yet happened. I shall be pleased if you can pursue this matter with the relevant officials in your Department.

Again, no statement was made for about a month. Then the department instituted a follow-up operation to ensure that the statement was made. It was only on 17 February 2005 that I received a copy of the 'announcement' note which read as follows:

> The Department of Justice and Constitutional Development hereby announce that new copies of Volume 6 of the Truth and Reconciliation Commission Report are now available. These copies *replace the print run of 2001*, which, on page 267, wrongly implicated Reverend Frank Chikane as an operative who appeared before the Amnesty Committee. The person, who, in fact, appeared before the Committee, is Mr Lazarus Chikane.
>
> The Department of Justice and Correctional Development expresses its sincere apologies to Reverend Chikane for the editorial error and the inconvenience it may have caused.
>
> All persons who received the erroneous copy of Volume 6 are invited to obtain the corrected version from the Department.

To date I have not seen any media report based on this statement and cannot confirm whether or not this statement was ever released.

The pain for me is that there is a record out there that still erroneously reflects my name in the place of that of Lazarus Chikane. In
the absence of a public statement by government, this will remain
fact and continue to be damaging to my person and integrity. Many
of my letters about this matter kept on emphasising my concern
about my integrity. To quote just one of the letters that was directed
to the Minister of Justice dated 16 July 2003:

> I also appeal to your Office to assist in correcting this grievous
> error. You will understand that this has to do with my integrity
> and person, and failure to expunge this erroneous record of
> history about me would mean that the texts will remain extant
> in private and public libraries worldwide, permanently testify-
> ing against my person and misleading generations to come.

The second emotional challenge was the fact that the person
who disclosed his activities to the TRC was one of my close relatives: Lazi Chikane, as the family calls him. Close family members
know that Lazi is one of those cadres who was involved in the
liberation struggle as part of MK, the armed wing of the ANC.
As a result, my contestation of the way I was reflected could be
seen as a denouncement of what Lazi had done. Fortunately, his
was a voluntary disclosure. He decided to take responsibility for
what he did by disclosing to the family so they could know who
carried out the attack on their father. This was part of a 'desire for
reconciliation' as the heading for the relevant section of the TRC
report suggests.

Under the same section, Mr Neo Potsane is more explicit. He says
that he 'jumped in' to take advantage of the opportunity granted
through the TRC process to 'extend my hand of friendship to the
victims or the people that suffered because of my actions in pursuit
of democracy and I'm happy today that I'm here ... explaining my

actions so that you know, other people can understand why I did those things'.[16]

As I said at the beginning, the error in Volume 6 of the TRC codicil did not only cause enormous pain to me but also threatened to wreck my relationship with Archbishop Tutu, a relationship that I cherish. The archbishop is one of the church leaders I could rely on any time during my tenure as general secretary of the SACC. Any historian would know that this was the most difficult time of our struggle. But the archbishop was one church leader who would abandon anything he was doing to respond to my emergency call. This is how close we were. I am pleased that we have not allowed a technical error to break our precious relationship. The misunderstandings in dealing with this matter and our divergent perspectives on the best way to deal with it simply showed that we are human, like all of humanity, and not God.

Through the TRC, a major milestone had been reached on the challenging journey of management of the transition from an apartheid society to a just, non-racial, non-sexist and democratic country. But as my personal struggle shows, as struggle veterans we should continue to defend our freedoms. Nothing should stand between us and our freedoms.

CHAPTER 16

Sela le Sela

There are other matters during my incumbency in the presidency that became so controversial that it would be surprising if I ended this book without dealing with or referring to them. Many of them occurred when I was engaged with the presidency, first as a special adviser to Deputy President Mbeki, and a year later as director-general in his office. Most of these matters were of such a strategic nature with national and international dimensions that they needed either to be driven from the presidency or the presidency had to have closer oversight over their conceptualisation, development and management.

Examples are the Strategic Arms Procurement Package; the GEAR strategy; and the Lesotho SADC military intervention led by South Africa.

I have decided to give this chapter the title of *Sela le Sela* ('this and the other') in my mother tongue, *Sepulana*, as I do not intend to deal with all the issues in full. As this is a book about my experiences in government, these matters belong to this book only in so far as I had some role in them, however limited. The account therefore cannot be considered as complete on these matters.

The Strategic Arms Procurement Package

The Strategic Arms Procurement Package, popularly known as the 'arms deal', is one of the most 'controversial' programmes the new democratic government was involved in. In hindsight the controversy should have been expected because, firstly, it was about arms – especially as it followed the demise of apartheid and ordinary South Africans expected an end to war and a period of peace. Secondly, it was about large amounts of money at a time when enormous resources were required for the reconstruction and development of the country. Thirdly, where a programme or project involves billions of rands one should expect corruption and fraud to follow.

The question is why the new democratic government prioritised the arms procurement in this context, which seemed to be militating against its focus on development.

The rationale of those involved in the programme was that security forces required special attention from the new government as it was inheriting apartheid forces, which had been used against the majority of South Africans, particularly blacks, to enforce the racist system of apartheid. In this regard the democratic government had to review the whole concept of defence and security in the country to bring it in line with a new reality.

The second reason for prioritising this programme was that there was a deal on the table that the apartheid government had already committed itself to. This was the acquisition of four corvettes from

Bazan in Spain. The process was intercepted and subjected to the general 'defence review' process by the new democratic government.

The starting point was the constitutional framework of the democratic government on security services, now contained in Chapter 11 of the Constitution, which identifies the 'primary object of the defence force' as that of defending and protecting 'the Republic, its territorial integrity and its people in accordance with the Constitution and the principles on international law regulating the use of force' (Section 200[2]). The process went through a 'White Paper' on defence in 1995, followed by an extensive consultative process on a 'Defence Review', which ran from February 1996 to April 1998. Amongst other issues, recommendations were made to retain an 'effective defence capability' and highlighted the need to 're-equip' the South African National Defence Force to be able to carry out its new responsibilities. Besides the need for 'effective defence capability' there was also a commitment by the new government to fulfil its international obligations.

Up to this stage there was general consensus on the matter amongst all parties in parliament and civil society, which was part of the consultative processes. The controversy started when the amounts involved in procuring arms to equip the force were made known.

The first line of attack was a moral one that queried the wisdom of spending so much money on arms during 'peace time' instead of spending the money on dealing with poverty and social needs, which went beyond the resources the country could muster. This position was supported by civil society groups, including the churches. The debate here was more about priorities in terms of a hierarchy of needs, rather than the need to maintain an 'effective defence capability'.

The second line of attack was a pacifist one, which was against any form of violence or even having an army as a matter of principle.

This attack is a universal one and was not unique to South Africa, except in our case, it also used the 'moral' perspective referred to above.

Government went ahead with the strategic arms procurement programme, despite these criticisms as it believed that it had a constitutional responsibility to ensure that the defence force was sufficiently equipped to defend the country as well as fulfil its international obligations. Government also believed that it could fulfil these objectives in a manner that balanced the needs of the country, especially in terms of the enormous social challenges the country was facing.

The agitation about this procurement package intensified once the contracts were approved. A tender system was used to assess the bidders and the final selection and approval of the contracts was at a cabinet committee level, which made recommendations to cabinet. Again, the attacks were at different levels. The first was from those with a commercial interest in the matter and who did not make it during the selection processes, including the Spanish bidders. This group with interests in the deals consisted of both national and international players. They launched and funded a massive national and international campaign against the processes followed and alleged that there was massive corruption involved in them not being selected.

The objective was to discredit the process and force government to reverse it so they could get a second chance to bid. Some engaged foreign intelligence agencies, former apartheid and liberation movement intelligence operatives, national and international investigation entities, and various individuals and groups in South Africa, to dig up dirt where they believed there was dirt. Some used smoke and mirrors, and mixing truth with falsehood, deception and unsubstantiated explanations, descriptions and stories to produce a concoction to discredit the players in this process.

They also fed information to the media, leaders of opposition parties, civil society groups, the police, prosecuting authorities, and other investigation entities within and outside the country. This information was also shared with other governments, like Spain, Germany, Britain and Sweden, which they thought would be interested in the matter. Various allegations were made against individuals and the committees that were responsible for the procurement processes.

In response the government explained that there were two levels at which the contracts were issued. The first was that of primary contractors for which the government was responsible. At this level the government argued that there was no corruption as this was handled by a cabinet committee involving four departments, namely, defence (technical defence requisitions), treasury (budgetary implications, affordability, fiscal and economic implications), trade and industry (industrial participation and economic implementation), and public enterprises (responsible for state-owned enterprises). The group representing these departments was chaired by Thabo Mbeki, then deputy president in Mandela's presidency. They argued that it would have required the four ministers and their department to collude, which they said was impossible. Besides, they knew it never happened – not at that level.

There was also a committee of officials including the above mentioned departments chaired by the economic adviser to the deputy president, but its function was to look at the issues and recommendations that came through to the special cabinet committee for action by cabinet. Again, it was argued that there was no corruption at this level.

For this reason cabinet was of the view that there was no need for it to review the decisions made as they were credible and reliable. In a formal statement on the matter it was argued that there was no room for any single person or minister to influence the others to make decisions that were corrupt or irregular.

But because of persistent accusations about fraud and corruption related to this arms procurement programme a decision was made to bring in the public protector (then Selby Baqwa), the NDPP (then Bulelani Ngcuka) and the auditor-general (then Shauket Fakie) to investigate this matter and report accordingly. It is at this level that I got involved and attended meetings between these agencies, institutions and government to lay the parameters for their work and clarify the modus operandi.

I remember an informal discussion with the chiefs of the three government entities at the end of one of the meetings during which I said that they should help us to find these corrupt people, whoever they may be, because the matter was impacting negatively on the integrity and credibility of the government. I also remember saying they should net us one 'big fish', if there was one, so we could act on it and show that government was committed to eradicating corruption and that positions and power would not deter us from acting against corrupt people in terms of our laws and the constitution.

The three agencies investigated and produced a report that concluded as follows in respect of the cabinet-level involvement with the programme:

> No evidence was found of any improper or unlawful conduct by the government. The irregularities and improprieties ... point to the conduct of certain officials of the government departments involved and cannot ... be ascribed to the president or the ministers involved in their capacity as members of the ministers' committee or cabinet. There are therefore no grounds to suggest that the government's contracting position is flawed.

This, as far as government was concerned, closed the matter at the level of cabinet and its cabinet committee.

The accusation against 'certain officials of the government departments' related to the departments of defence and trade and industry. In the Department of Defence accusations were levelled
against the chief of acquisitions, Chippy Shaik, who denied such
allegations and no charges were brought against him. Although he
did resign, it was over the release of classified information to his
lawyer in the process of defending himself from the allegations of
corruption. There were also allegations against an official in the
Department of Trade and Industry who was responsible for the
National Industrial Participation Programme (NIPP), which was
part of the arms acquisition strategy. He also resigned. Furthermore,
there is not one official of government who was involved in this
project who has been charged and convicted. If there are any guilty
parties, then I am as interested as I was then to find such officials,
and let them be charged.

Where there was corruption was at secondary-level contracts,
that is, at the level of the sub-contractors to the main contractors.
Once government had made the decision on the contractor, it was
the responsibility of the contractor to sub-contract other entities
necessary for it to deliver on its contract. Government had a framework and certain regulatory requirements to be met such as black
empowerment or the use of as much South African expertise as
possible, but the final decision of the sub-contractor was that of the
main contractor. In this sense, government did not have responsibility for decisions made at that level.

At this level the investigators found that 'there may have been
individuals ... who used or attempted to use their positions im-
properly ... to obtain undue benefits in relation to these packages'.
Interestingly, besides allegations against Chippy Shaik and the trade
and industry official, all other allegations of corruption related to
people who were far from the actual decision-making process of
awarding the primary contracts and had no way of influencing it.

Schabir Shaik, Chippy's more famous brother, who was convicted of fraud and corruption and sentenced to fifteen years' imprisonment, had no chance of influencing the process either.

Some argued that such influence could have been made through his brother, Chippy, or his relationship with President Jacob Zuma, then an MEC for economic affairs and tourism in the KwaZulu-Natal provincial government. But none of them could singularly influence the special cabinet committee on the Strategic Arms Procurement Package. In any event, Chippy Shaik's recommendations, as the acquisitions chief, would have had to have gone through the Armament Acquisition Steering Board within the defence department and the defence secretary (who is responsible for all acquisition activities), the Minister of Defence, and the interdepartmental officials committee before it reached the special cabinet committee for the Strategic Arms Procurement Package.

Whatever allegations were made against Zuma and Schabir Shaik were also outside the decision-making processes involved in the awarding of the contracts. The case of Tony Yengeni, the former ANC chief whip who was also convicted of fraud, was so peripheral that it was actually totally irrelevant to the procurement process itself. As some of these cases surfaced it became clear to many of us that the bidders for the packages targeted anyone and everyone they thought would have some influence and they focused mainly on targets within the ANC rather than in government. I am of the view that they also had no understanding of the ANC and how it operated. Anyone who had known the ANC would have known that trying to influence any of the people mentioned would not have achieved their intended objectives.

The other way to think about it is that the bidders went out like the sower in Matthew 13 who caused some seeds to fall on the path. The birds came and ate them up. Other seeds fell on rocky ground, where they did not have much soil, and they were scorched; and since they had no root, they withered away. Other seeds fell among thorns, and the thorns grew up and choked them. In business terms this would be considered a waste of money. Nevertheless, someone benefitted in a corrupt manner. But there are still people who believe that there were 'seeds' that fell on good soil and brought forth positive results for undeserving people in terms of influencing decisions on the primary contracts. This is the evidence we are all interested in.

At the time of writing this book a judicial commission of inquiry on the 'arms deal' had started its work. The country will await the outcome of the commission with interest. Hopefully it will help us better understand shenanigans involved in this matter.

'Asiyifuni iGear'

Whenever I think about 'GEAR', that is, the 'Growth, Employment and Redistribution' strategy of the first democratic government of South Africa led by President Nelson Mandela, I cannot but recall the joke that Inkosi UButhelezi, the leader of the IFP, used to make when he was a minister in government. He used to say that there were many people out there who chanted the slogan, 'Asiyifuni iGear', while protesting but had no clue as to what 'iGear' was. Some thought 'GEAR' was a name of a person in the same way others thought of 'Prerogative' in my earlier book *Eight Days in September*. The 'prerogative' debate related to the question about the 'prerogative' of the president to release Zuma, then as deputy president of the country, and appoint another. Some thought 'Prerogative' was a person. In the case of GEAR, generally workers understood 'iGear' as something bad for them and for the economy, and that it 'took' jobs away from them.

At an ideological level, that is, at the level of the battle of ideas within the ANC alliance family, GEAR has been given many names. Some call it a 'neo-liberal' policy based on the Washington Consensus, which brings back the worst images of the Washington-based institutions, namely the IMF and the World Bank, including the US Treasury, and the negative policy prescriptions for developing countries that caused enormous pain for those countries in the 1970s and 1980s. In economic or academic cycles this was called 'market fundamentalism' as the Washington Consensus was based largely on a strongly market-based approach. The prescriptions included macroeconomic stabilisation, opening of trade, and allowing market forces to expand within the domestic economy. The real pain of these policy prescriptions was that they were enforced during the Cold War period to impose the capitalistic system on developing countries, which were turned into battlegrounds for the superpowers.

I arrived at the GEAR policy from a completely different perspective but related to the concerns of the workers in its overall thrust. During the 1970s and the 1980s the churches worked in tandem with the liberation movement to resist the unjust global economic system imposed on us. As part of the liberation movement, activists within the churches believed that the capitalist system was the worst type of economic system (then coupled with an apartheid ideology) and we generally accepted a socialist perspective as the best solution for our societies at the time. In general the churches embraced some form of socialism, which was more compatible with what they learnt from the Scriptures.

This perspective was reinforced by the fact that those who supported apartheid – mainly Western powers within the UN Security Council – were promoting the capitalist system at the expense of the poor and oppressed. And those who supported South Africa against apartheid were either communist or had some socialist orientation. Among these were the Soviet Union and China.

It is a known fact that leaders of the liberation movement in South Africa first approached Western countries to support them against the apartheid system but did not find joy with them as they supported the apartheid government. Our leaders turned to the East where they found support and understanding. One could call this a form of camaraderie. The story of Comrade Oliver Tambo is often told in this regard. On leaving the country to go into exile, he first approached Western powers for assistance without any success. This took him to the Soviet Union, which was ready to help. The exceptions, however, were the Nordic countries, which were ultimately very supportive in terms of the struggle for liberation.

Generally, radical Christianity embraced various forms of liberation theologies, some of which used Marxian tools of analysis, and had no difficulties in embracing socialist ways of thinking. The language and practices of the early church of the Book of Acts lent themselves to these perspectives and approach.

In one portion of this Book it states: 'Awe came upon everyone, because many wonders and signs were being done by the apostles'; and 'All who believed were *together* and *had all things in common*; they would sell their possessions and goods and *distribute proceeds to all, as any had need*' (Acts 2:43–45). And in chapter 4:32 and 34 there is reference to 'the whole group of those who believed' who were of 'one heart and soul' and that '*no one claimed private ownership of any possessions*, but *everything they owned was held in common*'. And, '*there was not a needy person among them*, for *as many as owned lands and houses sold them and brought the proceeds of what was sold*. They laid them at the apostles' feet, and *it was distributed to each as any had need*' (emphasis added).

Paul – the theologian *par excellence* – defends this approach of giving and equality in a more analytical way. He says: 'I do not mean that there should be *relief for others* and *pressure on you*, but it is a question of a *fair balance* between your present abundance and their need, so that their abundance may be for your need, in order that there may be a fair balance' (2 Cor 8:13–14).

From this perspective the IMF and the World Bank of the 1970s and the 1980s were like swearwords to us – instruments of the global capitalist economic system that promoted the interests of the rich and powerful against those of the poor and downtrodden. They were monsters that had to be resisted. The pain they had occasioned in many poor African countries in pursuit of the interests of major Western countries was beyond any description. The stunted bodies and scarred minds of the people told the story.

As the new democratic society was born in 1994 these radical and negative views about the IMF and the World Bank and their related neo-liberal policies persisted, and in the main their representatives have not helped to change these views.

In this regard, I will not forget the encounter we had with one young Washington technocrat who was part of the IMF team that visited South Africa in the early 1990s to offer assistance to the liberation movement as it prepared to take over government. They were eager to be involved as part of the preparatory teams to finalise economic policies and programmes. This was part of the 'Ready to Govern' preparations. There was no doubt in our minds that their interest in assisting had other objectives: to try to influence our policies and programmes to advance their own ideological interests.

I was among those who resisted the IMF's involvement – given its history and ideological perspectives – and argued that we had enough qualified economists and professionals in South Africa with the correct political orientation to formalise our policy perspectives and programmes without the direct involvement of the IMF. Many agreed. This angered one of these young IMF technocrats who said to us in a very arrogant way, that they would leave us alone, but he reckoned that five years later we would call on them to 'come and fix the economy', or something to that effect.

This encounter and the arrogance of the IMF technocrat made us more determined than ever to make sure that the IMF never got called to come and 'fix' our economy. We had to fix it ourselves in a manner that left us in control to radically change the living conditions of our people, particularly the poor, and better the lives of all South Africans. This was what we struggled for and many of our comrades died for and we were not about to subject ourselves to economic prescriptions that were going to worsen our situation. If the IMF had to come it would be on our terms rather than theirs.

The challenge, of course, was enormous. We had to restructure the apartheid economy, which was geared to benefit the few – whites in particular – rather than the black majority. We understood that capital, which we needed to invest in the economy, was in the hands of the privileged (who were mainly white) and were not necessarily interested in using their money to change the economy in a way that seemed to threaten their interests. But at the same time they understood that without change the economy could be destabilised, as happened recently with the labour unrest of 2012 and the tragedy of the Marikana massacre. At the time of the discussions with the IMF officials the memories of many were still on the 'wildcat' strikes of 1973.

A two-year programme of consultations and engagement, particularly with big business in South Africa, was undertaken with the intention of changing these attitudes. This led to the establishment of, among other initiatives, the National Business Initiative.

Other challenges included a racially skewed national budget, which also had to be restructured in favour of the poor and poorer regions. The budget of the apartheid government had distributed resources in a manner that created deep pockets of poverty where blacks lived. We needed to structure the budget in a way that re-distributed resources to the areas (provinces, regions and localities) that were historical affected by apartheid policies.

We needed to reduce the budget deficit to manageable levels and understood that loans would only be made either to grow the economy or for productive activities with the possibility of financing themselves. All social expenditure was to come from our revenues rather than from loans. We committed ourselves to reducing the budget deficit but not at the cost of social expenditure, as the IMF and the World Bank might have dictated.

Our graph of social expenditure from 1996 to date indicates a steady growth rather than a decline. Some representatives of our alliance partners might have wanted a steeper rate of growth of social expenditure, but this would have required us to keep a larger budget deficit. My view has always been that debt can only make sense if it helps one to be better off rather than live beyond one's means. Debt makes sense only in terms of the capacity of the borrower to pay, otherwise it is unsustainable. We also had to deal with what was called the 'apartheid debt', which was the debt accumulated during the time of the apartheid system and sanctions against the system. The challenge we faced was that most of this debt was against pension funds of South Africans, and as a result we could not just write it off.

Another task facing the new government was the restructuring of state assets, which had previously been used to improve the quality of life of poorer whites and provide pension systems for white workers.

Restructuring also involved dealing with the country's parastatals. It made sense to keep some of the functions carried out by parastatals within government while others were best placed outside of government. This issue became controversial as it touched on the sticky subject of privatisation. In this regard, and to avoid misunderstandings between labour and government a national framework agreement on the restructuring of state assets was signed between the government (represented by the Ministry for Public Enterprises) and labour (represented by COSATU, the Federation of South African Trade Unions and the National Council of Trade Unions). The status of the national framework agreement was defined within the mandate of the National Economic Development and Labour Council (NEDLAC).

The agreement makes it clear that 'state institutional reform must be a major element of the Reconstruction and Development Programme' (paragraph 3). Paragraph 4 states it even more explicitly: 'The initiative to restructure State Assets is part of the process of implementing the RDP.' In the same paragraph the NFA states:

> Government has concretised some of these objectives in its so-called 'six pack' programme namely: belt tightening; reprioritisation of state expenditure; restructuring of state assets and enterprises; restructuring of the public service; building new inter-governmental relations; developing an internal monitoring capacity for the above programmes.

The 'six pack' was part of our plan to restructure the economy in a manner that would ensure we never had to call the Washington IMF technocrat to come and 'fix' our economy.

There are those who argue that GEAR was a substitute for the RDP. This question was adequately answered by Trevor Manuel in his article entitled 'No Contradiction between RDP and GEAR' published in COSATU's *Daily Labour News* (extra) on 11 August 2006, but was originally from *ANC Today* (Vol. 6, No. 31, 11–17 August 2006). Manuel relies on the 1997 ANC National Conference resolution, which read:

> Conference reaffirms that our *macroeconomic framework policies must be directed to advance the RDP.* We are not pursuing

macro balances for their own sake, but to create the conditions for sustainable growth, development and reconstruction. *The Strategy for Growth, Employment and Redistribution (GEAR) is aimed at giving effect to the realisation of the RDP* through the maintenance of macro balances and elaborates a set of mutually reinforcing policy instruments (emphasis added).

To be fair, the ANC alliance partners have consistently raised the issue of what they considered as the 'conservative fiscal policies' in GEAR but GEAR has always been considered as being within the policy framework of the ANC.

Others argue that closing the head office of the RDP in the president's office in 1996 was part of the process of substituting the RDP with GEAR. As I was in the presidency then I can attest to the fact that the motivation to close the RDP ministry and specialised office had nothing to do with GEAR. The case for closing the ministry and relocating the RDP fund to Treasury had to do with mainstreaming the RDP. It was aimed at encouraging all state departments to consider everything they were doing as part of the RDP, rather than having them run some projects outside their core business to show that they were involved in the RDP.

President Mandela announced this change and assigned Mbeki the task of overseeing the reallocation of the various RDP programmes, projects and institutions. Mbeki in turn formed a task team consisting of myself and Moss Ngoasheng (deputy president's office), Professor Jakes Gerwel (president's office), and Dr Bernie Fanaraoff and Tanya Abrahamse-Lamola (RDP office) to execute this task. A press statement issued by the office of the deputy president on 18 April 1996 states:

Government re-iterates that the decision to close the RDP office was done as a result of the positive evolution (of the RDP)

... to ensure that the various Departments of State make the realisation of the objectives spelt out in the Reconstruction and Development Programme the centre of all their activities (emphasis added).

There is no doubt that GEAR achieved many of its objectives, especially in the areas of growth and redistribution, reduction of the budget deficit and so forth, however much people may differ about it. Measuring the policy against its objectives of growth, employment and redistribution, one could argue the policy was partially successful in growing the economy although it did not reach the target of 6 per cent. There was effective redistribution of resources to benefit the poor but this happened mainly in the areas where government was involved and not in the rest of the economy. This is one of the reasons we have not been able to close the gap between the poor and the rich in the country. But where it really failed was in the area of employment. We experienced 'jobless growth' as some would say. Here again it is clear that where government relied on the private sector the objectives were not realised.

This lesson learnt within the first ten years of democracy was that where government did not depend on other parties, it achieved its objectives to some reasonable levels. But where it depended on other parties there was total failure. This conclusion was contained in the government's review document entitled 'Towards a Ten Year Review: A Synthesis Report on the Implementation of Government Programmes'. The report noted that there were weaknesses 'in those areas that are least dependent on direct government action'.[17]

Nine years later we are still where we were and this requires a radical examination of our policies and programmes, including the matter of the development of a strong developmental state, on the one hand, and the mobilisation of other sectors of our nation, on the other.

Whatever the case and whatever the pain involved in the implementation of some of the GEAR programmes, I am pleased that we did not have to call the young technocrat from Washington. We must find our own solutions while being informed by others who have gone through similar experiences and faced similar challenges.

A desperate call from Lesotho

In the early morning of 22 September 1998 the South Africa National Defence Force entered Lesotho. They were followed by the Botswana Defence Force as part of the SADC intervention force to stabilise the situation in Lesotho at the invitation of Prime Minister Pakalitha Mosisili, following a takeover of the command of the Lesotho Defence Force by junior officers.

Some described this as a 'creeping coup', others called it a 'creeping insurrection'. Yet others called it a mutiny. A classical definition of a mutiny would be an open rebellion against the proper authorities, usually within the force or unit they were serving. In this case the mutiny had gone beyond the classical definition of mutiny to a takeover of the command of the army and running it outside the constitutional authority of the country. In this sense it was quickly progressing towards a fully fledged *coup d'etat* with a threat to some of the leadership of the country and military commanders.

Efforts were made to talk to the junior officers and appeal to them to reverse their illegal actions. I attended most of these meetings as part of the team facilitating negotiations to deal with the primary cause of the unrest, which was the national elections held earlier that year. The 'mutiny' occurred while these peacemaking processes were in progress. Following the 'mutiny' we were joined by some of our military commanders and intelligence officers and asked to find a resolution of the crisis. Meetings were also held with the King, Letsie III, who was seriously concerned about the situation and wanted it resolved as a matter of urgency.

We had a rough time with the representatives of the 'mutineers' at the beginning as the commanders on the South African side took them on at a military level in terms of military culture, conduct and discipline. The 'mutineers' were led by four young junior officers, one of whom was the commander of the 'mutiny'. We engaged them with the objective of making them understand the implications of their actions and to persuade them to abandon their disastrous mission, which was bound to end tragically.

We did everything possible to change their perspectives with a commitment to help them normalise the situation and their relationship with their commanders, whom they had dismissed, as well as the political leadership, some of whom were effectively being kept in a state of house arrest. We were also ready to deal with the implications of what they had done and their future. These discussions took place over many days and involved a number of trips to and from Lesotho. Our aim was to avoid a military intervention, which could be very costly in terms of life and material resources. We would only intervene militarily to save the lives of the people of Lesotho as well as normalise the situation if everything failed.

Having now read and reread news reports about these events, I can understand how our concern to 'save lives' was questioned. But most of the reports were so far from the truth that it hurt. Many called it an 'invasion' rather than an 'intervention'. Others call it an 'attack' on a tiny country rather than a rescue operation to normalise the situation. Some called it 'illegal' action in terms of international law and others even questioned whether or not it was a SADC mission.

Even though it was unable to disclose all the information it had at its disposal on the crisis in Lesotho, the reality is that the government did not communicate effectively to help South Africans understand the action it took. My reading of this material now has made me believe that it would be in the interests of the South African government to declassify some of the information to be able to tell the story as the government understood it at the time.

I know that there are challenges to what I am suggesting, especially in relation to laws that govern the declassification of information as this could risk people's lives or national security. But there is much that can be said to demystify this story. The reality is that if the intervention had not been made there would have been more lives lost and more dire consequences.

The unfortunate thing about our interaction with the 'mutineers' is that at the time when we thought that we had an agreement that would have avoided the worst-case scenario, the 'mutineer' commanders somehow lost control of their forces. Urgent intervention became unavoidable. I still remember vividly that fateful Saturday afternoon standing in the command centre and feeling that I was losing it. No, I was not losing my mind; I was losing the battle to avoid a military intervention. My hope faded away as our interlocutor did. He faded away. Slowly, but surely, he faded away! In the end we lost him in his capacity as commander.

From there on one had to be a realist rather than an idealist. I also had to move quickly. A military strategy had to be devised to neutralise 'the boys' (mutineers) and save their lives. We had to secure a commitment that the army would do everything possible to avoid loss of life.

One of the major challenges was that the people of Lesotho themselves were a very divided people so that whatever course we followed would be open to critique. What was also challenging was the relationship of South Africa and Lesotho. We were like a family separated by an imaginary border that the colonialists chose to put between us. So, what happens to the Basotho affects us equally and what affects us affects them too. And, it is not just the Basotho in South Africa but all the language and ethnic groups because we have inter-married across all the historical boundaries, culture, nationalities and so forth.

As 22 September dawned calls began to come in to government at various levels. Some expressed disbelief and others concern. Some felt the government was doing the right thing while others felt it was wrong. In the midst of all this I had to keep my cool and do what was expected from the head of the office of the deputy president. Thus, I was constantly in contact with the deputy president outside the country and with President Mandela's staff, then in another part of the world. I worked with the acting president, then Inkosi Buthelezi. I kept in contact with the military command, intelligence and the Department of Foreign Affairs. I kept in contact with the communicators, lawyers and political strategists and fielded calls from political leaders and civil society groups from Lesotho.

Later, reports began to come through about loss of life on both sides. What was also painful was the death of members of the medical team who were attending to the injured on both sides in terms of the Geneva Conventions. By late afternoon there were still pockets of resistance and the risks became higher. Breaking the resistance before sunset, which had to be done, could be costly.

At that point, I started to receive calls from ordinary citizens of Lesotho, who were now addressing me as 'Reverend Frank Chikane' and not as the 'director-general in the office of the deputy president'.

'Please save our children!' 'My child is in that military base under siege. Please ask them not to bomb it!' The call I cannot forget came from the acting general secretary of the Christian Council of Churches in Lesotho who was also fielding pleas from the parents and relatives of those who were in that particular military base.

Their children were calling from that base and begging their relatives to intervene on their behalf.

We agreed to do our best on both sides to avoid any further loss of life. She acceded to communicate with those at the base and persuade them not to offer any further resistance so we could end it all before nightfall. I undertook to interact with the military command on the South African side. A strategy was devised to neutralise the resistance without losing another soul at the military base.

Shew! If you can, avoid war at all costs.

This is 'Sela le Sela' in my mother tongue – Sepulana.

Mokone wa mankobola

Mokone wa mokokona pola

Batho ba magana go tlholwa

Maduma go retwa

Morokong, Chikane.

Conclusion

The Things that Could Not be Said has been a long journey dealing with twists and turns from A(ids) to Z(imbabwe). The question could be asked whether or not I have said all 'the things that could not be said'? And my answer is an emphatic 'No!' I have said what could be said in this book given the constraints of space and time. More about some of these topics will come in the future.

I also accept that there will be things I will never be able to say because of confidentiality and the secrecy laws. Those things that could risk other people's lives are better not said.

Experience shows that even the best cadres of the glorious movement of the people (that is, the ANC) are corruptible – something that some of us never thought would happen. In this regard we might have been too innocent and lived in a utopian world. I am one of those who believed that the ANC is not 'capable of being lost' because of its strong convictions and revolutionary morality rooted in the legacy of O.R. Tambo. Today it is clear that it is as vulnerable as any other party.

Reality also shows that this is not only a problem of the 'new cadre' who needs to go back to 'political school' but it is often a problem of the 'old cadre' whose politics were shaped in the furnace of the struggle. Old cadres are often the leaders or centres of the rot and cancer that is eating up the soul of the people's movement.

A leading business leader who attended the Mining Indaba in Cape Town in 2013 expressed a concern about the possibility that the ANC could become more radical, to the extent that it would be difficult to invest in South Africa. My response was that reckless radicalism is unlikely to survive within the ANC government. The real threat for me is corruption, which can make leaders pursue their self-interests – be these of self, family, friends and/or factions – to the extent that the majority of the people are excluded. This is a recipe for another revolution.

In my opinion, the greatest risk this country faces is the danger of compromised (and corrupt) leaders who not only serve their own interests but also those of the people who compromised them – be these individual businesspeople, foreign and intelligence entities, or even countries.

This is a force capable of negating our strategic objectives of ending poverty and changing the quality of lives of all South Africans. It is this threat that we must fight by all means to ensure that we achieve the strategic objectives of the NDR.

I have tried in these pages to present as honestly and as accurately as possible my experiences in government in relation to controversial issues at the time. These are highly emotive issues, which provoke radically different views, but I think there are very important lessons to be learnt. Chapter 14 for me presents an example of intricate manoeuvring through a landmined debate to craft a policy that is lauded by the international community. And Chapter 12 shows the ability of a country, however small, to change the world's perspectives for the better.

Sadly, on the global stage, my impression is that lies, dishonesty, double standards and distortion of reality are often the order of the day. Those who claim to be 'old democracies' and champions of democracy often support the worst autocrats or sabotage emerging democracies in pursuit of their national interests.

What is worse for me is the fact that today's world is still constructed in a manner that perpetuates the old imperial and colonial thought systems, institutions and structures. I chose to call this 'Colonialism in a New Guise' but, in fact, it is just the old monster clad in modern garb. Current international institutions such as the UN Security Council, IMF and the World Bank are the best representations of the vestiges of these old colonial systems that are still with us.

This is what we need to change and I believe that those countries on the receiving end of these institutions and attitudes are the only ones who will be able to facilitate this change. And this is where the African Renaissance comes in. We need to renew ourselves and our systems and practices as Africans and all marginalised communities in the world as we strive to change the world. We need the world of the powerful to know that they can no longer make decisions that affect us without consulting us and that they can no longer simply impose their will and wishes on us.

We need to make the world of the powerful understand that power cannot guarantee peace, especially when it is used to impose the will of the powerful on others. In fact, our current experience of global politics is that those who are more powerful are more vulnerable.

My thesis is that the only way to ensure peace, stability and prosperity for all in the world – from families to communities, and from religious groupings to business, labour and countries – is the pursuit of the common good. In this ideal world, the powerful use their power to ensure that the common good is achieved without any hindrance. In this ideal world, national interest is achieved by guaranteeing the common interest of all. It is a lofty goal that is worth striving for.

Record of Orders for Chemical and Biological Substances, March–October 1989

AANHANGSEL "A"
VERKOPE

Datum gelewer	Stof	Volume	Prys
19.03.89 **JK**	Phensiklidien	1 x 500mg	Teruggebring
	Thallium asetaat	50g	
23.03.89 **JK**	Phensiklidien	5 x 100mg	
04.04.89 **C**	Aldicarb – Lemoensap	6 x 200mg	
04.04.89 **C**	Asied – Whisky	3 x 1,5g	
04.04.89 **C**	Paraoxon	10 x 2ml	
07.04.89 **C**	Vit D	2gr	
15.05.89 **C**	Vit D	2gr	R300,00
15.05.89 **C**	Katharidien	70mg	R150,00
15.05.89 **C**	10ml Spuite	50	
16.05.89 **C**	Naalde 15Gx10mm	24	R18,00

Datum gelewer	Stof	Volume	Prys
16.05.89 C	Naalde 17Gx7,5mm	7	R7,00
19.05.89 C	Thallium asetaat	1g	
30.05.89	Fosfied tablette	30	
09.06.89	Spore en Brief	1	
20.06.89 K	Kapsules NaCN	50	
21.06.89	Bierblik Bot	3	
21.06.89	Bierblik Thallium	3	
21.06.89	Bottel bier Bot	1	
21.06.89	Bottel bier Thallium	2	
22.06.89 K	Suiker en Salmonella	200gr	
27.06.89 C	Wiskey en Paraquat	1x75ml	
20.07.89 K	Hg-sianied	4gr	
27.07.89 K	Bobbejaan foetus	1	
04.08.89 K	Vibrio cholera	16 bottels	
10.08.89 K	Asled 4 x gr	Kapsule sianied 7	
11.08.89 C	Sigarette B anthracis	5	
C	Koffie sjokolade B anthracis	5	
C	Koffie sjokolade Potulinum	5	
C	Pepperment sjokolade Aldikarb	3	
C	Pepperment sjokolade Brodifakum	2	
C	Pepperment sjokolade Katharidien	3	
C	Pepperment sjokolade Sianied	3	
16.08.89 K	Vibrio cholera	6 bottels	
16.08.89 K	Kapsules Propan NaCN	7	
18.08.89 K	Formalien en Piridien	50ml x 30	
	Naalde 10cm x no 16	12	

Datum gelewer	Stof	Volume	Prys
18.08.89 K	Katharidien – poeier in sakkie	100mg	
18.08.89 K	Metanol	3-30ml	
C	Vibrio cholera	10 bottels	
08.09.89 K	Slange	2	
K	Mamba toksien	1	Teruggebring
13.09.89 K	Digoksien	5 mg	
18.09.89 C	Whiskey 50ml + colchicines	75mg	
06.10.89 K	B.melitensis c	1 x 50	
	S.typhimurium in deodorant	1	
11.10.89 K	Kulture vanaf briewe	2	
21.10.89 K	B.melitensis c		
	S.typhimurium in deodorant	1	

Frank Chikane *City Press* Article, 18 August 2007

NPA role in Vlok matter offers a lesson for our country

The decision by the National Prosecuting Authority (NPA) to prosecute Adriaan Vlok, Johan van der Merwe and others triggered robust debate.

Although it was clouded by the much-publicised issues concerning me and Vlok, it was about how our country deals with the unfinished business of the Truth and Reconciliation Commission (TRC).

Given the nature of the issue, it was not surprising that people responded to the debate in an emotional way. Perhaps they were not fully aware of the prescribed post-TRC processes. Questions were raised about whether this was a witch-hunt by the ANC and/or government against Afrikaners? Others wondered why we didn't send the perpetrators of apartheid who did not get amnesty to prison. Some wanted to know why we didn't forget the past and move on.

I emphasised the importance of a healthy and informed debate on all matters affecting our society, including those pertaining to the post-TRC era. Our democracy could not have been achieved in the absence of dialogue and robust engagement.

I appealed to opinion-makers to focus on the fact that the TRC was the result of a collective resolve by South Africans that the nation needed to talk, tell the truth, reconcile and strengthen its efforts in building a united post-apartheid society. I called for caution so that we would not undermine the spirit of nation-building in which the TRC hearings were carried out.

This brings me to why I welcomed the court's decision to accept the plea-bargain agreement between Adriaan Vlok, Van der Merwe and others and the NPA. I have always said I have no interest in sending anyone to jail for the political crimes of the past. Like others, I needed full disclosure.

Relating to my poisoning, I now know how decisions were made at the highest level to use execrable and extra-judicial means to eliminate some of us considered to be a thorn in the flesh. I also know how the operation was carried out, the chain of command and the people involved. I have a full picture of what happened and my family are left with no questions. The chapter is closed and I am pleased that a legal resolution was found.

That I have forgiven Vlok and others is well known. However, the court case was separately important. The information that surfaced in court two days ago serves a bigger purpose and takes our national quest to come to terms with our past to a higher level.

I am particularly pleased that Vlok and Van der Merwe approached the NPA on their own to provide information regarding what they knew about the case. This was an extraordinarily bold step they took, being aware of the possibility of serving a jail sentence, a fact which Vlok publicly stated when he visited me.

Undoubtedly, I would not have completely healed had they not taken this step. Likewise, I am certain Vlok would not have had peace of mind if he did not have the conviction to come clean. We both enter the future with determination never to allow the past to spoil the future.

Yet I believe the Vlok trial is of national importance for reasons other than my personal interests.

The outcome of the court process gives practical expression to the spirit of the 2005 NPA guidelines that regulate the handling of outstanding TRC-related matters.

A day before the court pronouncement, some people were still speculating that Vlok could be jailed. One hopes they, but most importantly, our Afrikaner brethren who may have been wrongly led to suspect that the NPA – through its guidelines – was an instrument to get some of them behind bars. An example was set on Friday. A great deal of uncertainty has been removed and legal certainty has been given to Vlok and his colleagues. That the new South Africa is a constitutional state has been demonstrated once again.

I want to believe that all perpetrators and victims during apartheid will follow this route. There is an opportunity for those who may find themselves in a similar situation. Now that a precedent has been set, one can only hope others will demonstrate Vlok's courage of conscience.

Also significant is the outcome of the court in reaffirming the importance of dealing with TRC-related matters within the confines of the law.

Hopefully, the outcome of the court will serve to renew our collective trust in the integrity of our legal system, particularity in its proven capacity to handle sensitive and complicated political matters in an unbiased manner.

The evidence that NPA guidelines can facilitate a win–win outcome is there for all to see. One can only hope that the wisdom of working within the law is recognised widely.

The uniqueness of our jurisprudence – however imperfect – to deal with conflicts of the past is a marvel for most of the world. I suspect the manner in which we handled the case related to Vlok and others will have important lessons inside and outside our country.

This, I hope, will further serve correctly to project ours as a country of people who have demonstrated that it is possible to make the law advance national unity and reconciliation.

Chikane is director-general in the Presidency and secretary of cabinet. He writes in his personal capacity

Notes

1 C.P. Snow. 1962. *Science and Government*. Signet.
2 *Guardian*, 16 September 2007.
3 *Washington Post*, 17 September 2007.
4 Allan Boesak. 1977. *Farewell to Innocence: A Social Ethical Study of Black Theology and Black Power*. Orbis Books.
5 John R. Boekenoogen. 2011 [2006]. *Farewell to Innocence*. Lulu.com.
6 Robert Brand, 'What the *Guardian*'s Journalism Tells us about the Media ... and Thabo Mbeki', *Mail&Guardian* online, 22 August 2007.
7 Marika Sherwood, '"There is no New Deal for the Blackman in San Francisco": African Attempts to Influence the Founding Conference of the United Nations, April–July 1945', *International Journal of African Historical Studies*, Vol.29, No.1 (1996), p.71.
8 Titus Alexander. 1996. *Unravelling Global Apartheid: An Overview of World Politics*. Polity Press, pp.158–60.
9 *Guardian*, 1 September 2011.
10 Reuters, 17 February 2011.
11 *Guardian*, 17 February, 2006.
12 See the APRM website, www.nepad.org/economicandcorporategovernance/african-peer-review-mechanism (accessed on 8 February 2013).
13 African National Congress. 1979. *The Green Book: Report of the Politico-Military Strategy Commission to the ANC National Executive Committee*. See

www.anc.org.za/show.php?id=79&t=Umkhonto (accessed on 8 February 2013).

14 Georg Meiring letter to Frank Chikane, 16 September 1996.

15 *TRC Report*, Vol.6, Foreword, p.2. see www.justice.gov.za/trc/report/index. htm (accessed on 8 February 2013).

16 *TRC Report*, Vol.6, p.267.

17 South African Government Discussion Document, 'Towards a Ten Year Review: A Synthesis Report on the Implementation of Government Programmes', p.103. See www.info.gov.za/otherdocs/2003/10year.pdf (accessed on 8 February 2013).